2888 2024

10/02 ✓

MANAGING INTEREST RATE RISK

Current and Forthcoming Titles in the IIA Series

MANAGING COMMODITY RISK
John J. Stephens

MANAGING CURRENCY RISK
John J. Stephens

MANAGING REPUTATIONAL RISK
Jenny Rayner

Series Editor: Andrew Chambers

MANAGING INTEREST RATE RISK

using financial derivatives

JOHN J STEPHENS

The Institute of Internal Auditors
UK and Ireland

JOHN WILEY & SONS, LTD

Copyright © 2002 by John Wiley & Sons, Ltd,
        Baffins Lane, Chichester,
        West Sussex PO19 1UD, England

        National 01243 779777
        International (+44) 1243 779777
        e-mail (for orders and customer service enquiries): cs-books@wiley.co.uk
        Visit our Home Page on http://www.wiley.co.uk

Other Wiley Editorial Offices
John Wiley & Sons, Inc., 605 Third Avenue,
New York, NY 10158-0012, USA

WILEY-VCH Verlag GmbH, Pappelallee 3,
D-69469 Weinheim, Germany

John Wiley & Sons Australia, Ltd, 33 Park Road, Milton,
Queensland 4064, Australia

John Wiley & Sons (Asia) Pte Ltd, 2 Clementi Loop #02-01,
Jin Xing Distripark, Singapore 129809

John Wiley & Sons (Canada) Ltd, 22 Worcester Road,
Rexdale, Ontario M9W 1L1, Canada

Library of Congress Cataloging-in-Publication Data
A Library of Congress record has been applied for.

British Library Cataloguing in Publication Data

A catalogue record for this book is available from the British Library

ISBN 0-471-48549-7

Typeset in Times 10/12 pt by Deerpark Publishing Services, Ireland
Printed and bound in Great Britain by TJ International Ltd, Padstow
This book is printed on acid-free paper responsibly manufactured from sustainable forestation, for which at least two trees are planted for each one used for paper production.

contents

preface

Interest rates represent the time value of money. It is the price to be paid for the privilege of having the use of money now rather than later. They are therefore also said to represent the price of money, although this latter concept must also include relative money values such as exchange rates. Since money drives economic activity, it stands to reason that having the use of money now must be worth more than having the same amount in the future. Conversely stated, a certain amount of money in the future will be equal to a lesser amount now. Furthermore, it follows that borrowing money, with its concomitant of lending, will always be a basic and fundamental element of economic activity.

Although this book is not intended as a primer on interest rates as such, it is intended for everybody who wishes to get to grips with the basics of managing interest rate risk. People with vast trading experience, knowledge and expertise in the field of interest rate derivatives might hardly benefit by much of the material contained herein. It is also not intended as a highly academic treatise on the subject. Rather, the book hopes to make a positive contribution to the general state of knowledge of internal auditors, managers, entrepreneurs and others. People who work at the coal face of modern commerce require practical know-how because they have to deal with the realities of daily business. Yet many such people are not experts in the financial discipline of financial derivatives, nor do they require the esoteric knowledge that is the preserve of trading floor boffins and financial quants. It is for these that this book has been written.

Although it may be unusual to regard money as a commodity, there is nevertheless a demand for money, just as there is for any commodity. As in the case of commodities, various factors constantly influence the demand for and the supply of money. Money markets consequently experience price volatility. That is to say, prices are constantly in flux. In this case, the prices are interest rates and there is consequently volatility in interest rates. Note also the use of the plural. There is not one price for money, but many. The market demands different interest rates for borrowings for different periods. There are thus different prices for money depending upon the period for which it is required. This fact results in the well-known and often mentioned yield curve, about which more will be said later.

Every business faces interest rate risk in one form or another. It would be true to say that businesses that consistently manage to outperform the cost of money will prosper, while those that do not, will not survive. It is thus crucially important for every businessperson to have a firm grasp of the fundamentals of interest rate risk and its management.

MODERN RISK MANAGEMENT AND THE NON-FINANCIAL SECTOR

As is evident from the title, the broad concern of this book is the management of risk, although it focuses on interest rate risk and financial derivatives in particular. Risk management is a relatively modern business activity. Indeed, in his excellent book on the history of risk, *Against the Gods,* Peter L. Bernstein argues that the idea that risk can be controlled is one of the fundamental distinguishing features of modern times. The development of that idea, through much iteration, led to the modern discipline of financial risk management.

The ability to understand and manage risk liberated humanity from its early enthralment by the oracles and soothsayer of the distant past. People ranging from gamblers through mathematicians and philosophers to psychologists and economists participated in that remarkable intellectual adventure. The results of that great journey are now available to us in the form of the powerful tools of risk management that were developed. These special and powerful tools of risk management are modern financial derivatives.

As it happened though, the idea of containing risk came to be identified more and more with managing the risks associated with investments and banking. It thus came about that the modern body of knowledge concerning the measurement, quantification and control of risk developed from needs arising from and questions concerning the expected returns on investment as well as the specific needs of investment bankers.

In the process of these developments, sight was often lost of the need that every business has of managing the risks it faces in its daily operations. Indeed, there is an influential body of opinion arguing that risk management is not a relevant activity at corporate level at all. This debate will be considered in more detail in a following chapter.

In non-financial business life as such, the risks incurred usually have very little to do with investment as such. Normally, the risks faced by businesses will be due to the nature of their activities such as buying, selling, borrowing, manufacturing, transporting and the like. The risks faced by businesses in the non-financial sector thus tend to relate more to adverse moves in the prices of commodities, adverse changes in interest rates and changes in the relative value of foreign exchange rates. They are also subject to the vicissitudes of supply and demand in the market for the goods and/or services they use and produce. Nevertheless, many non-financial businesses also invest, often quite substantially.

The modern techniques of risk management are equally applicable to non-financial businesses as to investment bankers and fund managers. The techniques are somewhat adapted for non-financial businesses in practice, but remain the same in essence and in principle. Their relevance is not restricted to the extent that non-financial businesses might engage in investing, but they address the very roots of their daily business activities.

THE SCOPE AND PURPOSE OF THE BOOK

This book is written as a practical guide for businesspeople who are not investment bankers or fund managers. The ultimate purpose is to make the use of financial derivatives a viable option for every businessperson to manage interest rate risk. Due to the mentioned historic development of risk management as a discipline, it represents a skill that is often not readily available outside of the large corporate and investment banking sectors.

As previously stated, the focus of the discussion in this book is the management of interest rate risk. Interest rates constitute a subject of such immense scope that certain limitations have to be imposed in order to serve and achieve the specific purposes of the book. Thus, in order to avoid raising expectations that cannot be met, it might well be easier to first spell out what is not the scope of the book, rather than what is.

The fundamental approach has been that this book is neither a primer nor an advanced text on the subject of interest rates as such. Extremely good and competent books already serve that purpose admirably. Although this book is intended as a practical guide to the non-specialist in finance, it will assume a certain basic knowledge and understanding of interest rates, as it must. Nevertheless, some fundamental concepts, practices and terms of the money markets, which may not be as well known to the uninitiated, will be mentioned and briefly discussed. The guiding principle throughout is, however, to keep things as simple and accessible as possible.

The purpose is further confined inasmuch as it is intended to demonstrate how interest rate risk can be managed using modern financial derivative instruments. This purpose has a very definite impact on the treatment of the subject and the range of issues discussed.

THE METHODOLOGY

Methodology must perforce follow purpose. Whereas there are very many fine books that discuss financial derivatives in great depth and detail, a similar discussion will not serve present purposes. Many businesspeople associate the subject of financial derivatives with highly developed and extremely involved mathematics. Such a view is indeed correct, as is shown by many books on the subject. However, the high-level math will not be dealt with in this book, for the reasons discussed hereunder.

The concern of this book differs somewhat from the concern of most derivatives textbooks. As mentioned previously, the present concern is rather with the needs of risk management in non-financial business concerns than with investment management normally associated with financial institutions. Interesting and essential as the mathematics of modern portfolio management theory may be, the vast majority of businesses outside the financial and investment sectors will seldom, if ever, need to use them. In the light of the usual mathematical treatment of this subject, the latter statement is in need of some explanation and motivation.

In order to deal with this question, it is necessary to examine and understand the reasons for the maths. The high mathematics associated with derivatives have a two-fold purpose: firstly to determine the overall size or value of the risk (risk quantification) and secondly to calculate the correct price of the derivative that would mirror that risk. This is a direct result of the requirements of investment banking. A bank will write a derivative instrument, for instance to meet the requirements of its client. However, the derivative that has just been written exposes the bank to risk. It must immediately set off that risk in the market, by creating a hedging derivative instrument. The ability to do this successfully requires a very keen knowledge of the marketplace as well as the ability to measure the risk of such an instrument very precisely. Then the instrument must be priced very accurately, or the bank will be unable to show a profit on the deal.

A non-financial company merely trying to manage the interest rate risk encountered in the course of its ordinary business should not have this type of problem. The methodology adopted in this book is thus intended to demonstrate that uncomplicated approaches to risk management with derivatives are possible for mid-size and smaller corporations, and even for large corporations. Safe and effective risk management in the non-financial sector can be a much simpler and much more straightforward process than many generally believe.

The discussions and examples in this book will therefore primarily deal with the management of single transactions involving interest rate risk. For most businesses, it will be adequate and beneficial to treat and deal with each of its borrowing or cash investment transactions as a separate risk. It will be suggested that even when a portfolio of interest rate risks is held by a non-financial company, it might be better served by treating each exposure separately. The 'portfolio of derivative instruments' that might be created in this way does not require to be treated separately as a portfolio of risks, since each derivative will be matched to another risk which mirrors it.

Some non-financial companies have such vast exposures and use interest rate derivatives to manage those exposures to such an extent that they actually qualify as market makers for certain derivatives. They need the same expertise as would be found in any investment bank. This is very different from the situation faced by more than 90% of non-financial firms.

A further determinant of the methodology adopted is the intention of being a practical guide to managing interest rate risk. Thus, this book seeks to explain and discuss the principles involved in managing interest rate risk more than the actual detail. There is so much detail in the vast field of interest rates that one might easily be lead astray, eventually losing sight of the wood for the abundance of trees. Not that the discussions will lack detail in clarifying and illustrating the principles discussed – they will be properly detailed and worked.

There are however too many interest rates and permutations thereof to be covered in this book. It is thus only practical to deal with the major interest rates, especially US money market and Eurodollar rates. Readers' indulgence is therefore requested should the particular set of interest rates applying to their situation not be dealt with. The principles dealt with apply to all rates. Derivatives can be engineered to deal with those rates also. Rates not mentioned or dealt with herein can be managed along exactly the same lines as those that are mentioned and detailed. The principles of managing interest rate risk are constant without regard to the exact interest rates or country where they are found.

The two facets of risk quantification and derivatives pricing are discussed hereunder in some detail in order to afford the reader a better understanding of the reasons for the methodology adopted in this book.

RISK MANAGEMENT AND RISK QUANTIFICATION

It stands to reason that before a risk can be properly managed, one must know how big it is. The risk must thus be quantified before it can be handled. The problem with the quantification of risk lies in modelling the total behaviour of a risk relative to an index or some other benchmark. Modern portfolio theory deals primarily with the risk characteristics of a basket, or portfolio of risks.

Modern risk quantification really starts with one Harry Markowitz. In 1959, he followed his original 1952, 14-page article titled *Portfolio Selection*, with a full-length book titled *Portfolio Selection: Efficient Diversification of Investments*. He was the first person to formalise the trite notion that not putting all of one's eggs in a single basket is a good idea. He then applied that good idea to financial instruments. His main point was really that the risk of holding a basket of securities is an entirely different matter from the risk of holding each of the separate securities in the basket. The whole does not equal the sum of the parts and he demonstrated why that would be so. Some more attention will be given to this matter in a later chapter.

However, without putting too fine a point on it at this stage, Markowitz can be summarised by the statement that he demonstrated that portfolio diversification lessened the totality of the risk of holding the portfolio: whence the title *Portfolio Selection*. The works of researchers such as Sharpe, Lintner, Ross and many others developed the ideas of Markowitz further. They presented the world with ideas on the quantification of risk and the tools with which it might be managed. As the ideas developed, so the mathematics became increasingly involved.

In order to demonstrate this proposition, consider a company that has borrowed money. Assume that it has not only borrowed money, but it also has investments in different stocks, further borrowings in foreign currency and owns inventories of different metals. The question of risk quantification now resolves itself into what the total value is that the company stands to lose over any given period. Some analysts would use the capital asset pricing model (CAPM) and others the arbitrage pricing model (APM) to resolve the issue. Others would argue that the question is really, what the value at risk (VAR) of the company is over any given period.

Many analysts would argue, with good reason, that none of these models is applicable to non-financial corporations where substantial illiquid assets generally form part of the total asset portfolio. Under such circumstances, many of the results of these models may be irrelevant at best and dangerously misleading at worst. Nevertheless, it is only when the question of the quantity at risk is answered that it will be possible to model a derivative that would mirror the behaviour of the total portfolio under the same market conditions.

As against the Markowitz proposition, it is straightforward to quantify any one particular risk on its own. Assume the above company borrowed $1,000,000. If the interest on the loan is at a fixed rate for its life, no direct interest rate risk is incurred. Indirectly however, the borrower will be in a worse position should interest rates decline, since it will be paying more for the loan than the value of the money borrowed as indicated by the rate of interest at that time. If the loan is at a floating rate, the borrower will be at risk of a rise in interest rates. Although the then higher market rate will be paid, the loan will be more expensive and will impact negatively on the cash flow of the company as well as its profit margins.

Whether one is concerned with the direct interest rate risk or the indirect one, the amount at risk remains the same. What then would be the measure of that risk? In this simple case, the measure would be the percentage change in the interest rate based on a capital of $1,000,000. The index or benchmark rate against which the risk would be measured would be the interest rate used at the time of the loan. To model a derivative that mirrors that risk is quite simple. This will be demonstrated in later chapters as each interest rate derivative is discussed.

It is at this stage that the parting of the ways comes for the purposes of this book. As was previously stated, the book is primarily intended for use by non-financial firms and businesses. Some businesses may of course be involved in a number of transactions, all of which exposes them to interest rate risk. It may well be that many such businesses are not exposed to the same interest rates on each transaction. Thus, a certain amount of diversification might exist inside such a business' portfolio of borrowings and investments.

The main point is however, that a business that incurs interest rate risk as a matter of course in the pursuit of its ordinary business activities does not have the luxury of portfolio selection. It would be short-sighted to borrow or lend money solely in order to balance a company's portfolio of interest rate risks. A business must borrow or invest money because that is what is required by its core business, not because its present interest rate risk portfolio requires it. After all, no sane manager is going to borrow $1,000,000 because the company could use another $1,000,000 exposure to 6-month Libor (London inter-bank offered rate).

It cannot be denied that a company with a very large number of transactions involving interest rate risk can be said to have a portfolio of interest rate risk. Although the word 'portfolio' actually refers to paper assets (L. *portare-* to carry + L. *foglio-* sheet or leaf), contracts such as those of borrowing and lending can be construed as paper assets and liabilities. There is therefore no reason in principle why such a portfolio could not be diversified and thus 'balanced out' by means of interest rate derivatives. However, as will be evident from the discussion in the following chapters, derivative instruments are not really used for portfolio diversification. They are used for the more direct approach to risk management that they make possible, namely the hedging of risks.

Obviously, a portfolio of risks can be hedged. Once the portfolio's value at risk has been determined as well as the variance and covariance of its performance as measured against some desired benchmark, a derivative instrument can be designed to hedge the portfolio. Very few non-financial firms require such sophisticated treatment of its risks. Indeed, some very enlightening research has been done, demonstrating that this type of risk management is virtually never undertaken in the non-financial sector. There is thus no need to burden this book with the abstruse mathematics required. Once the basic principles discussed herein are understood and practised, a person wishing to conquer the heights of stochastic calculus will find many excellent books to guide such an expedition.

THE ROLE OF PRICING DERIVATIVES

The second facet that requires involved mathematics, is the need to price derivatives correctly. Derivatives are paper assets that carry risk. Because they are assets, they have value. Like all items of value, market forces determine their value. In this respect, derivatives do not differ from other assets. The real difference between derivatives and other assets is that derivatives have no inherent value of their own. They derive their value from some other asset. The asset from which a derivative derives its value is known as the underlying. It is the asset underlying the derivative. Every derivative instrument is created with a particular underlying asset. The underlying is its whole reason for existence. For the purposes of this book, the underlying will always be a currency and the value will relate to a rate of exchange between a pair of currencies. This concept will become clearer as the discussion progresses.

Since a derivative's value is derived from the value of some other asset, it stands to reason that the value of a particular derivative must be linked to the value of its underlying. The problem in pricing a derivative is that its value is not equal to the value of its underlying. The value of the underlying is only one of the elements that determine the value, or price, of a derivative instrument.

Before Messrs. Fisher Black and Myron Scholes presented the world with their option pricing model in the May/June issue of *The Journal of Political Economy* in 1973, derivatives were valued by gut feeling and seat of the pants calculations. Their model for pricing options was soon developed and expanded to include models for the pricing of every possible derivative. Once derivatives could be confidently priced, the way was open for general trading in financial derivatives. Their seminal work thus allowed the explosion in derivatives trading to take place.

Because derivatives are in essence contracts, they always involve at least two parties who act as counterparties to each other. Derivatives are traded on public exchanges and in private deals. Realistic pricing is obviously the key to finding two parties who are willing to contract. Once there is confidence that real value is reflected in the price of a product, it will be accepted in the market place.

In the public markets or exchanges, counterparties are obviously found in the same way that buyers and sellers are found in any public auction situation. All financial exchanges are really locations for regular public auctions. Buyers and sellers come to the market because they know that they will be able to trade there at the current market price.

However, derivatives do not trade only on public exchanges. An extremely large market exists for derivatives that are bought and sold 'over the counter' (OTC). OTC derivatives developed because the particular risks faced by many clients wishing to risk manage their positions will often be unique and specific for an appropriate derivative to be found on a public exchange. A derivative with the appropriate specifications will then have to be designed in order to meet the particular need. Since these derivatives are so specific, where will counterparties be found?

The short answer is that banks and brokers are usually approached under these circumstances. Either they will be able to find another company with opposite needs, or they will themselves assume the role of counterparty. They will do so for a fee, or to receive a bid/offer spread. That means that banks and brokers will lend at a higher rate of interest than they are prepared to borrow or to take in deposits. That difference is known as the bid/offer spread. Because not all banks are the same, different banks will price the same derivative differently. It will therefore pay the user to shop around when dealing in OTC derivatives.

Banks and money brokers can afford to take on these risks as speculators because they can diversify their risk. They can select risks from a large database of customers with differing requirements. Investing in paper assets is what their business is all about. It is therefore essential for such institutions and persons to be able to assess their total risk exposure accurately and to price their derivatives correctly, because their core business requires them to do so.

Looking at the situation from the point of view of business management, which is the point of departure for this book, a different scenario presents itself. Although it is always an advantage to be able to calculate what good value would be for whatever it is that one is trading, one is bound to either accept the market price or not to trade at all. This is the essence of what buyers and sellers do in the marketplace. It does not matter whether the transaction is done on a public exchange or privately with a bank. One's alternatives remain the same: accept the price or don't trade at all.

The concern of a risk manager does not lie in buying and selling the derivative for the sake of profit. Her only concern must be to weigh the price she is being asked to pay for the derivative against the value of the risk she intends to manage. Not trading at all will therefore have very different consequences for the risk-manager than for the speculator. Her question resolves itself into what the consequences will be if she does not manage her interest rate risk, versus overpaying (in terms of a pricing model) for the derivative. On the other hand, the effective markets theory suggests that the market price of a product is always the correct price, whatever it may be.

Treasurers, financial and other business managers are quite capable of making that decision without resorting to a calculation of the price of the derivative. For the purposes of the practical use of currency derivatives in managing currency risk it is thus neither essential nor necessarily desirable to digress into the mathematics of pricing derivatives. However, there are extremely good textbooks on this question for the benefit of those readers who wish to master that particular element of derivatives.

STRUCTURE OF THE BOOK

The structure adopted for the book is thus to start off, in Chapter 1, with a discussion of all the basic concepts involved in managing interest rate risk. This covers a discussion of the nature and general characteristics of interest rate risk and its derivatives. Chapter 2 deals with the general principles of interest rate risk management. This chapter is intended to serve as an introduction to the subject matter of the book and to give a general overview of material that is to be dealt with in greater detail in later chapters.

Chapter 3 will discuss the value of managing interest rate risk at corporate level followed by a discussion of interest rate risk management strategies. Each following chapter will be devoted to the discussion of one particular interest rate derivative, illustrated with fully worked examples of how they are used to manage the risk. In discussing each derivative, no reliance will be placed upon any prior knowledge on the part of the reader. The purpose is to make the material as accessible as possible to everybody, while at the same time giving sufficient explanation, information and detail as to be of value even to the knowledgeable reader. Since the overall purpose is practical guidance, use will be made of case studies and examples of the practical applications of each currency derivative.

Each chapter is devised as a stand-alone unit. This structure enables the reader who is familiar with certain currency derivatives, but not with others, to ignore familiar material and to concentrate only on more unfamiliar ones. This also offers the advantage that the reader can use the book to dip into from time to time to refresh the memory or perhaps simply to obtain some stimulation for creative problem solving. Nevertheless, it must also be emphasised that the book is specifically designed as one that can be read through from the first page to the last. This may prove to be an advantage to those readers who have no previous knowledge and are new to risk management techniques involving financial derivatives.

Chapter 7 deals with various strategies that can be employed with derivative instruments to reduce the direct cost of risk management and also some profit retention strategies that are compatible with sound risk management. They will be related to the strategies that are available using particular interest rate derivatives and combinations thereof. In Chapter 8, specific interest rate risk situations will be dealt with. Some common as well as some uncommon business situations involving interest rate risk and their possible handling will be examined and analysed.

Some appropriate risk management strategies will be suggested and demonstrated for each situation. The purpose thereof is not to prescribe solutions to particular problems, but rather to demonstrate and encourage some creative thinking in the use of interest rate derivatives

Interest rate derivatives is one of the fastest growing areas of finance. New ones are being invented almost daily. It will be a worthwhile investment for any manager or company to keep a close watch on these developments. Every innovation is made to address some situation not adequately addressed previously or to improve on the risk management possibilities of existing instruments. It is an area of development ignored at a company's peril.

one

interest rate risk, interest rate derivatives and the management function

INTRODUCTION

The ideal of every financial analyst is to find some interest rate model or system that explains but especially one that forecasts the behaviour of interest rates. Alas, none presently do so. That is not to say that interest rate behaviour cannot be explained. Various historical, political and economic factors explain some of the behaviour of interest rates over history. However, all that can be said with certainty is that the behaviour of interest may vary quite significantly over time.

Interest rates can be seen to fluctuate from day-to-day and intra-day. Not only do they fluctuate continuously, changes of interest rate regimes also occur over time. This can be demonstrated by observing, for example, the behaviour of 3-month Libor (London Inter-Bank Offered Rate) over the last decade of the previous century. The rate fluctuated around 15% between the end of 1989 and the end of 1990 before shifting down to fluctuate around 10–11% between September 1991 and September 1992. Thereafter the rate drifted downward, levelled off and started drifting upward from September 1994. In between, spikes occurred in the rate that went as high as 14%, while sterling overnight rates went as high as 150%.

The implications are clear. Corporations and businesses with debt can rely only on uncertainty as far as their payment schedule and cost of funds are concerned. Investors with portfolios of bonds will also have to manage their risk in order to protect the value of their investments. Managers have to learn very quickly how to cope with this constant volatility in interest rates that greatly complicate and hamper the successful conduct of business.

FUNDAMENTALS OF INTEREST RATE RISK

Interest rate risk is the risk to a person or business that interest rates may change adversely given the individual's or business' exposure to such rates. Adverse in this sense is obviously a relative term. What constitutes an adverse change for the borrower will constitute a favourable change for the lender/investor and *vice versa*.

A person or a firm is exposed to interest rate risk when that person or firm has either lent or borrowed money. However, that only deals with direct interest rate risk. One may also face indirect interest rate risk, such as when interest rates change substantially, they tend to affect the prices of goods and products as well. Interest rates also determine the available amount of money in the economy. This is the much-vaunted money supply, which can be manipulated through adjusting interest rates. Because of the impact interest rates have on economic activity as a whole, it has always been a favourite tool of governments and reserve banks by which to steer the economy.

economic impact of interest rates

It might be appropriate at this stage to take note of the ever-present danger of assuming things will always remain as they are and have been for a long time. Interest rates have always been an important tool of economic policy, but that does not mean that they will remain so. At least one economist, James W. Paulsen, chief investment officer at Wells Capital Management in Minneapolis at the time of writing, is of the opinion that things have already changed. He is reported in the *New York Times* of March 25, 2001 as having come to the conclusion that the Federal Reserve's two major policy tools may not be as effective today as they have been over the last 40 years.

He has made a study of the economic impact that these two interest rate related tools have had on the US economy over the last 40 years. According to the *New York Times* report, the study has led him to the conclusion that, after 1990, the relationship between real economic growth and changes in the money supply and the Federal Reserve funds rate has virtually disappeared. Apparently, this has to do with the increasingly dominant role of technology in the economy.

While interest rates hugely affect on the fortunes of big borrowers, such as manufacturing concerns, car and home buyers, technology companies and their consumers are apparently not so dependant on borrowings. Rather, their success has everything to do with new product introductions, he is reported as saying. The report also quotes Mr. Paulsen as saying that 'although the Federal Reserve (of the US) traditionally has had strong influence on the economic cycle, this (study) suggests that coincident with the substantial growth in the technology sector, the Federal Reserve's ability to manage the economy has been greatly reduced'.

If Mr. Paulsen's conclusions prove to be correct, this development will have far-reaching implications for interest rate risk. It might mean greater interest rate volatility, or it might translate into a more continuous market harbouring less volatility. It could also impose further stresses and strains on the international economy as the factors influencing the US economy start diverging substantially from less technology driven economies. Only time will tell what the actual effects will be. All that can be said with certainty is that things will change. Thus, vigilance is strongly advised.

FINANCIAL DERIVATIVES

Interest rate derivatives form part of the class of financial instruments known as financial derivatives. As such, they share the vital characteristics of other financial derivatives. They have been developed and adapted especially to serve the specific needs of managing interest rate risk. Since these derivatives must be viewed within the context of financial derivatives as a whole, a brief discussion of financial derivatives follows.

derivative fundamentals

In the modern world of financial derivative instruments, the essential idea underlying the concept is that one can buy and sell all the risk of an underlying asset without trading the asset itself. Thus, instead of investing in a 30-year US Treasury bond, one can buy a US Treasury bond futures contract on the Chicago Board of Trade (CBOT).

Buying the futures contract will allow one to enjoy the same profit, if bond prices rose, or suffer the same losses, should they decline, that one would have done had one owned such bonds to the same face value. In addition, the advantage would be that the trade would be leveraged by margin, thus avoiding the outlay of capital that would have been required to actually purchase the bond. All this will become clearer as the discussion progresses.

Any financial derivative is a paper instrument that has no value of its own. It has a derived value, hence its name. Its value is derived from the value of its so-called underlying instrument or asset. An example of a derivative instrument is an option to purchase, say, a property. The value of the option is obviously determined by the value of the property in question. Of course, exactly how the value of the option will relate to the value of the property is a rather involved question, which is not relevant to the discussion now. It must be clear, however, that if the property were valueless, the option would be valueless also. Contrariwise, the more valuable the property, but subject to a number of factors, the greater the value of the option would be.

It is quite apparent that a property can have value by itself. However, an option has no value by itself. As such, an option without some underlying asset means nothing and consequently has no value. That is why it is an instrument with a derived value. It will be apparent from the discussion that follows that numbers of other instruments exist that have no value of their own, but only have a value derived from the value of some underlying asset or instrument.

Obviously, the underlying of the derivative need not be an asset such as property. It could be anything that has value, including a legal right such as stocks and bonds. In the case of interest rate derivatives, the underlying values are interest rates and the underlying instruments can be any one of a multitude of interest bearing instruments.

Having a derived value is not the only distinguishing element of a financial derivative. Another important element is that the underlying is never traded. Although the underlying can be traded indirectly or even directly as part of the outcome of a derivatives trade, the exchange of the underlying never forms part of the essence of the derivative itself. It is for this reason that currency swaps, for example, are not regarded as true derivative instruments. Nevertheless, they are treated by the financial markets as such.

the fear of derivatives

It might be as well to admit and address the fear of derivatives right at the outset. Although trading in derivatives is experiencing an exponential growth rate, there are still very many ordinary businesspeople who view them with suspicion. In fact, the term 'suspicion' may be a euphemism. In some quarters, 'derivatives' is a downright dirty word. This opprobrium is entirely undeserved.

A derivative instrument is in essence financial paper that creates risk. It creates risk in a number of ways, some risks being inherent in the paper itself and others being a product of the way the instrument has been put together. In order to make the explanation slightly clearer, one might say that the inherent risk in a derivative instrument is the risk that it is intended to create. For example, an interest rate swap is intended to create interest rate risk and a commodity option is intended to create commodity risk. Any derivative instrument is created and designed to create a particular financial risk.

The exact mechanics of how this is achieved in each type of derivative and to what purpose will be fully discussed in the chapters dealing with the different interest rate derivatives. Suffice it to say at this stage that no matter what particular interest rate derivative one holds, be it an interest rate swap, option or futures, that derivative holds interest rate risk for the holder. In essence then, the first thing that one must understand about all derivatives is that they are intended to carry risk, in the same way that ammunition carries both a bullet and an explosive charge in the cartridge. It is the explosive charge behind the bullet that makes it potentially deadly. A bullet without an explosive charge is not deadly, but it is useless as ammunition. So it is with a derivative: if it were not charged with risk, it would be totally useless as a tool of financial risk management.

Thus, like a charged bullet, the value or otherwise of a derivative lies in the way it is used. If it is used to play Russian roulette or if it is used negligently, you are going to hurt, maim or kill someone you love. However, if you use it properly in self-defence, it will protect from harm those whom you love. Don't fear the ammunition; fear the user.

Contrary to what many people believe, derivatives are not the new-fangled inventions of financial whiz kids. Derivatives, in one form or another, have been around for hundreds and sometimes even thousands of years. Indeed, options to purchase and options to sell were very well developed instruments of Roman law. During Mediaeval times, when the Church prohibited the charging of interest on loans since it viewed virtually all interest charges as usurious, merchants got around that by creating what were basically mortgage-linked annuities. These annuities, styled *censi* (*census* in the singular) resembled the modern market for interest rate swaps in their scope and variety. What is new is the combination of these instruments with the modern concept of risk management.

Of course, risk management is largely what derivatives have been about all these many ages, although it was not seen as risk management at the time. However, risk management in the modern sense has suddenly resulted in the exponential proliferation of derivatives. It was suddenly realised that these old instruments of commerce could be restructured, manipulated and compounded to suit the involved purposes of modern commerce. They could be structured to meet any set of particular circumstances, thus the explosion in their popularity and their often-confounding structural complexity.

So why do derivatives have such a bad reputation? It is simply because they've had such a bad press. The bad press resulted from, *inter alia*, the shocks and scandals of the Bärings Bank disaster, Proctor and Gamble's woes, as well as the German Metallgesellschaft AG and Gibson's Greetings cases. The shock and the bad press resulted not from the fact that things went wrong, but from the fact that things went so horribly wrong with such very respected and high profile companies. Strangely enough, when it appeared that their problems all originated from losses they sustained on derivative positions, derivatives were seen as the danger rather than the purposes to which they had been put and the manner of their use. The real problem was overlooked in favour of the more sensational story about the new evil that has come to dwell among men – derivatives trading.

Analysing those case studies is certainly beyond the scope of this book. Yet, it is significant for the idea of risk management using financial derivatives that an understanding is reached of what went wrong. Although the facts in each case differed greatly, they all had one common element. That element was speculation with derivatives.

Speculation, as is generally known and accepted, is the voluntary assumption of risk in the expectation of profit. That is in fact what all business is about. One can speculate on so many things: fixed property, stocks, bonds, metals and cattle, to name but a few. Buying any of the aforementioned with the purpose of selling them at a profit involves the risk of loss. Each of the items mentioned above is a risk-carrying asset. In fact, it would be hard to find any real asset that does not carry any financial risk. The price may go down and the speculator who bought it will make a loss. It is a fundamental principle of business that you cannot expect to make a large profit if you are not prepared to risk a loss.

Although there is the essential concept of the risk-free return on capital, there is alas, very few truly riskless investments in the real world. The potential profit and loss on any one transaction are not even necessarily of equal magnitude. A great part of the art of investing is to balance the positive value of the potential profit against the negative value of the risk run. This is known as the risk/return profile of the investment. A long and interesting history lies behind the search to place an objective value on the risk that could be appropriate given a particular expected return.

All of this serves only to state that a financial derivative is merely another risk carrying asset. If you speculate with derivatives, you run the risk of loss. Thus, investing in derivatives can be a valid business enterprise. However, if you own or manage another business, don't branch out into speculating with derivatives. That is essentially, what got these formerly mentioned companies into trouble. Instead of using derivatives to manage the risks incurred in the normal running of their core businesses, they started taking speculative positions in derivatives. They actually turned the Treasurer's office into a profit centre. If a company's guess or expectation of the market is wrong, it can sustain losses – very severe losses. Don't bet the business on market expectations, unless that is the business. If calling the market is not one's business, don't make a business out of doing that.

Financial derivatives therefore play an extremely important role in modern finance and business. Any firm, whatever its size, that withholds from making use of derivatives in managing the risks inherent in its business is doing itself a great disfavour. How to use the derivatives that have been especially designed to manage interest rate risk is the proper purpose of this book.

classes of derivatives

Financial derivatives may be classified in many ways. They can be classified with reference to the platforms from which they are traded, namely over the counter (OTC) or public exchange. They can also be classified, *inter alia*, according to whether they are long- or short-term instruments, or whether they concern future transactions or whether they are options on transactions.

Generally, two types of derivatives are distinguished: futures and options. This over-simplification may be confusing, since one of the derivatives falling into the first category is called futures contracts. Futures contracts are standardised contracts that trade on public exchanges.

Nevertheless, the classification is not without merit. It stresses the fact that a whole class of derivatives only consists of variations of the same basic idea, namely future transactions involving interest rates. The three instruments concerned are forward rate agreements interest rate futures contracts and interest rate swaps. They all represent the unconditional buying and selling of interest rate risks. The second class consists of option contracts on any one of these derivatives as well as on any other cash or spot interest rate instrument. This class of instrument represents the conditional buying and selling of interest rate risks.

The classification thus forces one to differentiate between spot and forward interest rates.

spot and forward interest rates

All markets consist of spot and forward markets. The single most important distinguishing feature between these two markets is that the spot market is for immediate delivery of whatever is traded, while the forward market is for delivery at an agreed future date. 'Immediate' is also a relative term. It does not precisely translate as 'on the spot'. There may be a delay in any transaction due to time constraints and other formalities that might take some time to settle. So, for example, a Libor rate settlement is accepted to take 2 days. That means that if a time deposit at 3-month Libor matures on December 16, actual receipt of the funds will take place on December 18.

Unless stated otherwise, interest rates reported in the financial press are spot interest rates. Forward rates are often also reported, but are clearly identified as such. As previously mentioned, an extremely wide array of interest rates are quoted in the media. Interest rates vary by the purposes for which the capital is sought to be borrowed (mortgages, vehicle financing, revolving credit), the credit standing of the borrower (prime rate, prime rate minus, prime rate plus) and the period for which it is required (overnight, 1 month, 1 year, 30 years). The reader will be well aware that the above examples do not even scratch the surface of the numerous variations and permutations of available interest rates. Nevertheless, the one common element of all these rates is that they are quoted for spot transactions. They are quoted as being available from a particular supplier if the money is borrowed now.

As opposed to spot transactions, another possibility also exists. Very often, if not usually, a person or a business will know beforehand that a loan will be required at some future time. What will that money cost to borrow in say, 3 months time? That question leads on to interest rate risk management and interest rate derivatives.

INTEREST RATE DERIVATIVES

forward rate agreements (fras)

The market for forward rate agreements was developed in the early 1980s in response to the needs of banks and their large corporate customers to hedge against future movements in interest rates. Before this market was developed, such hedging could only be done by actual deposits, which inflated both the assets and the liabilities side of the balance sheet. It also required large sums to be tied up in deposits. FRAs provided a ready facility to achieve the same end without tying up large parts of the balance sheet.

Today, a very liquid market exists for FRAs. The market is centred in London, but it is active throughout the world. Like most interest rate derivatives it involves the concept of notional principal. The concept is essential since interest rates only have meaning when they are applied to a principal or capital sum of money.

❐ THE NOTIONAL PRINCIPAL

What was said regarding the fundamentals of derivatives at the beginning of the chapter might now become clearer. The principal amount of money involved in a derivative instrument is never traded. Thus, the principal to which a rate of interest is applied in an FRA is called the notional or nominal principal. The purpose is merely to arrive at a quantitative amount of interest.

In an FRA, two parties agree to a rate of interest that will be applied to a loan of money to be taken out in the future, for a period extending further into the future. There is no actual loan and the principal sum is thus notional. Both parties are merely seeking protection against an adverse change in interest rates, or perhaps one or both of them are speculating on their view of future movements in interest rates.

❐ THE FORWARD/FORWARD RATE

In simplified terms, the FRAs agreed rate of interest is calculated from the applicable spot interest rates, say 3- and 6-month Libor, and the result is known as the forward/forward rate, or simply as the forward rate. If the FRA is for a loan to be taken out in 3 months time for a period of 6 months, it will be called a 3 × 6 FRA. The settlement date of the FRA will usually be on the day the notional loan would have been taken out. The forward rate at which the FRA was agreed is compared at that date with the 6-month Libor rate. If that Libor rate is higher than the FRA rate, the notional lender will pay the difference to the borrower and *vice versa*.

All of this will be explained in detail in Chapter 3. However, the concept of the forward rate is an important one when dealing with interest rate derivatives, since it is also encountered in the following derivative instrument – the interest rate futures contract.

interest rate futures

Interest rate futures contracts are standardised contracts that trade on exchanges such as the Chicago Mercantile Exchange (CME), the London International and Financial

Futures Exchange (LIFFE), the Chicago Board of Trade (CBOT) as well as many others. Since their introduction on the CME in 1972, the market has grown exponentially. Today, a vast array of futures contracts allows managers to manage interest rate risks ranging from 1 day to 10 years into the future.

One of the differences between contracts offered on different exchanges is that minor users can select those that meet their particular needs best. Like all derivative instruments, futures have an underlying interest rate instrument. As mentioned in the discussion on FRAs, the underlying cannot be an interest rate as such. While an FRA has a notional amount of principal linked to a selected interest rate as its underlying, futures contracts have a particular number of interest rate instruments that trade in the spot market as their underlying. Examples of such instruments are US Treasury bills, 5-year US Treasury notes, Eurodollar time deposits and 30-year US Treasury bonds.

◻   ESSENTIALS OF FUTURES CONTRACTS

A futures contract is really a standardised, exchange traded FRA. The major feature of a futures contract is that it is a standardised commitment where the essential terms of the agreement are prescribed by the exchange on which the contract trades. The essential terms of an interest rate futures contract are:

- The underlying instrument, i.e. a time deposit, Treasury bill, Treasury note, bond or the like. The description will be very specific stating the issuer (US Treasury, Mexican par Brady Bond), the maturity period (3-month maturity, 1-month maturity, 13-week maturity), and the face value at maturity ($1,000,000, $3,000,000).
- The price quote protocol, e.g. prices may be quoted in points where one point is shown as 0.01 equalling $25.00 given the notional principal of the contract;
- The delivery date, i.e. the date on which the notional investment or borrowing will start, but this is generally referred to as the contract month or the futures expiration date.
- The delivery mechanism – in most cases the contracts are cash settled, although there are contracts where specified issues of the underlying bill or note can be delivered.

The standardised terms detailed above are by no means exhaustive. Futures contracts typically contain many more terms than those stated. The full terms and conditions of every futures contract are published by the exchanges on which they trade. It is advisable to examine these terms and conditions before entering futures trades. Many exchanges have extremely helpful websites on which full contract details may be found.

In order to trade successfully on a public exchange, which operates as an auction, there can only be one variable in the contract, namely the price. All other terms and conditions must of necessity be prescribed. It may seem strange to refer to an interest rate as a price, but the easiest way to structure a futures contract is to create a price for it. This is the reason why most interest rate futures are quoted in terms of a points system as indicated above. The points quoted for a contract is referred to as its price and an interest rate is implied by the points. The system is in fact quite simple.

In a points system, a futures contract is considered to have 100% of its face value if interest rates were zero. The interest rate is then regarded as a discount from full value. Thus, if such a futures contract is quoted at 94.46, an interest rate of 5.54% is implied. It follows naturally that the price of a futures contract will react inversely to interest rates. If the interest rate rises, the price of the contract declines and when the rate of interest declines, the contract price rises. This has important implications for taking positions in interest rate futures. The matter is fully discussed in Chapter 4.

☐ PRICE DISCOVERY IN FUTURES TRADING

The points value of a contract is agreed upon by means of bids and offers on an open outcry exchange as in any auction. On electronic exchanges, bids and offers are broadcast to exchange members on-line in an electronic auction. All trading then takes place electronically. Most exchanges in the world offer regular trading hours (RTH) and after hours trading (AHT). RTH is conducted by open outcry and AHT is done electronically.

☐ CONTRACT MONTHS

Futures contracts trade with cyclical expiration dates. In the case of interest rates, they typically trade in quarterly cycles, but some interest rate futures have monthly expirations. The expiration dates of these contracts always fall on a regular business day of the expiration month, such as the last Friday, or the third Wednesday or the seventh last business day of the month in question.

☐ MARGIN ACCOUNTS

Whereas FRAs are done on credit, futures trades are done against a margin account. Futures contracts are 'marked to market' daily. This means that the value of every futures position is adjusted to reflect its value at the price of the futures contract at the end of each trading day. Thus, between the date that the futures trade is done and the expiration date of the contract, gains and losses on futures positions are settled in cash on a daily basis.

The cash settlement is achieved by debiting losses against the losing position holder's margin account and crediting the gains to the gaining position holder's margin account. The losing position holder must then top-up her margin account to the minimum level required by the exchange. Through the mechanism of margin, credit risk is thus all but eliminated from futures trading. Also, by means of this daily process of 'marking to market,' the sum of all the daily profits and losses will equal the net change in the futures price over the life of the contract.

☐ THE FORWARD RATE AND THE FUTURES PRICE

There is obviously a relationship between the spot interest rate, the FRA rate and the implied interest rate of the futures price for the same periods. One might expect the forward rate and the futures rate to be equal for equal periods into the future and they do approximate each other. However, they are not necessarily identical. Small differences in the rates will be apparent from time to time, due to certain influences that prevail in the futures markets, but do not prevail in the forward exchange markets.

☐   CONCLUSION ON INTEREST RATE FUTURES

In summary, it can be stated that futures are undoubtedly one of the most effective and straightforward risk management alternatives available on the money markets. It is a highly liquid instrument that trades on well-established exchanges. It is easy to enter and liquidate positions and the whole process is transparent. It eliminates counterparty credit risk as well as legal risk.

The downside is, however, that because contracts trade in fixed quantities, contract sizes will seldom equate to the capital amounts of the interest rate exposures being hedged. This quantitative disparity creates basis risk. Basis risk is a lesser risk than naked interest rate risk, but it does influence the effectiveness of the tool marginally. These matters will receive greater attention in Chapter 4.

interest rate swaps

The swap market is the fastest growing financial market in the world. As with FRAs, the swap market really took off during the early 1980s. The currency swap market started first, but the concept was soon applied to interest rates and later also to commodities. As was previously mentioned, there is some disagreement between the market and academics whether currency swaps can be regarded as true derivative instruments. However, it will be demonstrated that interest rate swaps are true derivative instruments in every sense of the word. Today, the interest rate swap market has overtaken currency swaps and outstrips the combined market for currency swaps and interest rate options.

This is also borne out by a 1995 survey undertaken by the Weiss Centre for International Financial Research at the Wharton School of the University of Pennsylvania. The survey was undertaken to determine the usage of derivative instruments among non-financial corporations in the US at that time. It was found that 83% of companies making use of derivatives make use of swaps to manage their interest rate risk. This does not of course mean that these companies use swaps exclusively for managing their interest rate risk. Nevertheless, it underscores the importance of interest rate swaps in managing interest rate risk for non-financial companies.

☐   THE FUNDAMENTALS OF INTEREST RATE SWAPS

At their core, all swaps are essentially an exchange of periodic cash flows. That is the prime purpose and distinguishing feature of swap transactions. It distinguishes them from the two other previously discussed derivatives, both of which essentially relate to single cash flow transactions. The exchanged cash flows of all swaps are based on some notional principal or asset, which forms part of the exchange arrangement.

Like all true derivative instruments, interest rate swaps thus have notional principal as its underlying value. This arrangement conceptually involves a loan and a deposit. The first party borrows a principal amount from the second party. As a consequence, the first party must pay interest on the loan to the second party. Simultaneously, the first party deposits the same amount of money with the second party as an investment for precisely the same period as the loan. The second party must now pay interest on the investment to the first party. The net result is obviously that no principal actually changes hands either at the start or at the end of the transaction. The principal remains in the hands of the second party at all times. The principal is thus notional.

What remains is the obligation that each party has to pay interest to the other party for the agreed period of the swap. It must be obvious that the two interest rate payments cannot be the same. Otherwise, the whole exercise would be pointless. Thus, the most common arrangement is that one party pays a fixed rate of interest while the other party pays a floating rate, usually, but not necessarily, 6-month Libor. It may also be that two floating interest rates are used, such that the one party pays 3-month Libor, while the other party pays 6-month Libor. While the possible permutations are endless, it is apparent that such arrangements create interest rate risk.

Exactly how such swap arrangements are employed to manage interest rate risk in a business will be fully discussed, illustrated and analysed in Chapter 5.

interest rate options

An option is an agreement between two parties giving one party (the option buyer) either the right, but not the obligation, to buy the underlying asset from the other party (the option seller, giver or writer), or the right to sell the underlying asset to the option giver at an agreed price. An option gives the right either to buy or to sell the underlying asset, never both rights simultaneously. Once the option buyer has bought the option, he/she is then said to be the holder of the option.

An option giving the right to buy the underlying asset is known as a call option, while an option giving the right to sell the underlying is called a put option. Interest rate options have interest rate related instruments as their underlying. The instrument may be a bond or a note, a bill, an interest rate or an interest rate related futures contract.

☐   THE OPTION PREMIUM

The buyer of the option pays a premium in return for the rights granted. The option writer receives the premium and gets to keep it. The effect, to be explained in greater detail later, is that the buyer of an option has the potential of unlimited gain on the option, while no more than the premium paid for the option can be lost. The option writer, on the other hand, has a potentially unlimited loss on the option and cannot gain more than the premium received.

The correct premium of an option was one of the great outstanding problems in finance until Messrs. Fisher Black and Myron Scholes initially solved the problem in 1973. The problem did not relate to options only, there was great difficulty also in pricing other derivatives, such as swaps. Only after the basic pricing problem had been solved could options and swaps be traded generally, thus becoming the powerful risk management tools that are known today. The premium not only reflects the price of the option at the time that it is created, it actually reflects the value of the option at any time during its life. Thus, it was a major undertaking to develop a model that would explain price behaviour at any time throughout the life of an option.

The foregoing cannot detract from the fact that option premiums, as are the prices of all other instruments, are determined by supply and demand in the market place. Thus, although option-pricing models greatly advanced the understanding of the factors influencing premiums, the market mechanism has the final say. This is because, in any price model, there is plenty of room for disagreement about the assumptions being incorporated in the model. Pricing options thus remain more of an art than a science. The basic factors that influence the value of an option are discussed below.

☐   THE STRIKE PRICE

Although the option premium is the price of the option and reflects its value from time to time, there is also another price involved in options. It is known as the strike or exercise price of the option. The strike price of an option must be clearly distinguished from the premium paid for the option. While the option premium is the price paid for the option itself, the strike price of the option is the price at which the underlying asset can be bought or sold by the option holder. In the case of an interest rate option, the 'price' will be the price of the underlying bond, futures contract or the rate of interest on a time deposit.

The strike price is also referred to as the exercise price of the option. When the right granted by the option is taken up by the holder, the holder is said to exercise the option. An option ceases to exist when it is exercised.

☐   OPTION EXERCISE AND MATURITY

It is an immutable characteristic of all options that they have a limited life span. This means that the rights granted by the option must be exercised within an agreed upon period of time or they lapse. There is no such thing as an indefinite period option; they all have an expiration date. The expiration date is also referred to as the option's maturity date and the time left to expiration is consequently known as the time to maturity.

It must be obvious that since the holder of the option has a right but not an obligation to take a certain action, the position of the counterparty to the option remains uncertain for the life of the option. The counterparty virtually lives at the behest of the option holder. Nobody would tolerate such a situation indefinitely. The period of validity of an option and the time left to its expiry at any particular moment are consequently important elements in determining its value.

An option's life can thus be ended in one of two ways: through its exercise or by the passage of time. The way in which options can be exercised also play a very important role in their value. Briefly, there are two exercise styles to options: American and European. An American style option can be exercised on any business day during the period of the option. A European style option can only be exercised on the expiry day of the option. The greatest numbers of OTC options are European style options, while options on futures are mostly American.

☐   OPTION PRICE AND THE PRICE OF THE UNDERLYING

Although this book is not intended to introduce the reader to the mathematics of option pricing, it is important to understand which factors influence option values and how they basically interact. Throughout the foregoing discussion, mention has been made of factors that have an influence on the price of an option, such as strike price, time to maturity and exercise style. The one outstanding element that has not yet been discussed fully is the price of the underlying. It was mentioned earlier that the value of any derivative is by definition influenced by the value of its underlier. This is especially true in the case of options, the relationship of which will now be given some attention.

For the purpose of gaining a basic understanding of the working of options, it is necessary to understand that an option may be in the money (ITM), at the money (ATM), or out of the money (OTM). These three conditions, along with a number of other factors, bear a direct influence on the value (premium) of an option and play an important part in option selection for risk management purposes.

The three mentioned qualities refer to the relationship between the strike price of an option and the prevailing price of the underlying. In order to facilitate the explanation, an example from everyday life will be used.

Assume you wished to purchase a home. You find one that you like, but you are not so familiar with the area and the market that you are sure that the price is acceptable. Assume the seller offers the house at $250,000. You now negotiate an option to buy the house for $250,000. The option is for 1 week only. It is doubtful whether the seller of a home will demand a premium for such an option under those circumstances, so the matter of the option premium can be disregarded for the purpose of the explanation. Nevertheless, the option is clearly a call option with a time to expiry of 1 week and a strike of $250,000.

The underlying asset of the option is the house and the purchase of the house is the underlying transaction. The value of the underlying is the market value of that house in that place, at that time.

In the first iteration of the example, assume you investigate the property market in the area thoroughly and you conclude that the strike price of your call option is fair market value for the house. The price of the underlying is thus equal to the strike price of the option. Consequently, the option is ATM.

Now consider the second possibility. Your investigation shows that the strike price is below the market price. You could in fact immediately resell that house for $280,000. You have an option to buy at $250,000 and the price of the underlying is thus higher than the strike price of the option. You could make an immediate profit. The option is ITM by $30,000.

The third possibility is that your investigation uncovers that the price the seller wants is far too much. The true market price of the house is no more than $200,000. Again, you have an option to purchase, but this time at a price that is greater than the market value of the underlying. You will not want to exercise such an option and the chances that the market price will rise within the 1-week period of the option are almost zero. You will therefore most likely allow the option to expire. The problem is that the option is OTM by $50,000.

The example illustrates that a call option is OTM when the value of the underlying is lower than the strike price of the option. It is ATM when the value of the underlying is equal to the strike price of the option and it is ITM when the value of the underlying is greater than the strike price of the option. It is important to keep in mind that the situation described up to this point describes a call option. Matters are entirely opposite when a put option is considered.

Everybody wants to make a profit and in order to do so one has to buy low and sell high. A put option is an option to sell the underlying at a certain price (the strike). It follows that when the value of the underlying is lower than the strike price of the option you can sell the underlying immediately for a greater price (the strike price) than you can buy it on the open market. In other words, you can realise an immediate profit. The put option is then ITM. A put option is ATM when the strike of the option is equal to the value of the underlying. There is no change to the situation compared to a call option. However, a put option is OTM when the value of the underlying is greater than the strike price of the option.

All the principles discussed thus far apply to all options. They are therefore applicable also to interest rate options. There is however, a complication. The complication relates to the underlying value that the strike of an interest rate option has to be compared to in order to determine whether it is OTM, ATM, or ITM. Nevertheless, as the above example demonstrates, the principle remains that the option will be ITM, ATM or OTM relative to the price of its underlying. Thus, an exchange-traded option on futures must be viewed in terms of the current price of the futures contract. An option on an FRA must be evaluated in terms of the applicable forward rate while the strike of an option on a swap must be compared to the appropriate swap rate.

Option values are further considered in Chapter 6.

◻   OPTION TRADING PLATFORMS

Interest rate options are traded on two platforms: OTC and on futures exchanges. OTC interest rate options are reported to be the most liquid options in certain markets. According to the findings of the previously mentioned survey done under the auspices of the Weiss Center for International Financial Research, OTC options rank behind swaps as the most popular derivative instrument for managing interest rate exposure.

An exchange-traded interest rate option is really an option on a futures contract. Its underlying is not an interest rate transaction, but a long or short position in a particular interest rate related futures contract. The value of an option on futures thus derives its value from the value of a futures contract. Since the value of a futures contract is a derived value, it is not an overstatement to say that a futures interest rate option is in fact a derivative of a derivative.

This may sound quite complex, but options on futures are often simpler than OTC options. An option on futures consists of a single instrument with a fixed, predetermined expiration date, which is much simpler than the multiple expirations and compounded cash flows that can be encountered with some OTC options.

Ever since the introduction of options on futures, a debate has been raging about the relative merits of OTC options and exchange traded options. Each trading platform has its unique advantages and relative disadvantages. OTC options can be tailored to suit the needs of the user exactly. They are also usually available for longer maturities. By comparison, exchange traded options have standard sizes, strike prices and maturities and they are often not liquid for more than 1 year forward.

On the other hand, options on futures are easily tradable while it is usually not as easy to resell an OTC option. One normally has to sell it back for fair value to the writer. The two types of options may also not be treated similarly for tax purposes. Intending users will have to inform themselves on this matter. An important advantage of exchange traded options is, of course, that they involve no counterparty credit risk. This is indeed a perennial issue with OTC options.

The debate will eventually not resolve anything. There is obviously a market for both trading platforms. The reality is that sometimes an OTC will be more appropriate to a company's needs and at other times it may be more advantageous to make use of exchange-traded options. A manager must keep abreast of what is available in the market and evaluate each particular need of the business on each occasion, to determine the most appropriate instrument.

THE INTEREST RATE RISK MANAGEMENT FUNCTION

Managing interest rate risk forms part of the greater risk management function of a business. Risk management is a growth industry. Companies outside the investment banking and financial sectors are becoming more and more aware of how essential it is that the risks of a business must be actively managed. Indeed, risk management and business management are becoming inseparable.

The first task in any risk management function is obviously to identify the risks that the company faces. As was discussed earlier in this chapter, direct interest rate risk is easily identified, but indirect interest rate risk may be somewhat more difficult to pin down and to manage. Once the risk has been identified, it must be assessed and evaluated. By that is meant that the company must determine, firstly, what the impact of the risk will be on the company and secondly, what impact the management of the risk will have on the company.

There are no free lunches. Managing risk has a cost. The financial instruments that are used may will have a cost, there may be trading costs, and there will certainly be an internal cost to bear in terms of time and resources spent on the activity. The company must then assess the impact of the risk faced with the cost of managing that risk. It may well be that the impact a particular risk can have on a particular business may be too insignificant to warrant the expense of managing it.

In adopting a proper approach to interest rate risk management, a business must assess the avenues that are open to it in managing the risk. There are five basic ways of dealing with interest rate risk: avoiding it, accepting it, leveraging it, diversifying it and hedging it. Each of these options will be examined in more detail in an attempt to provide a better synopsis of the scope that is available in managing interest rate risk. Their practical uses will be more fully discussed and illustrated in Chapter 7.

avoiding interest rate risk

This is always the first option in any business situation. Whether it is a viable option will depend on the totality of the circumstances in each particular case. In discussing this alternative, it must be kept in mind that the primary concern of this book is with businesses for which interest rate risk will be incidental to their ordinary business. In other words, a firm that incurs interest rate risk as part of its main business, such as an investment bank, searches out the risk in order to profit from it. However, the present purpose is to deal with non-financial businesses, whose risk-focus for the purposes of profit will be elsewhere.

Since interest rate risk is an incidental risk, it can be avoided to an extent. The price of money is a factor that every business has to contend with. If a business requires money than it has on call, it needs to borrow. On the other hand, if it has more cash available than it can presently employ in the business, it needs to invest the cash, even if only temporarily. In addition, a manager with even a passing familiarity with economic principles, knows that a certain amount of gearing is essential to optimise the performance of a business. Thus, a strategy of absolutely avoiding interest rate risk is unlikely to be viable or achievable.

Nevertheless, it cannot be rejected out of hand as a strategy. Avoiding interest rate risk can be used to limit a business' interest rate exposure rather than allowing it to grow unabated and unchecked. In effect, a strategy of avoiding interest rate exposure amounts to contracting out of interest rate risk. In avoiding interest rate risk, a course of action is followed whereby the risk is transferred to the other party to the transaction. An example of such a strategy would be to borrow or invest only at fixed interest rates. It will be effective in avoiding direct interest rate risk for a firm in respect of every completed transaction. The cash flow of a company cannot then be adversely influenced by changes in interest rates.

That, however, is not the end of the matter. Although direct interest rate risk is avoided by only doing transactions at fixed interest rates, there is a substantial downside to the strategy. During the life of such fixed rate transactions, the business will be precluded from gaining any advantage from favourable interest rate moves. Of course, the same result is achieved through a hedge. A hedge fixes the outcome of a transaction that is otherwise subject to fluctuation.

The problem is that there is usually a penalty to pay for dealing at a fixed rate. The longer the period of the loan or the investment, the greater the penalty will be. However, there is in any event also a cost to managing risk. Thus, it is suggested that a better strategy would be not to take any rigid policy decision in this regard, but rather to evaluate each transaction on its merits. Sometimes, fixed interest borrowings may be the best solution to manage interest rate risk, but very often, better alternatives will be possible. This is demonstrated by practical examples in later chapters.

Active interest rate risk management strategies could provide a competitive edge for a company where its competitors are so totally risk-averse as to avoid interest rate risk altogether. Thus, even if interest rate risk-avoidance is a company's preferred strategy, it could be counterproductive to follow it too rigidly. It is therefore advisable for a firm to be always willing and able to employ other active interest rate risk management strategies.

accepting interest rate risk

In general, only risks which are not cost effective to manage, or which are run for the sake of profit can be accepted. It would be totally wrong and counterproductive for a business in ordinary commerce to try to turn its treasury into a profit centre. This has been amply demonstrated through some spectacular failures. Therefore, if the business is not one of dealing in interest rate for the sake of profit, interest rate risk should never be accepted for the purposes of profit.

Interest rate risk can be managed with very little cost, so the exposure must be minor if it would be more expensive to manage the risk than to suffer any loss that might eventuate. Given the volatility of the interest rate markets, it would need very careful evaluation and consideration before it is decided merely to accept interest rate risk.

Nevertheless, a number of interest rate exposures will undoubtedly not be deemed worthy of active management. The permutations of risks faced by a business in its day to day functioning are endless. If a business were to hedge every permutation of risk that it encounters, the risk management cost would outstrip any possible advantage that could be gained by hedging.

Therefore, the first important principle of risk management is to ensure that one is fully aware of all the risks to which one's business is exposed. The second is to have the ability to evaluate which risks are big enough to worry about and thirdly, to have the knowledge and expertise to handle those risks properly and adequately. It follows that a business must develop the expertise to be able decide between which risks to hedge and which risks to accept. This decision-making ability will be crucial to the success of the business.

Not only must one be able to decide which risks to manage and which to accept one must be aware of the effect of the importance of correct timing. The timing of risk management strategies may be very important. For example, interest on borrowings is favourably affected when interest rates decline. Thus, when interest rates are undeniably in a downtrend for sound economic reasons, then accepting the interest rate risk is probably the most advantageous strategy even if the exposure is large enough to warrant active management under other circumstances.

There is no denying that such a course of action (accepting the risk) is speculative in nature. Great care should thus be taken before it is embarked upon. Once taken, the situation will need to be carefully monitored because other action can be taken at a later stage if matters do not develop as expected.

leveraging the risk

Leveraging an existing risk in a business can only have one purpose – profit. If the risk concerns the core business of the company, leveraging it may be a sound business decision. In the case of interest rate risk however, what has already been said before, regarding the inadvisability of turning a firm's treasury into a profit centre, can merely be reiterated.

When derivatives are used for risk management purposes, they usually involve a substantial amount of leveraging. That is one of the reasons that they are so cost-effective in risk management. Very large amounts of notional capital may be involved against the investment of very little by way of premium or margin. The use of derivatives thus involves leveraging a dampening or neutralising risk in respect of the core risk the business is exposed to. This leveraging is essential to make risk management feasible.

Leveraging the original business risk with derivatives is not an option in the premises of this book.

diversifying the risk

The principle of risk diversification was brought to the forefront of risk management by the previously mentioned work of Harry Markowitz. He formalised the notion that a basket of risks, actually known as a risk portfolio, has a different risk/reward profile than the mere sum of the risks and rewards of the individual assets in the portfolio. The principle of diversification actually comes down to the fact that each asset can be said to have two components of risk: diversifiable risk and non-diversifiable risk. Diversifiable risk can be made to disappear through a judicious combination of risks. The residual, non-diversifiable risk is all that will have to be borne by the investor. The result is that the reduction of overall risk, or portfolio risk, by a well considered spread of money across a wide range of alternatives remains central to all sound financial practice.

At the start of this chapter, it was stated that the primary concern is not with portfolio management as such. Yet, certain companies may have such a mix of risk-bearing assets, that the totality could be regarded as a portfolio of risks that can be managed according to the principles of modern portfolio theory.

It is this core observation that has led many companies into the trap of speculation under the guise of risk management. Portfolio diversification is such an attractive and definite way of dampening risk that some companies find it irresistible. One problem of this approach has already been mentioned, and that is that a business incurs risk in the ordinary course of its operations. It does not have the luxury of selecting risks in order to obtain a more balanced portfolio of risks. Portfolio selection, or the ability to judiciously select risks, is what the principle of diversification is all about.

The complication inherent in a strategy of diversification is that increasing the overall size of a portfolio does not diversify it, even if it is increased by means of uncorrelated risks. Only by means of diversifying the assets within a given a risk portfolio can it be diversified. Adding new risks to a portfolio of risks merely increases the total risk, even if the new risks are diversified risks relative to the risks already in the portfolio. This matter will also be investigated in Chapter 2. The only reasonable conclusion is therefore that a non-financial company does not actually have the facility of judiciously selecting other risks for the purposes of diversifying a portfolio of business risks. Therefore, in the past such companies have sought other ways of dampening their business risks through diversification.

hedging the risk

Hedging is probably the simplest risk management tool next to avoiding the risk. Hedging is not the same thing as avoiding risk. It involves the purposeful taking on of another risk that is negatively correlated with the risk being hedged. Mention has previously been made of risk correlation. It is time to have a quick look at what is meant by this.

Risk correlations can be calculated mathematically. If the risk on two assets is entirely uncorrelated, they have a risk correlation of zero. The two interest rate risks would then tend to dampen one another. This is the principle of diversification. If two risks are negatively correlated to a value of -1, they move in an exactly opposite fashion. That is the correlation of heads and tails in a coin toss. If heads win, tails inevitably loses and *vice versa*. If a business is exposed to interest rate risk, that risk can be hedged by taking on another risk that is negatively correlated with the first one. The two risks will neutralise each other. The example of the coin toss will illustrate the principle

In a game of coin toss, the probabilities are 50/50 for either heads or tails to show, if the coin is 'fair'. On any bet, the fair odds would therefore be one for one. If one thus bets £1 on heads and win, one must get the £1 stake back plus an additional £1 as winnings. If one wanted to hedge the bet on heads, one would also have to bet £1 on tails. One's total capital at risk is now £2. Now it does not matter what happens, the position will be the same in the end. If tails come up, one wins on the tails bet and gets £2 for one's trouble, but one loses the £1 bet on heads. I brought £2 to the game and I walk away with £2 pounds. If heads come up exactly the same thing happens. So what's the point? Either way one neither wins nor loses.

There is no point in playing the game since one cannot win. One also cannot lose. That is the principle of hedging. You do not hedge a risk on which you wish to profit. You hedge a risk that you are forced to take for other reasons, but that you prefer not to take a loss on. In hedging interest rate risk, the strategy with derivatives is thus to create or to construct a derivative that is negatively correlated with the primary risk being hedged. If the hedging risk has a correlation of exactly -1 with the primary risk, there is no chance of loss or gain on the transaction.

The outcome of an uncertain event has thus been made certain. The downside is that all opportunity for profit has also been lost, or hedged away. Hedging with options will ameliorate the latter situation. However, a company must decide what its real business is, focus on that and make its profits on that activity. As previously stated, it is exceedingly dangerous to turn the treasury department into a profit centre. Where the opportunity of profit invites, the risk of loss lurks.

CHECKLIST FOR THE REVIEW OF CHAPTER 1

General overview of the subject matter of the book: the overall control objectives of the material dealt with in this chapter are to gain a basic understanding of what interest rate risk is, how it can be identified, what derivatives are available to manage it and the basic strategies that can be employed in its management.

	Key Issues	Illustrative Scope or Approach
1.1	Does the firm borrow and invest only on fixed interest rates?	If this is true, then the business does not face any direct interest rate risk. It does not exclude the possibility that the firm may face indirect interest rate risk
1.2	Does the firm conduct at least part of its business floating interest rates?	If any part of a firm's borrowings or investments are linked to floating interest rates, it faces direct interest rate risk

continued

	Key Issues	Illustrative Scope or Approach
1.3	Has the firm identified all transactions that expose it to interest rate risk?	These include all transactions that involve fixed or floating interest rates
1.4	Has the firm analysed its exposure to indirect interest rate risk?	Indirect interest rate risk is faced when a business is unable to take advantage of favourable moves in interest rates. This may result in a serious competitive disadvantage for the company The risk may not be limited to amounts borrowed or invested, but may be related to market conditions influencing the demand for the company's products or services
1.5	Has the impact of managing the risk of each transaction creating direct interest rate risk, or of each source of indirect interest rate risk, been assessed?	Managing interest rate risk has a cost implication for a firm. It impacts on the organisation in terms of staff training, creating a risk management culture and even by increasing the employee head count Managing interest rate risk must also be assessed in terms of the direct cost of the derivatives used, such as premiums, margins and trading costs. The benefits to be gained must be assessed against the costs to be incurred. There is inevitably a trade-off between risks that are managed and ones that are accepted
1.6	Does the firm repeat the steps outlined in 1.3, 1.4 and 1.5 above on a continuous basis?	Business and the interest rate markets are constantly in a state of flux; Especially indirect risks can develop quite quickly and virtually undetected. Developments on world markets create new risks and new risk management tools. These tendencies require a firm to assess its interest rate risk situation on an on-going basis
1.7	Does the firm have the knowledge and facilities to make use of all interest rate derivatives?	The interest rate derivatives are: ● FRAs. This contract involves counterparty credit risk. The firm will have to establish proper lines of credit with a bank or other financial institution. It is not only the credit of the firm that has to be established: the credit of the bank or institution should also be good for the cumulative transactions that the firm requires ● Interest rate futures. The firm will need to establish an account with a Futures Commission Merchant through an introducing broker, before any trades can be done on the futures markets

continued

Key Issues	Illustrative Scope or Approach
	• OTC swaps. Counterparty credit risk is involved. Proper reciprocal credit lines will have to be established with banks, financial institutions or brokers
	• OTC options. This again involves counterparty credit risk. Reciprocal credit lines need to be established
	• Exchange traded interest rate options. An account will have to be opened and margin paid in before any options trading can be done. There is virtually no credit risk. It is advisable to go through an introducing broker
1.8 Does the firm, with respect to each source of direct or indirect interest rate risk, consider all the major strategies of dealing with each of the risks?	The major risk management strategies are: • Avoiding the risk – e.g. by contracting out of the risk by establishing only fixed interest rate credit or investment lines • Accepting the risk – if the impact of accepting the risk does not have substantial financial consequences for the business and if the cost of managing the risk is not warranted by the advantage gained • Leveraging the risk – increases the total risk and the likelihood of profit and loss. In terms of interest rate risk this is not advisable and should never be contemplated unless the core business of the company has changed to speculating on interest rate movements • Diversifying the risk – when it is possible to disinvest partially or wholly from some interest rate risks and then to reinvest in an interest rate risk that is uncorrelated with the remaining risks. This is highly unlikely with interest rates as their dynamics are all correlated to some extent • Hedging the risk – when another risk that is negatively correlated with the first risk can be assumed so that the two risks neutralise one another

two

interest rate risk management in the non-financial sector

INTRODUCTION

It is trite to say that interest rate risk is a factor of the volatility of the money markets. If volatility were zero, there would be zero risk in having interest rate exposure. The greater the volatility in the markets, the greater the risk incurred through exposure to interest rates. Interest rate risk management has consequently come to mean a deliberate process whereby interest rate risk is dampened, reduced or neutralised in order to stabilise cash flows within a company.

Managing interest rate risk is only one facet of the general activity of managing financial risk. Financial risk is a product of the general volatility of prices and rates. Price volatility results in volatility in the cash flows of a company and consequently in its profits. The primary purpose of risk management is consequently to neutralise such price volatility, thereby smoothing out and stabilising the cash flows of the company.

Since the value of a company is directly related to the net present value of its expected future cash flows, neutralising or 'smoothing out' such volatilities would only make sense if value were thereby added for the existing shareholders of the company. Obviously, if no value were added by the activity, it would be so much wasted effort. Consequently, the first question that arises in discussing interest rate risk management strategies, is whether the risks should be managed at all. Is a complete *laissez-faire* attitude towards interest rate risk, and perhaps all financial risk for that matter, not perhaps the best strategy?

This question has been the subject of long and intense debate over many years. To this day, many academics and business professionals are of the opinion that it has not been proven that risk management at company level adds any value to a company. The purpose of this book is to demonstrate how interest rate risk is managed with financial derivatives and not to argue whether or not it should be managed. Thus, no attempt is made herein to contribute new insights to this debate.

Nevertheless, it is appropriate to point out and discuss some of the salient points of the debate, so that the practitioner of risk management is at least granted the opportunity of an introduction to the major points of view pertaining to the activity he or she is engaged in. Knowledge of the different points of view will contribute to an understanding of the issues involved and help shape a manager's approach to the whole process of managing risk. It is therefore trusted that this necessarily condensed discussion of the issues involved will nevertheless allow the reader to gain certain insights that will be of assistance in making risk management decisions under real life conditions.

THE CRITIQUE OF CORPORATE RISK MANAGEMENT

As was pointed out earlier, price volatility reduction as a company strategy has been the subject of severe criticism and debate over many years. A paper published by Franco Modigliani and Merton Miller in 1958 started the debate. In their paper entitled *The cost of capital, corporation finance and the theory of investment*, they argued that the value of a business is determined solely by its operations and real investment decisions. Its value is consequently independent of its capital structure and of how the company finances those investments. It follows that an investor will be unwilling to pay a premium to participate in the equity of a company that has undertaken an action that the investor himself can undertake. This idea is central to much of modern financial theory.

modern financial theory

Since the sole purpose of risk management is to dampen or neutralise the volatility of returns, an investor can take that action himself. It does not matter whether the risk management is undertaken by means of portfolio diversification or through hedging with financial derivatives, the argument remains the same. The investor can spread his investment portfolio in such a way that the volatility of the portfolio will dampen the volatility of the returns on each of the equities in the portfolio. Thus, no value is added for the investor when an individual company follows a strategy of diversification in order to stabilise its cash flows. The paper by Modigliani and Miller was delivered before the explosion in financial derivatives. However, the criticism is as applicable to hedging with derivatives as it is to volatility reduction through portfolio diversification.

As a simple example, consider the case of an investor who purchases shares in an airline company. Assume that its major operating risk is the volatility of the price of fuel. When the price of oil rises, the profit of the airline shrinks and improves again when oil prices decline. The investor can protect himself against volatility in the expected returns from the airline company's profit by diversifying his investment through investing in an oil producing company. The oil producing company's profits will tend to react oppositely to the airline company's profits when changes occur in the price of oil. Alternatively, the same result can be achieved by means of financial derivatives. The investor could take a position in oil futures contracts, which would likewise have the effect of neutralising the profit volatility of the airline due to oil price volatility.

The argument is thus that, as far as the investor is concerned, the airline company adds no value to its shares by hedging the price of oil or by diversifying its business into oil production. Such activities at company level are consequently irrelevant to the value of the airline's equity. Since volatility reduction is irrelevant, it should not be indulged in since it uses company facilities and resources non-productively.

It is worth noting that the critique does not concern the issue of whether there should be risk management or not. In the whole debate the issue is not and has never been whether cash flow volatilities should be managed, the question is rather whether it serves any purpose, or adds any value, to manage risk at corporate or company level. It should also be noted that most analysts also agree that the critique applies mainly, if not solely, to large publicly traded companies. Their view is that such publicly traded companies are themselves risk sharing vehicles. That is why a portfolio of judiciously selected listed stocks will result in less risk. This aspect will be more fully discussed under the strategy of portfolio diversification.

discussion

In effect, the critique concludes that managers, at least of large publicly traded corporations, should not be risk averse, because investors are. Everybody thus seems to be agreed that people who are in business, be it as investors or otherwise, are there to make a profit. That statement seems to be eminently true. Thus, it must follow that the net result that a businessperson wishes to attain is a net positive cash flow – which is all that profit is at the end of the day. If a particular course of action improves the probability of a net positive cash flow rather than a negative one, every sensible businessperson would take such action. The debate is consequently merely concerned with whether the action should be taken at company level or at investor level. Corporate risk management is argued to be irrelevant, not risk management as such.

The critical assumption that underlies the Modigliani–Miller view is that capital markets are perfect. That implies, *inter alia*, that there are no taxes, that there is perfect symmetry of information between management and investors and that volatility reduction strategies are without cost. When these assumptions do not hold, or are relaxed, the conclusion is not warranted. Indeed, Messrs. Modigliani and Miller published a later article wherein they considered a world with corporate taxes, but without personal tax. They concluded that hedging at corporate level was relevant under such circumstances.

It would be wrong to jump to the conclusion that, because we do not live in a world with perfect capital markets, the critical view is not applicable to the real world in which we live. Theories are often developed under 'ideal' circumstances, because 'ideal' circumstances often enable principles to be identified that are otherwise hidden by the daily 'noise' of the real world.

The proposition can be illustrated by considering a company that expects a profit of £20 million or a £10 million loss with equal probability. The expected cash flow of the company is therefore £5 million [(£20,000,000 × 50%) + (−£10,000,000 × 50%) = £5,000,000]. Assume that the company manages to hedge its risk in such a way that it has a guaranteed profit of £5 million after the hedge. All that has happened is that the risk has been reduced, since the expected cash flow remains the same as before. The question that now arises is whether, by merely by reducing the risk, the hedge has increased the value of the company.

In order to answer this question, it has to be kept in mind that the value of a company is essentially the net present value of the expected future cash flows of the company. As every student of finance knows, the net present value of future cash flows is calculated by discounting the flows at a certain rate over the expected period. The only possible way to increase the net present value of a given set of future cash flows is therefore to decrease the rate at which the set is discounted over that future period. It is an accepted fact that investors will discount future cash flows at a lower rate, the lower the risk attached to the expectation. Alternatively, to put it differently, the greater the certainty of the future cash flows, the lower the rate at which they are discounted will be.

Based on the above assessment, the company in the example has seemingly succeeded in adding value for the company's existing shareholders. This is consequent upon the fact that the discount rate of the company's expected future cash flows have been lowered. Thus, the present share price must have increased. The problem is that the example assumes that the hedge costs nothing. Surely, the counterparty to the hedge that assumed the company's risk would not have done so without charge. The protagonists of the corporate anti-hedging view will argue that in general, any reduction in the rate at which a company's future cash flows are discounted will only result from a reduction of the systemic risks faced by the company. Any such reduction in systemic risk is likely to be offset by a reduction in the expected future cash flows, due to the cost of the hedge. The cost of the hedge is represented by the compensation that the party assuming the risks from the company will demand for doing so. In the result, the increased equity value derived from the lower discount rate should be exactly neutralised by the lower total cash flow due to the cost of the hedge.

The contrary view holds that the above objection is again based on the assumption of perfect capital markets, where arbitrage never occurs. Even assuming perfect capital markets and no arbitrage, there can be no general principle that excludes another party from facing the exact opposite systemic risk. Simply put, assume that if the DOW declines, a certain company A loses money; why should there not, in principle, be a company B that gains an equal amount of money? If each company were to hedge by assuming the systematic risk of the other, they would both be perfectly hedged. There should be no cost to either company since they each gain equally from the hedge. What remains true however, is that an investor in any one of the companies could have achieved the same result by also investing in the other company. Would it be as easy for the investor to know or to find the second company as it is for the management of the first company to do so? Probably not, is the realistic answer. Assuming perfect markets and thus perfect information, there can be no difference in the information that management has and that the investor has, is the reply of the anti-hedging advocates.

The commentators that grant the relevance of hedging at corporate level, hold the view that the decision to hedge or not should be based only on cost effectiveness. The cost of every hedging action should be weighed against the advantage to be gained therefrom. This is purely a common-sense reasoning that applies to all business activity. The matter that can thus only be assessed and decided upon in each particular case of identified risk in a company. As will appear from a later part of the discussion, this seems to be the generally held view in the marketplace.

IN DEFENCE OF CORPORATE RISK MANAGEMENT

The whole debate is actually short-circuited by the fact that company managers do indeed manage risk. Not only are risks vigorously managed at corporate level in the financial sector as well as the non-financial sector, but risk management is an explosive growth industry. Indeed, notwithstanding the fact that the weight of the critique against corporate risk management is specifically aimed at large publicly traded companies, these companies are now specifically required to do so in the UK.

The Combined Code (the Code) and the Listing Rule of the London Stock Exchange (LSE) require listed companies to manage risk or to explain annually to their shareholders why they have not done so. Principle D.2 of the Code states that 'The board should maintain a sound system of internal control to safeguard shareholders' investments and the company's assets'. Principle D.2.1 requires listed companies to conduct a review of the company's system of control 'at least annually' and report that to the shareholders. The principle specifically requires that 'the review should cover all controls, including financial, operational and compliance controls and risk management'.

Of course, the fact that companies actually engage in risk management activities and are even required to do so, does not really answer the objections raised by the arguments of those who hold opposite views. At most, it might suggest that practical experience demonstrates that companies do obtain added value through managing risk. Consequently, there has been a lot of academic research and debate regarding the reasons for, as well as the extent and results of company risk management. Some of these findings will be dealt with somewhat later in the chapter.

A number of analyses and research papers have seen the light which, to some extent or another, shows that hedging at company level may add value under certain circumstances. It is not proposed to enter into any detailed discussion of these views. It will suffice for the purposes hereof to attempt a condensed overview of some of the research that has been done. The theoretically inclined reader will find a vast reservoir of material to study on this subject. It is trusted that the present necessarily truncated version does not do an injustice to any of the views concerned.

prospect theory

In the real world, real people invest in and manage companies. Any theory purporting to describe or prescribe human behaviour, whether in a purely social or economic context, must take into account the reality of human nature. Determining what human nature is, is of course the catch.

There is reason to believe that regarding economic or financial value in mere monetary numerical terms may be a misconception of how human beings generally perceive such value. Granted that if asked whether an asset with an accepted worth of $200 has greater value than another with an accepted worth of $100, every rational person would be expected to answer in the affirmative. However, when the element of risk is added to the monetary values, the answer is not so simple. At present, the most influential theory on how human beings perceive and react to risk and uncertainty is known as Prospect Theory.

Prospect Theory was not developed as part of or in response to the debate on the relevance or irrelevance of corporate hedging. However, its findings are pertinent to some of the arguments raised in the debate, especially those arguments that relate to adding value through risk reduction.

Two Israeli psychologists, Amos Tversky and Daniel Kahneman developed the theory. Their interest was first sparked by the observation that people generally tend to err in their evaluation of probabilities by ignoring the phenomenon of regression to the mean. That led them to conduct numerous experiments to determine the ways in which people err in forecasting future performance from past performance. They discovered human behaviour patterns that were never previously recognised and that seriously aggravate the proponents of rational behaviour.

Should we really be surprised that as a rule people do not behave strictly rationally? Indeed, the most surprising finding methinks is that human beings sometimes do behave rationally. Consider for a moment the frenzied purchase of state and national lottery tickets with adverse odds of millions to one. This behaviour moved Stephen Pinker, in his book *How the Mind Works,* to observe that lottery ticket prices amount to no less than 'stupidity tax'.

The most important observation of Prospect Theory in the context of the present discussion is the asymmetrical way that decisions are made when gains and losses are involved. The research shows that when significant sums of money are involved, most people will reject a fair gamble against a certain gain. Tversky and Kahneman found that for the vast majority of subjects, $100,000 for certain, is much preferred to a 50/50 chance of gaining $200,000 or nothing. In one of their experiments, reported in their first paper on the theory published in *Econometrica*, volume 47, 1979, entitled 'Prospect Theory: an analysis of decision under risk', they found that 80% of their subjects preferred a smaller, but certain return, over a return with a mathematically higher expectation. To put some numbers on this experiment, the choice offered to the subjects was between a 100% chance of receiving $3,000 and an 80/20 chance of receiving $4,000 or nothing. The expected return of the second choice is $3,200 ($4,000 × 80%), but it was rejected by 80% of the people.

The result of the converse experiment is equally interesting. They offered the subjects a choice between a certain loss of $3,000 and an 80/20 chance of losing $4,000 or breaking even. The second choice has an expected return of −$3,200, yet 92% of the respondents preferred it. It appears that the prospect of a certain outcome is given greater weight in the human decision making process than mathematical probabilities. The experiments and findings of these two gentleman go much further than the present discussion allows and the reader is invited to explore this really fascinating subject.

The question is what implications these findings have for modern financial theory. Most of modern financial theory is founded upon the idea that investors and managers will make rational investment decisions. Rationality in this sense meaning mathematically rational. There is no hard empirical evidence to support this assumption of strict rationality, yet it is strictly held, regardless. When the demonstrated asymmetry in decision making is considered within the context of adding value, a different perspective may be achieved. If the choice offered to the respondents were slightly altered to reflect the present context, the result could upset some widely held views.

Assume that instead of the choice Kahneman and Tversky offered their subjects in the first experiment, there were two listed companies. The one company offered a guaranteed return of $30 million, while the second company offered an 80/20 chance of a $40 million profit or nothing. The expected return of the first company is thus $30 million against the expected return of $32 million of the second company. The rational approach would thus be that the stock of the second company should be preferred to the stock of the first. Yet, based on the results of their experiment, we can expect the demand for the stock of the first company to be four times as great as the demand for the stock of the second company. This represents a striking asymmetry of value.

Given this asymmetry in valuation, can the assertion that the lower discount rate applied to value a guaranteed return will be strictly symmetrical with the cost of the hedge resulting in the guaranteed cash flow, be supported? The evidence of over 30 years of empirical research gainsays any such assertion. This may be one of the reasons that companies find that hedging risks is relevant in practice and why industry leaders, such as the LSE demand risk management practices from listed companies.

corporate hedging – adding value in monetary terms

Apart from any of the above considerations, many of the 'rationalist' financial academics and professionals have found reasons why hedging at corporate level makes sense and does add value.

They argue that when the basic assumptions of modern financial theory are relaxed, risk management does add value for existing shareholders. When they refer to the basic assumptions, they are referring to the basic explicit assumptions relating to perfect capital markets and not the basic implicit assumption of strict 'rational' behaviour. Reference has already been made to the paper by Modigliani and Miller that acknowledges the value added by corporate hedging under conditions of corporate taxes. A number of other circumstances have also been identified.

An important consideration is the asymmetry of information between investors and management that was mentioned earlier. The passive investor of a company can never be as well informed about the day-to-day exposures and risks of a company as its management is. The investor could thus never be in as good a position to hedge or dampen the risks of his investment. At best, an investor would know the general major risks run by companies operating in a particular sector and dampen the risk accordingly. Such action may be much less efficient than similar action taken by management.

In addition, there is also the cost of financial distress. Too much negative cash flow can and will cause financial distress. Financial distress and bankruptcy carry severe cost penalties. Apart from all of these, management have their own selfish motives for hedging company risk that have everything to do with their own monetary and non-monetary investment in a business.

The argument has been raised that managers can hedge their positions in the market as much as investors can. They therefore have no need of risk aversion when it concerns company value. This argument seems somewhat facile and artificial. Apart from all other considerations, a manager has a reputation as a manager. Managers are employees. Their own value rests on their ability to be employed. Thus, a manager's reputation as a successful manager is probably worth more than any immediate remunerative prospects, because reputation affects employability and market value. Reputational risk is thus an extremely high priority concern of any manager. A manager invests a lot of human capital into a company. This capital investment cannot be diversified across a wide portfolio of businesses. The manager's value as an employee thus sinks or swims with the results of the activities managed.

CONCLUSION ON CORPORATE RISK MANAGEMENT

Today it is generally acknowledged that risk matters. Companies and managers are rightly concerned about managing a company's risks, for a plethora of reasons, including those discussed above. There is also a better understanding of why it matters and how the risks should be managed. It is realised that in today's business environment every enterprise is subject to risk and a sound system of risk management must form an essential part of every business.

It is also worthwhile to note at this stage of the discussion what a sound system of control is considered to be. It is unwise for any business, whatever its size or capital structure, to jump willy-nilly into risk management without proper preparation. The first and foremost risk management strategy is to establish and maintain a sound risk management system. Even if interest rate risk is the only risk worth managing in a business, it must nevertheless take place within the context of a sound system of internal control.

MAINTAINING A SOUND SYSTEM OF CONTROL

This question has enjoyed consideration by some of the world's leading financial specialists and professionals. After the introduction of the mentioned Code of the LSE, the Institute of Chartered Accountants in England and Wales (the Institute) put together an Internal Control Working Party under the chairmanship of Nigel Turnbull, executive director of Rank Group Plc. Their purpose was to develop guidance for the directors of companies in order to assist them in complying with the code. This task required the working party to consider closely what the role of risk management in a modern company is and how a sound system of internal control might be developed and maintained. Their eventual report, now known as the Turnbull report, is published by the Institute as guidance for directors of companies on the Combined Code.

Although produced for the specific purpose as stated above, this group of eminent professionals considered the very wide implications of the provisions of the code. In the result, they addressed themselves so well to the requirements and principles of a sound system of internal control that their recommendations are of equal value for businesses all over the world. One can thus do no better than to condense and quote the report on this matter as it is the most valuable insight available for businesses embarked upon the management of its risks.

The report states that it is the responsibility of the board of a company to create the system of control. It must seek regular assurance that the system is functioning effectively, but it is the responsibility of management to implement the policies of the board. Notwithstanding the responsibility of management, the report is adamant that *all* employees have some responsibility for internal control as part of their accountability for achieving objectives. The employees should, collectively have the necessary knowledge, skills, information and authority to establish, operate and monitor the system. It is part of management's function to ensure that the employees are so endowed and empowered.

Very importantly, when the board considers its policies on control, the factors that must be considered are the following:

- the nature and extent of the risks facing the company;
- the extent and categories of risk which it regards as acceptable for the company to bear;
- the likelihood of the risks concerned materialising;
- the company's ability to reduce the incidence and impact on the business that do materialise; and
- the costs of operating particular controls relative to the benefit thereby obtained in managing the related risks.

Broadly speaking, there are two strategies available to dampen and reduce risk: diversification and hedging. A general redux of both strategies is undertaken below.

DIVERSIFICATION

Ever since the seminal work of Harry Markowitz, *Portfolio Selection: Efficient Diversification of Investments*, 1959, diversification has been a cornerstone of modern portfolio theory. His work was the first to formalise the principle of diversification, applying it to financial instruments. The idea was not new, but the tools were then forged with businesses which might systematically select assets for investment. This type of portfolio selection is ideally suited for companies in the financial sector, since their asset portfolios tend to consist overwhelmingly of liquid paper assets.

Without delving into the mathematics of modern portfolio theory, the main principle demonstrated by Markowitz is that the risk of a portfolio of risks will be less than a simple weighted average of the individual risks making up the portfolio. This phenomenon is due to asymmetry of the correlations between the different risks in the portfolio. It also follows that the lower the correlations between the constituent risks are, the lower the portfolio risk will be.

risk correlation

For the purposes of the above principle, risks can be viewed as vectors. That is, risk acts like a certain force that is exercised in a particular direction, which is what a vector is. It therefore has a quantitative value (the amount of force used) and a directional value (the direction that the force will move the object on which the force is exerted). Two risks can thus be compared much as two vectors can. Two forces of equal size, working in the same direction on the same object will exert twice the amount of force on that object in the same direction. Two equal forces that work in opposite directions on the same object will cancel one another out and will thus not move the object at all. The object will thus not experience any force in any direction and will be at rest.

Simple single factor risk equations can be solved in the same way as vector equations. What follows is an extremely simplified explanation, but one, which will nevertheless serve to explain the principle involved. When a single factor, such as say, the change in an interest rate such as 3-month Libor, may or may not affect the value of two assets, their risks may be compared in this manner. If, for example, one basis point increase in the interest rate increases the value of asset A and the value of asset B by $1, their risks are identically related. They react in an identical manner to an upward change in the 3-month

Libor rate. If, when 3-month Libor declines by one basis point, both assets devalue by $1 each, their risks are also identically related to a downward change in the exchange rate. Since their risks are identical to the extent that they are in lockstep with each other, the conclusion must be that the two risks are perfectly correlated. Such a perfect correlation is given a numerical value of 1. If one were to hold both assets simultaneously in one portfolio, the two assets would give one double the exposure to 3-month Libor than holding only one of the assets would.

On the other hand, should one basis point increase in 3-month Libor increase the value of asset A by $1 without affecting the value of asset B at all, the risks of the two assets are unrelated. They are unrelated, at least, as far as a rise in 3-month Libor is concerned. Should the same result be obtained with a one basis point decline in the rate, the conclusion must be that the sensitivity of the value of the two assets to 3-month Libor are totally unrelated. Hence their risk correlation regarding this single factor (3-month Libor) is zero. In fact, asset B does not expose the holder to any 3-month Libor interest rate risk. Thus, holding both asset A and asset B in one portfolio does not expose the portfolio to any greater exposure to 3-month Libor than merely holding asset A alone.

Finally, suppose that one basis point increase in 3-month Libor causes asset A to increase in value by $1, but causes asset B to decrease in value by $1. Similarly, suppose that a decline of one basis point in the rate decreases the value of asset A by $1, but increases the value of asset B by $1. The risk of these two assets are thus perfectly correlated, but negatively so. They have a risk correlation of −1 to changes in 3-month Libor. Their values behave oppositely to a change in the rate. It is obvious that if one were to hold both assets A and B simultaneously in one's portfolio, the portfolio's total value would be unaffected by any change in the value of 3-month Libor.

Risks with a correlation of 1 thus leverage one another, i.e. they double the total risk, while risks with a negative, −1 correlation, hedge one another, and they neutralise the total risk. Financial risks in a portfolio of risks will have correlations anywhere between 1 and −1. The trick is thus to spread the investments in a portfolio in such a manner that the net portfolio correlations are as close as possible to zero. Add the total correlations in a portfolio and you will get the net correlation of the portfolio. The lower the result, the lower the risk of the portfolio will be.

The gravamen of the argument is not that there will actually be no risk in the portfolio at all. If this were so, there would only be a very small return, which is known as the risk-free rate of return. The point is really that each and every asset can be conceived of as having two risk components: one component can be neutralised through a judicious combination of that asset with other assets, while the second risk component must be borne by the investor.

The first component is known as the diversifiable risk. Diversifiable risk actually consists of those risks that are specific to any one particular company. It is also called company specific risk. It excludes those risks to which a specific company is exposed due to general market-wide economic factors. Investing in a broad category of businesses can eliminate company specific risk. There is no reward for exposure to company specific, or diversifiable risk. Why should an investor be compensated for carrying unnecessary risk?

The element of market risk cannot be diversified away and thus represents the limit of the power of diversification. Investors demand compensation, in the form of returns, for carrying market risk. The market risk exposure of companies differs and therefore the riskiness of owning their stock differs. Investors are risk averse and they therefore require the prospect of a return greater than the risk-free rate of return for taking on market risk. The more market risk they are asked to take on, the greater the return they expect.

The innate sense of the idea of diversification, coupled with its practical and theoretical difficulties, ensured an explosion in the development of modern portfolio theory. There was, and still is to this day, a great deal of effort being put into the development of portfolio selection models based on this theory, its refinements and updates. The most popular current tool to estimate the risk adjusted cost of capital is still the Capital Asset Pricing Model (CAPM), but it is seriously challenged by Arbitrage Pricing Theory (APT), which is an extended CAPM model, but factors in multiple sources of risk and return. Various versions of these models are in daily use in all the sectors of the corporate world.

diversification in the non-financial sector

For non-financial companies, the theory presented very different practical difficulties of implementation. The actual management practices that have been employed by non-financial companies to dampen the volatility of cash flows and profitability are poorly documented. Nevertheless, it is generally accepted that non-financial companies conduct risk management by engaging in activities that aggregate less volatility than each activity displays when evaluated individually.

It thus amounts to a discrete selection of business projects to establish a portfolio of projects that, taken as such, results in less volatility of cash flows and profits than the volatility exhibited by the individual projects. A further dimension of diversification strategy in non-financial companies is illustrated by companies that embark upon diversifying the portfolio of businesses operated by the firm. It is a strategy of diversification by conglomerate merger.

Nonetheless, a revolution has taken place in the practice of risk management in non-financial businesses. Diversification through conglomerate action has fallen out of favour. This is not due to the criticisms levelled as discussed above, but is due to fundamental problems with the implementation of the strategy, as well as concurrent developments in the financial markets.

Over the many years that diversification across industries through conglomerate mergers as well as other means was in vogue, companies actually learned that they do not necessarily have the expertise to add value in more than one area. Companies have generally found it extremely difficult to prosper across industry lines. At the same time the financial markets started coming up with alternative risk hedging financial instruments such as forwards, swaps, options and futures. Those managers that were concerned about the volatility of cash flows and earnings consequently started favouring the more direct approaches to risk management that these financial instruments allowed. It was no longer necessary to invest directly in activities that reduce volatility indirectly.

a pitfall of diversification

Before the subject of diversification can be concluded, a basic pitfall needs to be highlighted. Diversification concerns the spreading of risks within a portfolio in order to dampen the volatility of the returns on the portfolio as a whole, compared to the volatility of returns of the individual portfolio assets. In order to give a very basic demonstration of the idea, one can resort to the comparison with vectors that was made earlier on.

Put very simply, and it must be stressed that this example serves only to demonstrate a principle and not how portfolio risk is calculated, the famous Pythagorean equation can be used: $A^2 = B^2 + C^2$.

Imagine the risk of asset B, as a vector: in this case, represented by a vertical line with direction North. Asset B might as well be a portfolio of risks for that matter. The risk referred to is not the asset or portfolio's vulnerability to any particular risk, but the aggregate volatility of its expected return. Assume also that the capital invested in the asset is $1 million. Although risk is normally described in terms of the standard deviation, which equates to the volatility of the expected return, in this instance just imagine the quantity of risk as having a value of 5. Let the length of the line represent the quantity of risk.

The holder of asset B wishes to dampen the risk by investing in asset C that has zero risk correlation with respect to asset B. Asset C represents a capital investment of $600,000 and has a risk value of 3. Imagine the risk of asset C as a vector lying at 90° with respect to the vector line of asset B. The risk of asset C is thus a horizontal line with direction East. The two vectors are at right angles with respect to one another because they have no correlation. There is no commonality in their direction. Let the length of the line represent the risk. Since they are to be incorporated into one portfolio, let the two vectors be joined at point p. The picture is illustrated in Figure 2-1.

The basic tenet of Markowitz is that the total risk of the portfolio will be less than the sum of the combined risks in the portfolio. The portfolio risk, after the addition of asset C, will thus be less than 8, which is the sum of the two assigned risk values. In fact, the length of the hypotenuse, line A in Figure 2-2, will represent the net risk of the portfolio. Thus from:

$$A^2 = B^2 + C^2$$

We derive the value of A as

$$A = (B^2 + C^2)^{1/2}$$

Substitute the values

$$= (5^2 + 3^2)^{1/2}$$

$$= (25 + 9)^{1/2}$$

$$= 34^{1/2}$$

$$= 5.8310$$

The total risk is thus 5.8310 as compared to the 8 one might have expected. Hold on a moment, though. The original risk attached to the portfolio was 5 and after diversification the risk is greater than 5. Something is amiss.

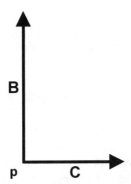

Figure 2-1   The uncorrelated risks on assets B and C illustrated as vectors.

Obvious as it may seem, many companies have nevertheless fallen into this trap. It is one of the reasons why risks are not as easily diversified away, as it might seem at first. In this case, the original portfolio was increased from its original capital investment of $1 million to $1.6 million. That will not diversify the existing portfolio. In fact, a second portfolio was created. However, the risk inside the original portfolio is still there at the arbitrary numerical value of 5. None of that risk has been dissipated. Granted however, that the second, enlarged portfolio has a better risk/reward profile than the first one.

Diversification therefore consists of a very careful and judicious selection of assets and risks in order to spread the investments in an existing portfolio in such a way that the total effect gives a desired risk/reward profile. Investments and projects can therefore not be valued solely on their own merit. Consideration must be given to the total effect that the incorporation of a particular asset or project will have on the risk/reward profile of the total portfolio of the business.

conclusion on diversification strategy

It would thus be fair to conclude that diversification, for all its advantages, proved a difficult, tortuous and ultimately inexact strategy for reducing the volatility of cash flows

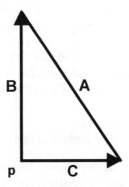

Figure 2-2   The net risk when assets B and C are incorporated into one portfolio equals the length of the hypotenuse.

and profits in the non-financial sector. For non-financial companies, hedging with financial derivative instruments thus superseded the earlier practice of diversification. This then is the opportune moment to investigate the strategy of hedging.

HEDGING WITH FINANCIAL DERIVATIVES

The action of hedging is taken when one risk is intentionally incurred in order to offset or neutralise another risk. Contrary to the just explained pitfall of diversification, it is justifiable to take on additional risk for hedging purposes. From the previous discussion on risk correlation, it must be evident that only a risk with a correlation of -1 relative to another risk will hedge that other risk. Thus the additional risk incurred will neutralise existing risk and it does not matter that the total value of the risk portfolio is effectively increased. Although mentioned in the previous discussion, it is necessary to investigate the correlation of -1 somewhat more intensively.

It has already been stated that two assets, whose values react oppositely to a change in some other economic variable, have a risk correlation of -1. It does not matter what the economic variable is. It can be anything such as an index like the FTSE 100, an interest rate or a particular foreign currency exchange rate; the principle remains the same. However, to have such a correlation, there must be no variance in the quantitative value changes. In other words, a one basis point change in the economic variable must always result in an opposite, but quantitatively equal change in value of both assets. The word 'always' in the previous sentence should also be noted. It denotes the element known as 'stationarity'. In practical terms this refers to the fact that two assets may have a risk correlation of -1 at one particular point of time, but over a longer period, their value changes start to diverge, resulting in a correlation greater than -1. This phenomenon is very often seen in assets such as in company stock that grow over time.

To find assets that are so correlated and that also display stationarity would be extremely difficult in real life. This is where financial derivatives enter the arena. As will be seen in much detail from the chapters that follow, these instruments can be tailored to suit any particular risk. In fact, their very popularity lies in the fact that risk correlations no longer have to be calculated and sought out over a wide range of assets. in order to hedge or at least dampen particular risks, a financial derivative can be tailor made to mirror the risk to be hedged. There are of course, also the standardised derivatives, such as futures and options on futures. They are not tailored to cover specific risks, but they are nevertheless extremely useful and popular in hedging risks. Because of their dynamics and structure, they can be made to approximate specific risks closely enough to make them eminently useful. This will appear more fully in the chapters that deal with these derivatives.

the perfect hedge

The technique of hedging thus has as its purpose: neutralising and eliminating risk, rather than dampening it as is the case with diversification. Neutralising risk means, by implication, that the outcome of an uncertain event is made certain at the start. A perfect hedge is established when the risk correlation between the asset being hedged and the derivative instrument used is exactly -1. This need not always be the case. It is possible and sometimes desirable to have a correlation that is slightly greater than -1. There must be a negative correlation however; otherwise, there will be no element of a hedge.

It is as well to understand the implications of a perfect hedge at the outset. A perfect hedge will not result in a greater profit being made on any transaction. A hedge protects against a loss on a transaction or on some other event that is hedged. It is thus not a technique primarily suited to improving profits. It is there to protect profit, value or budget. This is the reason for the debate traversed at the start of the chapter. Hedging is not a way of making profits or enhancing expected cash flows. If the expected return on a share is $5 million with a 50% probability, hedging cannot change it to $6 million. Hedging can only change the expectation to a slightly lower return (due to the cost of the hedge), but fully guaranteed.

For the purposes of this book, interest rate derivatives are narrowly defined. They are limited to FRAs, interest rate futures, interest rate swaps and interest rate options. The broader derivative contracts that contain combinations of these basic derivatives will be dealt with under strategies with derivatives, in a later chapter.

the benefits of managing interest rate risk

The question is thus what managing interest rates exposure will allow a company to do. What benefits can be expected from hedging interest rate risk with derivatives? There are a number of things that a company will be empowered to do through a policy of effective interest rate risk management.

Broadly speaking, hedging interest rate exposure will allow a company to achieve the expected and budgeted outcomes of transactions or business operations, the success of which are dependant upon, or influenced by changes in particular interest rates. Other techniques will allow a company to lower interest rate cost of borrowings or to improve yields on cash instrument investments.

Given these broad purposes, a closer investigation of the most commonly cited rationales for managing interest rate risk can be undertaken. What follows is not intended to be an exhaustive description of all rationales for hedging interest rate risk. The intention is merely to mention some of the most commonly cited rationales for managing interest rate risk.

the rationales for managing interest rate risk

The main motivation for managing interest rate exposure using financial derivatives appears to relate to financing activities by companies. Most projects that are financed from sources other than retained income are financed through debt. Debt necessarily implies exposure to interest rates. Companies often prefer fixed rate debt to floating rate debt due to the ease of budgeting. However, fixed rate borrowing is not always available and when it is, it may be at too high an interest rate. Companies can use derivatives to swap floating for fixed interest rates without increasing the cost of capital.

The second most important motivation seems to be doing exactly the opposite, namely swapping fixed interest rates for floating interest rates. This activity might be related to floating interest rate investments that are being exchanged for fixed rate incomes. Or, it might relate to companies that take the view that interest rates are going to move favourably for their exposures. They therefore exchange their fixed rate investments or borrowings for floating rate in order to avail themselves of the expected favourable changes in interest rates.

A further motivation is that companies need to fix the interest rate spread on new debt issues. Related to this is to lock in borrowing rates in advance of a debit issue. The latter action might be based on the view a company takes on the interest rate market at a particular time. Derivatives also allow companies to adjust their interest rate exposures based on their view of the markets. The result of a company's view of the market may influence it to alter the size or the timing of hedges. Only very few companies sometimes take up speculative positions because of their view of interest rates.

Finally, it is possible to manage investment return or cost of capital by means of some currency/interest rate derivatives. This does not constitute hedging activity, but forms part of risk management. By lowering the cost of capital by lowering the interest paid on loans or increasing the return on investments by using interest rate arbitrage, the riskiness of holding the assets or the liabilities involved are lowered.

These rationales will be more thoroughly discussed and analysed in the final chapter of the book when the management of specific interest rate risks is considered.

interest rate risk management rationales – their relative importance

It is interesting to take note of the rationales of companies that are actually using currency derivatives to hedge interest rate risk. As was mentioned previously, the Weiss Center for International Financial Research conducted a detailed survey of derivatives usage and practice by non-financial corporations in late 1995. The Weiss Center is attached to the Wharton School of the University of Pennsylvania. The survey was done with the support of CIBC Wood Gundy and more than 2,000 US businesses in the non-financial sector were sampled. The survey is reported and discussed in an article by Richard Marston, Gregory S. Hayt and Gordon M. Bodnar entitled 'Derivatives as a way of reducing risk' and published by FT Prentice Hall in *Mastering Finance*, 1998.

It appears from the survey that 73% of those businesses that use derivatives to manage risk use interest rate derivatives to manage their interest rates risk. The interest rate swap contract is by far the most popular derivative instrument, followed by structured derivatives, OTC options and futures. It appears that 78% of companies listed swaps as their first choice among interest rate derivatives, while 95% rank it as one of their three top choices.

It is interesting to note the conclusion that the authors of the article come to. The conclusion they reach is that derivatives are primarily used to reduce risk rather than to take risk. This is not surprising, given the purpose, history and development of derivatives. They also conclude that the use of derivatives will increase due to price volatility in the markets and as companies' knowledge of them improves. The public's negative perception of derivatives was also found to be an inhibiting factor in the use of them by some non-derivative user companies. This is also bound to improve as investor and public knowledge of the real nature of these instruments grows.

conclusion

Even though only 41% of the respondents in the survey said that they used derivatives, the conclusion was that notwithstanding several widely publicised financial debacles related to the improper use of derivatives, there was no real fall-off of users. In fact, the evidence seems to suggest that there was a small increase in the numbers of businesses using derivatives in 1995 over 1994. It must also be kept in mind that the sample represents only businesses in the non-financial sector, which is not traditionally the largest users of derivative instruments.

From the fact that the vast majority of users link their use of derivatives to hedging contractual obligations and changing the nature of their interest exposures, some useful conclusions can also be drawn. It seems that all the theorising concerning the value of hedging away risk, companies find value in treating risks on an individual basis. As was earlier suggested, it seems that hedging judgements are not made in the context of hedging company value as such. Rather, it seems that hedging decisions are made on a transaction by transaction basis. These findings, taken with the large percentage of 'sometimes' responses, may suggest that companies tend to weigh the advantages to be gained against the costs incurred in hedging in each separate transaction.

It is suggested that such an approach cannot be faulted. That seems to be the best and proper way to approach the principle of hedging and the proper use of derivative instruments. Neither a policy of always hedging every interest rate risk exposure, nor a policy of never hedging any interest rate risk exposure can ever give as satisfactory a result as a transaction by transaction consideration of risk exposure will give. Company practice seems to bear out this evaluation.

CHECKLIST FOR THE REVIEW OF CHAPTER 2

General overview of the strategies of managing interest rate risk: the overall control objectives of the material dealt with in this chapter are to gain a basic understanding of the value of interest rate risk management as a corporate strategy as well as of the application and value of the strategies of portfolio diversification and hedging with interest rate derivatives.

	Key Issues	Illustrative Scope or Approach
2.1	Does the firm currently manage its interest rate risk?	If not: • The company should regularly evaluate the nature and extent of its direct and indirect exposure to interest rate risk • The company should regularly investigate the different alternatives that are available to hedge the exposures and the cost of each alternative • A cost/benefit analysis should be considered at least annually to determine whether not managing the risk continues to be more beneficial to the company than doing so

continued

	Key Issues	Illustrative Scope or Approach
		If yes: • The company must regularly evaluate whether its risk management and internal control policies are as effective as they could be • The company should consider the effect of its risk management strategies on company value at least annually
2.2	Does the business currently have a system of internal control coupled with a set policy on managing its interest rate exposure?	It is the responsibility of the board of directors to establish a system of internal control and to set appropriate policies therefor. The board must ensure that the system is effective in managing risks in the approved manner
2.3	Does the company consider all the major rationales for managing interest rate risk when determining its risk management policies?	• To hedge the company's contractual commitments • To protect the company's cash flows from interest rate volatility • To take advantage of favourable movements in interest rates • To fix the cost of capital or the yield on investments • To lower the cost of capital • To increase the yield on interest rate related investments
2.4	Does the company consider the use of all available interest rate derivatives when considering its risk management policies?	The major interest rate derivative instruments are FRAs, interest rate swaps, interest rate futures, OTC interest rate options and options on interest rate futures Research indicates that interest rate swaps are by far the most popular choice of interest rate derivative A company should not develop a natural first choice or select a particular derivative purely from habit. Every risk situation should be analysed and the best derivative chosen on the basis of the best horse for the course Management must ensure that there is sufficient knowledge and expertise within the company to enable it to make an informed choice in every instance. That may ensure that the most appropriate derivative is used to manage every particular instance of interest rate risk

continued

	Key Issues	Illustrative Scope or Approach
2.5	Does the company encourage a risk management culture among all its employees?	All employees have some responsibility for internal control and risk management as part of their accountability for achieving objectives
2.6	Does the company ensure adequate training of employees in the basic requirements of risk management?	Management must ensure that employees collectively have the necessary knowledge, skills, information and authority to establish, operate and monitor the prescribed control and risk management system
		All employees require an understanding of the company and its objectives, the industries and market in which it operates, and of the risks it faces

three

interest spot and forward rate agreement markets

THE SPOT INTEREST RATE MARKET

introduction

Every article of commercial value, be it corporeal or incorporeal, trades on a market. Articles of commercial value are often referred to by their Latin term, *merx*, to indicate everything of commercial value. Although every *merx*, by definition, has a value sounding in money, money itself is also a *merx*. Money has a value and thus it has a price.

It is often said that interest is the price of money. Of course, money in the sense of a particular currency also has another price, which is reflected by its value in terms of other currencies. It is also true that every currency has a particular interest rate applicable to it at any particular moment, which rate of interest is not necessarily applicable to any other currency. It can therefore not be said that money as such has a particular price. Every currency has a particular price at a particular time, which is distinct from other currencies' prices at the same moment of time.

Nevertheless, the exchange rates of currencies are interrelated and arbitrage keeps them so. The value of any currency against every other currency will be such that if these rates of exchange are known, then the rate of exchange between any other two currencies can be calculated therefrom. In that valuation system, the interest rate differential between currencies play a vital role. Although the differential is by far not the only factor that influences the relative values of currencies, it plays an important and irreplaceable role therein.

How then is the price of money determined? In a free market system, the price of money is determined by the market. It is determined in the markets where money changes hands, and the markets are loosely referred to as the money markets. All the major industrialised countries have money markets with broadly similar operating structures, especially since the general liberalisation of the world's financial markets which was completed in the 1990s.

Although this book is not intended as a primer on interest rates and the money markets as such, it is necessary to undertake a brief redux. The purpose is to cover those principles and aspects of the money markets that will be essential to a proper understanding and appreciation of interest rate derivatives and their uses in managing interest rate risk. Readers who are well versed in the principles and workings of the money markets might wish to skip the next section and continue to the section of the chapter following thereon.

the money market

The money market in its broadest sense, is the cash or spot market for money. Cash and spot have the same meaning in this context. They refer to the market where money is traded for immediate delivery. The trades are done and settled on the spot. This distinguishes it from the futures markets where deals are struck for trades that will be done in the future.

The term 'money market' is a technical term, and indicates a market that meets two conditions. The first condition is that the term refers to the spot market on which a single currency is traded. It is the market on which a particular currency is 'bought' and 'sold' for spot delivery. Buying and selling in the money market translates as 'borrowing' and 'lending'. Spot borrowing and lending thus means that the money that is borrowed and lent is handed over at the time of the deal and not at some agreed future date. 'Immediately' must also not be taken too literally. It can sometimes mean a delay of up to 2 days before the money actually changes hands.

The second condition is that only the market for short-term funds is referred to as the money market. The term 'money market rates' thus indicates those interest rates that are applied to money borrowed and lent out for a short time. What exactly constitutes a short term will be dealt with presently.

The role of the money market can thus be said to be to facilitate the flow of short-term capital from investors to borrowers. A borrower today may literally be an investor tomorrow, so money flows between market participants continuously. It is also important to note the term 'single currency' as used above. In that sense, it is intended to distinguish the domestic money market from the international currency market, where currencies are traded against one another. The money market will thus normally be the 'home' market of a particular currency.

❐   SHORT-TERM RATES

Although what exactly is considered short-term for borrowing is rather nebulous, it is generally accepted to refer to periods of less than 1 year. Nevertheless, it sometimes extends out to 18 months. Since borrowing and lending is the activity on a money market, it stands to reason that time periods are the essence of the price mechanism.

Money is borrowed and lent only for a time. It may be for periods ranging anywhere between a number of years and a few minutes, but the concept of lending and borrowing is inseparable from time. It is for this reason that the price of money is expressed in terms of an interest rate per period. Consequently, the term 'money market rates' thus generally applies to interest rates for borrowings for periods of less than 1 year. That is the sense in which the terms 'money market' and 'money market rates' will henceforth be used in this book.

The money market is itself obviously also a component of the financial markets. The market in longer-term interest rate instruments forms an indistinguishable part of the financial markets. However, it would be a misconception to regard the money market as a single entity. It really consists of a series of interlinked pools of money that are used for investment and borrowings using different investment instruments.

Different interest rates are applied to different investment periods, for reasons of risk exposure that are mentioned later. It is important to note also that different interest rates are applied to different investment instruments. Not all investment instruments hold the same risk for the investor. Thus, interest rates will differ even for same-period investments. The difference will then be related to the difference in the risk associated with the instrument concerned.

Money market instruments are cash instruments, there are several of them, and they differ from country to country. Nevertheless, they are similar in essence and in purpose. They are also referred to as cash instruments or paper and they represent investments and borrowings where the entire sum of interest plus principal is due at maturity. There are thus no interim cash flows. Some of the more commonly encountered instruments are discussed below.

❐ MONEY MARKET INSTRUMENTS

The key money market instrument in the US is Federal Reserve funds. Although some longer-term transactions involving Federal Reserve funds do occur, most are for overnight maturity. Federal Reserve funds that are traded for longer periods than overnight maturity are called term Federal Reserve funds. These funds are central to the money market and the rate is keenly observed by the market as it serves as an indicator of the US Federal Reserve's monetary policy.

Commercial paper (CP) is another important money market instrument. CPs are in fact promissory notes, issued by large corporations, typically maturing in 30 days or less. Companies that issue them are rated by a rating agency such as Standard&Poor, thus establishing the credit quality of the paper. CPs are generally issued on demand from investors on a continuous basis and are generally considered safe investments for short-term money.

Bankers acceptances are also highly rated paper. These are usually for smaller sums of money than in the case of commercial paper. They arise from forward dated bills drawn on companies in the course of trade. If the bill is presented to a bank and the bank accepts it, the bill becomes a high quality, negotiable instrument. The bill then inherits the credit standing of the accepting bank rather than the credit standing of the company on whom the bill is drawn. Bankers acceptances trade at a discount rate, rather than a direct interest rate. The rate is generally lower than that for CPs, because of the low risk involved.

The final instrument to be discussed here is a certificates of deposit (CDs). They are negotiable paper issued by banks in maturities that range from 14 days up to 5 years or more. However, the vast majority of CDs are for 6 months or less. They are sometimes also referred to as time deposits.

❐   THE EUROMARKET

At the start of this discussion, the money market was defined as the spot, short-term domestic market of a single currency. While the definition is quite correct, there is also a transnational market for short-term loans and deposits in the major currencies. The transnational market is really an offshore pool of money where a particular currency is traded offshore. This transnational market is referred to as the Euromarket, but it is somewhat of a misnomer. The derivation is historical rather than geographical and has no connection with the Euro currency unit, which is a much later development.

The Euromarket is an extremely important market internationally and its interest rates will feature prominently in the examples used in later chapters. It is really a professional, wholesale market that is accessed and used almost exclusively by banks. Through banks, the facilities and rates of the Euromarket are available to their clients. Many derivative instruments have Eurocurrencies and interest rates as their underlying instruments and understanding this market is thus a prerequisite for managing interest rate risk.

The offshore markets originally developed in response to the requirements of international money market participants, especially the requirements that arose due to cold war politics. The domestic market for any currency is obviously subject to domestic political control, a situation that often does not suit international users of a currency. This is especially true of such very widely used international currencies as the US dollar and the Japanese yen.

Political control was not the only issue that played a role in the creation and success of these markets. The monetary authorities in a country impose rules and regulations on domestic banks to suit their own purposes. For instance, in every country there are different requirements as to the reserves that banks have to place with the central bank of that country. If banks have to place in reserve with the central bank say, 10% of the deposits they hold, they can only lend 90% of each deposit on to its customers. This obviously limits the money available to domestic banks for investment and would consequently make them uncompetitive with banks that do not have to comply with a similar requirement. Thus, the offshore money market began.

The practice began by the placing of US dollar deposits with banks in London. Banks operating out of London were thus placed in a position where they could take in and lend out US dollars without the restrictions of the US Federal Reserve faced by US banks. The US dollar is the most widely traded currency in the world and so other banks outside the US quickly jumped on the bandwagon. Lots of short-term borrowing and lending of US dollars was soon taking place outside of the US and the centre of that trading activity was in London. The name 'Eurodollar' was coined to describe dollars that were placed on deposit outside the US and that were not subject to the restrictions of the US Federal Reserve.

Since Eurodollars were being lent and borrowed subject to different conditions from those that prevailed in the US, it follows that these transactions were differently priced. In addition, since the Euromarket was initially restricted to inter-bank trading in London, the appropriate interest rates became known as London inter bank rates. As in all trading, the banks have bid rates, at which they are prepared to borrow Eurodollars as well as offered rates, at which they are willing to lend Eurodollars. The London inter bank offered rate thus became known as Libor, while the bid rate is known as Libid. Only the Libor rates for different investment periods are important outside the banking world. They are used as international benchmarks for floating interest rates.

The US dollar was not alone in the Euromarket for long. It was soon joined by the Japanese yen as well by other European currencies. Consequently, the markets also trade other currencies 'offshore' such as Euroyen. Libor thus also gained additional meanings as it became necessary to specify the maturity period as well as the currency in Libor based transactions, such as '3-month US dollar Libor', and '6-month yen Libor', etc.

Today, the main offshore centres are London, Singapore and Bahrain. These locations are primarily trusted to provide facilities for Eurotransactions that are exempt from domestic reserve requirements. London is still the single largest location for Eurotransactions. Eurotransactions are, however, not totally unsupervised.

In London, Eurotransactions were always supervised by the Bank of England until its responsibilities were taken over by the Financial Services Authority (FSA) in 1998. Internationally, the Bank for International Settlements (BIS) also acts as a central bankers bank. Although it has no supervisory powers, it does act as a vehicle for international monetary co-operation and thus influences the control of Euromarket trading.

❑ EUROMARKET INSTRUMENTS

The vast majority of Eurotransactions involve time deposits. A time deposit usually consists of the taking and placing of unsecured funds for a specified or fixed maturity date. The credit risk of such deposits is thus totally dependent on the credit rating of the borrowing bank. During the 1990s, repos have also become important in the Euromarket. This involves the purchase and sale of secured paper at a given repurchase rate. This brings the Euromarket more in line with the trading practices of 'domestic' money markets.

A second market instrument that has developed is the CD and they play an increasingly important part in the market. A CD is usually created by large international corporations that place their temporarily excess dollar funds on deposit with an offshore bank. The bank then issues a negotiable certificate of deposit to the company that specifies all the terms, including the maturity date of the deposit. The company can then assign the CD by negotiating it to a third party for value. The onward negotiation of the Eurodollar deposits constitutes a very liquid secondary market for these securities. The largest part of this market consists of negotiable Eurodollar CDs. Although a CD can be issued for any amount, the minimum size for the secondary trading of these instruments is usually $1 million.

The third instrument of the Euromarket is true Euro-commercial paper (ECP). The market for this instrument has only recently matured into an important short-term source of finance for global borrowers. Like domestic commercial paper, it is an instrument issued by an international corporation for Eurocurrency borrowed for a specified term.

the yield curve

The yield curve is an important concept in the totality of the interest rate markets. It brings together all the interest rates that pertain to a particular currency at a particular time. It thus integrates the short-term rates of the money market, with the long-term rates that are determined in the financial markets as a whole. As has been discussed, rates in the true domestic market of a currency will differ from the rates for the same currency in the Euromarket. Two curves thus result: the first is derived from interest rates in the domestic market of a currency while the other results from the interest rates in the Euromarket.

In addition, to make the yield curve meaningful, the curve should be derived from comparable instruments. This means that bank deposits should be considered separately from Treasury bonds. The latter yield curve can become quite complex as the yield curve for securities often are. The reason is that apart from interest earnings, their yields are influenced by capital gains, which are treated differently from interest earnings by most tax regimes. The yield curves discussed here will thus refer to simple deposit or investment interest rate yield curves. It also needs to be mentioned that overnight rates are normally excluded from the yield curve. Overnight rates are often subject to very different pressures of supply and demand than prevail generally. Their inclusion might then distort the total picture more than clarify it.

The yield curve arises from the following considerations. Due to the basic phenomenon that different rates are applied to different investment periods, it follows that there ought to be some discernible pattern, related to the length of the period of investment. If one were to plot at any particular moment, the current interest rates against increasing periods to maturity, the resulting graph might be enlightening. In fact, the result is what is known as the yield curve or the term structure of interest rates. Figure 3-1 illustrates a steep, normal yield curve.

Normally, the yield curve would be an upward slanting curve, indicating that the longer the maturity period, the higher the interest rate applied to the loan/borrowing.

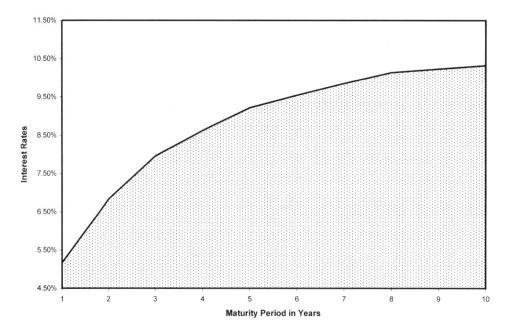

Figure 3-1   Normal yield curve.

This is regarded as normal since the longer the exposure to a single investment, the higher the risk. Thus, under normal circumstances an investor would demand compensation in the form of a higher interest rate for accepting the higher risk.

This does not mean that the normal upward slanting curve is usual. The curve is seldom smooth. It often is spoon shaped and may exhibit bumps and dips. It also varies from a steep upward slope as depicted in the illustration above to an inverted downward slope, where long rates are lower than short rates. Although there are many examples of inverted yield curves, they are atypical and are relatively seldom seen. Flat term structures, on the other hand are often found, especially in times of lagging economic growth. It must also be apparent that due to differences in local economic conditions, the interest rate term structure will be different for each currency.

The yield curve contains a lot of useful economic information. Most importantly, for the purposes of this book, it contains the information required to determine the forward interest rate that is used to price interest rate derivatives like FRAs and interest rate futures contracts.

FORWARD RATE AGREEMENTS

introduction

A forward rate agreement is an agreement between a borrower and a lender on an interest rate to be charged on a future loan of a notional amount of principal, for an agreed period of maturity. The date on which the future loan is to be taken up forms part of the agreement.

The important factor to keep in mind is that the agreement is essentially concerned with a future interest rate. An interest rate is only meaningful if it is applied to a sum of principal. Thus the principal in an FRA must be agreed, but its is only notional. This means that its sole function is to provide a basis that allows the quantification of the amount of interest that will be settled at the maturity of the contract. Indeed, it can be said that the agreement is notional, except for the interest, which is the only 'real' thing about the agreement. This will become clear presently.

The whole point of an FRA is that it is cash settled at maturity or, more usually on the settlement date. It means that the agreed interest rate will be compared to the agreed interest rate index, such as Libor, on a particular date. The difference, if any, between the two rates will be quantified using the notional principal as base and the party found to be owing the difference, would settle with the other party in cash. The precise mechanics of achieving this will be explained in this section.

A number of technical terms are involved in dealing with these derivatives. These terms will be dealt with individually in order to illustrate the function of each. Although each term forms a necessary part of the whole, the multiplicity of terms should not be taken to indicate an extremely involved concept. The basic idea underlying an FRA is extremely simple. This will be apparent once whole structure is viewed and when the case studies are discussed.

the notional parties

It may seem strange to refer to two actual parties to an agreement as 'notional' parties. However, as far as the agreement itself is concerned, the parties are very real, as are their legal rights and obligations. Since the future loan is merely notional, one party would be a notional borrower, while the lender would be a notional lender.

The notional borrower will be the party who undertakes to pay the agreed rate of interest on the notional loan. Should interest rates rise to higher than the agreed interest rate, this party will be in a better position, because his obligation to pay the lower interest rate remains fixed. The notional borrower is thus protected against rising interest rates.

The notional lender agrees to lend the notional principal at the notional interest rate. Should interest rates drop, this party will benefit, as he will still receive the higher interest rate. The notional lender is thus the party protected against a drop in interest rates by the agreement.

In the case of both parties, the converse is also true. Both parties cannot gain from a favourable movement in interest rates. Because they have fixed the future interest rate, no change in the applicable interest rate will affect them, at least as far as the contemplated transaction is concerned.

the contract rate

The contract rate is that agreed interest rate that will be applied to the notional amount to be borrowed. The rate is usually one of the standard Libor rates, such as 3-month or 6-month Libor.

However, the current Libor rate will not be used as the contract rate. At the time that the FRA is entered into, the applicable Libor rate will be calculated forward to arrive at the contract rate. It is thus the forward 3-month Libor rate, for example, that will be the contract rate. This calculation of the forward rate will be examined at the appropriate time.

the contract amount

The contract amount is the amount of the notional principal. As has been mentioned, a forward rate agreement is not an agreement to borrow or to lend any amount of money at any time. It is not a necessary result of the agreement that any of the parties will lend or borrow any money from any person at any time at all. The point of the agreement is merely to fix a rate of interest at an agreed time in the future. Since no actual loan is contemplated, the contract amount is thus purely notional.

In essence, an FRA is a contract particularly suited to managing interest rate risk. It is an extremely efficient way of hedging against interest rate risk. Its efficiency can be compared only to interest rate futures contracts if they are available for the same underlying rates. FRAs are not an alternative way of securing a loan in the future. The purpose of the contract amount is to provide a mechanism to allow for the quantification of the interest due in terms of the agreement.

the contract period

The contract period refers to the period of the notional loan. This is represented by the length of the period from the date that the notional loan will be made to the date that the principal and interest will be repaid. It is thus the period from the settlement date to the maturity date of the notional loan, as is explained below.

Although the contract period can obviously be for any period that the parties choose, the period usually consists of a 'standard' period, such as 3 months, 6 months, 1 year or any multiple thereof.

❐ THE SETTLEMENT DATE

The settlement date is that agreed upon date in the future when the notional loan is to be made and taken up. It is thus the start date of the period of the notional loan. It is called the settlement date, because it is the date on which the settlement sum is normally payable. As is discussed later, the settlement could also be payable on the maturity date, but that would be a departure from the practice in the FRA market.

❐ THE MATURITY DATE

The maturity date is the date on which the notional loan must be repaid. It is usual to refer to that date as the maturity date of the loan or the investment. It represents the final date of the period of the contract.

In FRAs the maturity date is the date on which the principal and interest is repaid as a single amount. There is no provision for interim interest payments and receipts. For this reason, FRAs are often also referred to as single-period interest rate swaps.

❐ THE FIXING DATE

The fixing date is an important date in the structure of an FRA. The settlement rate of the FRA will be fixed on that date. It is thus the date on which the agreed interest rate index will be compared to the contract rate in order to determine the settlement sum.

the settlement rate

The settlement rate is the interest rate against which the agreed contract interest rate is compared. Assume that the contract rate is 3-month US dollar Libor. When the FRA was established, the appropriate forward rate would have been calculated and that would become the contract rate. Assume that that rate was 7.5%. Assume further that when the fixing date arrives, 3-month US dollar Libor is quoted at 8%. This latter rate is the settlement rate. The contract rate will be settled against the 8% rate.

the settlement sum

The settlement sum is the quantified amount of interest that one party will be paying to the other party. Given the assumptions used in the previous paragraph, the settlement sum would be calculated on an annual percentage rate of 0.5%.

The normal practice is to pay the settlement sum on the settlement date, thus extinguishing the FRA. However, given the nature of interest rate calculations, this implies that the settlement sum would have to be discounted back to its net present value, using the contract rate. This is required because settlement of the interest now takes place at the start of the loan rather than at maturity, when the full interest would normally have been payable. These calculations will be demonstrated in due course.

Nevertheless, it is in the interest of all parties to finalise the contract at the soonest date rather than at the latest date. It limits exposure to credit risk and it serves no further purpose to keep the deal on the books once the result is known.

fra market conventions

As in all markets, there are certain conventions. Knowing what they are makes it easier to use the markets properly. The FRA markets are not fraught with difficulties, but a few pointers may be in order.

☐   BUYING AND SELLING

One of the most important conventions to keep in mind is that the market refers to the buying and selling of FRAs. Up to now, they have been treated as agreements in this book. Indeed, they are agreements and normally one enters into an agreement. Normally, one is not said to buy an agreement, unless it costs money. Nevertheless, FRAs are agreements that do not have a price as such, but which are regarded as things that are bought and sold. The same situation arises when futures contracts are dealt with.

The buyer of an FRA is the notional borrower. The buyer is thus the party seeking protection against a rise in interest rates. The seller of an FRA is the notional lender. The seller is thus the party seeking protection from a drop in interest rates.

☐   STANDARD PERIODS AND QUOTES

The second matter that should be noted is that the periods dealt with in the market are standard periods of 3 months and multiples thereof. This facilitates communication and pricing in the market. It also means that when quotes are asked for and given, they imply months into the future.

To understand the quoting system correctly, it must be kept in mind that the FRA is basically an agreement to take out a loan at a date which is a fixed period into the future, for a loan that will last for a further fixed period into the future. However, the periods should be kept to standard quarterly periods.

Thus, one might request a quote for a $5,000,000, 3 × 6 FRA. The periods mentioned are always calculated from the present time forward. Thus, the request is interpreted as meaning an FRA that will start in 3 months time and end in 6 months time, measured from the present. The request is consequently shorthand for an FRA agreement with a contract amount of $5,000,000, a settlement date 3 months hence, a maturity date 6 months hence and consequently a contract period of 90 days. The implication will further be that the underlying interest rate will be 3-month US dollar Libor.

☐ INTEREST RATE QUOTES

A further important convention is the manner of the quoting of interest rates. The applicable rates of interest are always annualised rates. This means that when a 3-month rate or a 6-month rate is quoted, it is not the effective rate for that shorter period that is quoted, but the annualised rate for that period is used. Thus, to quantify interest payable or receivable, the annual rates must be converted to rates for the specific period or periods in question. In order to do the necessary calculations one has to know what the applicable interest rate conventions are.

There are two bases for calculating the number of days in a standard year. A 360-day and a 365-day year is used, depending on the currency. In the Euromarkets, the 360-day year is used for virtually all currencies. The only exceptions are sterling and the Kuwaiti dinar, for both of which the 365-day year is standard.

☐ TERMS AND CONDITIONS

In the Euromarket, FRAs are usually traded on the terms and conditions agreed to by the British Bankers' Association (BBA). This makes for legal certainty, while uniformity of terms creates international familiarity with the instrument. All of this leads to liquidity in the market because traders and clients know exactly what they are dealing with and what the implications of the deals are. These standard terms and conditions for FRAs are known in the market as FRABBA terms.

One of the very important terms of FRABBA is the so-called BBAISR, or the British Bankers' Association Interest Settlement Rate. The Association has an appointed information vendor, which supplies financial market information to market participants. The BBAISR provides that the offered rate the information vendor calculates at 11 A.M. on any day is the interest settlement rate for FRAs with a 'fixing date for settlement-date value' on that day. How the vendor should fix the rate is also detailed by the regulations.

calculating the forward-forward rate

A forward-forward interest rate is used in the deposit market. It involves the making of actual deposits of money for the periods concerned. It is called a forward-forward rate, because at the time when the agreement is made, the date at which the deposit will be made and taken is on a future, or forward date. The maturity date of the deposit will then be at a deferred forward date. This market was in existence long before FRAs came into existence. Forward-forward agreements oblige the parties actually to place and take large sums on deposit. That obviously has an impact on the assets and liabilities of the parties as well as their cash flows. FRAs are a meaner and leaner way of obtaining the same benefit without the disadvantages.

It is thus not surprising that the rate used in forward-forward deposits, are also applied to FRAs. The concepts are identical. When FRAs are dealt with, the rate is merely referred to as the forward rate. Although, no actual principal changes hands in an FRA, as it does in a proper forward-forward deposit, the notional loan in an FRA equals a forward-forward deposit in all respects, except that it is notional rather than actual.

Although the calculation of the forward-forward rate seldom needs to be done by the non-financial client of a bank or financial institution, it is quite straightforward. The purpose of discussing it in the present context is to facilitate better insight into the structure of interest rate derivatives as such. Once the method of calculating the rate is understood, the derivatives and their uses become more apparent. In addition, this insight might be useful later, when risk management decisions need to be taken in a business context.

There are two ways of arriving at the forward-forward, or merely the forward rate as used in FRAs. The first method is the easy route. Assuming we need to know the rate applicable to a $5,000,000, 3 × 6 FRA, we need look no further than the price of the 3-month US dollar Libor futures contract, with expiry date 3 months hence. The rate at which it is trading will approximate the forward rate for the above FRA. Incidentally, the futures rate and the forward rate will not be the same. The futures rate needs to be adjusted for convexity in order to convert it into the proper forward rate. That particular calculation does not require further elaboration in this book.

The second method is by actual calculation, using the yield curve for Eurodollar cash deposits. On the yield curve appropriate rates for a 3-month Eurodollar deposit and a 6-month Eurodollar deposit is read. Applicable formulas are used to calculate the forward rate from the yield curve. From the curve the 3 × 6 month forward-forward rate, or any other forward-forward rate, can be calculated.

However, there are a number of very basic and very practical methods used in the marketplace. The step-by-step method is the easiest one and it will be used in this discussion. The issues involved in the whole system might be better explained and understood if the whole problem is systematically explored.

The calculation requires the matter to be approached from the point of view of the bank or institution giving the quote. The bank or institution granting the loan must take into account the cost of funds in order to determine a profitable rate at which it could do the deal. Therefore, the bid/offer spread is relevant, as is the actual number of days in the 3- and 6-month periods as is shown hereunder.

From the point of view of the bank, it must raise the $5,000,000 for the full 6-month period. It must consequently pay for the funds at the 6-month offered rate. The client requesting the forward-forward rate is only prepared to borrow the money for the last 3 months of the 6-month period and will thus only pay interest for the last 3 months. The bank cannot charge the client interest for the first 3 months, as it does not have the use of the funds then. In addition, it cannot charge so high an interest rate for the last 3 months that the charge covers the cost of the funds for the full 6 months, plus a profit. The bank thus approaches the matter differently.

The first consideration of the bank is that it will be able to lend out the $5,000,000 for the first 3 months. It will be able to lend it out at the 3-month offered rate and thus recoup part of its cost of funds. Assume, for the purposes of illustration, that the 6-month period has 182 days, while the 3-month period consists of 90 days. Further, assume that the 6-month offered rate is 5.5%, while the 3-month bid rate is 5.25%. This suggests a rather steep yield curve.

The interest rates are annual rates, so they must be reduced to rates for 90 days and 182 days, respectively. The US dollar Libor convention works on a 360-day year. To convert the 6-month offered rate to a rate for 182 days, the annual rate must be divided by 360 days and the result multiplied by 182. Thus:

$$\text{Rate} = \frac{0.055}{360} \times 182$$

$$= 2.78\%$$

Similarly, the 3-month bid rate is converted as follows:

$$\text{Rate} = \frac{0.0525}{360} \times 90$$

$$= 1.31\%$$

The total cost of funds to the bank would be \$139,000 (\$5,000,000 × 2.78%), less the \$65,500 (\$5,000,000 × 1.31%) income from the investment of the funds for the first 90 days. The net cost is thus \$73,500 (\$139,000 − \$65,500). Consequently, the interest charged for the second period must at least equal the outstanding balance of the cost of funds. However, the bank is not in the business of lending out money at cost. The only reason a bank opens its doors in the morning is to make a profit. Thus, a further perspective is required.

In order to avoid errors that arise from too much rounding off, the above result can be recalculated somewhat differently. The net cost calculated above, is merely the difference between the interest received for the first 90 days and the total interest paid by the bank for the fund. In order to determine the percentage of the principal that the difference represents, the actual interest earned is subtracted from the actual interest paid. The calculations done above are then merely combined and subtracted, as follows:

$$\text{Rate} = \left(\frac{0.055}{360} \times 182\right) - \left(\frac{0.0525}{360} \times 90\right)$$

$$= 1.468\%$$

The result of the subtraction can be tested by calculating the actual cost by using the percentage obtained above. The result is \$73,400, which is virtually the same as the amount calculated previously. The difference arises from the rounding of the percentages used in the earlier calculation. First, in order to determine what the interest rate is that must be charged to cover the outstanding cost, the previous calculations must be turned on their heads. In other words, the bank must now calculate the annual percentage that it must charge to recoup its outstanding cost of funds over the 92 days that the client is actually going to borrow the money. Thus, it has to divide the percentage by the 92 days to get the daily rate and then multiply that result by 360 to get the annual rate. The calculation is as follows:

$$\text{Annual Rate} = \frac{1.468}{92} \times 360$$

$$= 5.744\%$$

The bank must charge the client an annual rate of 5.744% for the second 3-month period in order to break even. This is not the correct forward-forward rate since the bank, as mentioned previously, does not wish to deal at cost. The interest rate must be brought back into line to reflect the profit margin, which is given by the bank's bid/offer spread. This is achieved by adjusting the interest rate required to make good the shortfall, upward by the actual interest accrual (expressed as a percentage of the principal) charged during the first 90 day period. It amounts to an interest charge on the interest rate. In the present example the interest accrual was 1.31% – more accurately, it calculated to 1.311/4%. This adjusted rate is the correct forward-forward rate. The adjustment is calculated as follows:

$$\text{Forward Rate} = 5.74456\left(1 + \frac{1.3125}{100}\right)$$

$$= 5.82\%$$

The process just described can be summarised in one formula, which does all the steps in one. For those readers who enjoy math, the formula is given hereunder. If the figures of this example are substituted into the formula, it will give the result obtained above. The formula as it stands, is applicable to calculating mid-term forward-forward interest rates. It thus caters for calculations up to 1 year. It needs to be adjusted to calculate interest rate periods of greater than 1 year. However, the logic of the process, as explained above, remains the same no matter what periods are involved.

There are always two periods involved in a forward-forward rate. The first period is always the shorter period, because the second period is always the total period, which automatically includes the first one.

The formula for calculating a mid-term forward-forward rate is as follows:

$$\text{Forward Rate} = \frac{(\text{LP} \times \text{LR}) - (\text{SP} \times \text{SR})}{(\text{LP} - \text{SP})\left(1 + \dfrac{\text{SP} \times \text{SR}}{100 \times \text{IC}}\right)}$$

For the purposes of the formula, the key is as follows:

- SP the number of days in the short period;
- LP the number of days in the long period;
- SR the annual interest rate for the short period;
- LR the annual rate for the long period;
- IC the interest rate convention: 365 days for sterling and Kuwaiti dinar, but 360 days for all others.

case study 1: using a forward rate agreement to lock in future borrowing rates

Luthor Homes is a residential housing construction company in the San Francisco Bay area. Its cash flow projections show that the company will require short-term funds totalling $3,000,000 in 3 months time. The funds will be required for a further 3 months, whereupon the company will be able to replace them from its own cash flow.

The company's treasurer is uneasy about interest rates, as short-term rates have been quite volatile. He decides to lock in present rates, using an FRA. Locking in future interest rates is in fact a hedge against a rise in interest rates. He contacts the company's bank as well as a few other banks in the area that the company has used from time to time, asking for quotes on a $3,000,000, 3 × 6 FRA.

❐   FINANCIAL INFORMATION

At the time of the request, the Federal Reserve reports that the 3-month US dollar deposit rate is 4.66%, while the 6-month deposit rate is 4.45%. Since the longer rate is lower, the yield curve is clearly inverted, at least in the short-term money market. The treasurer would like to take advantage of this favourable situation.

Bay Tech Bank offers him the best deal. They structure their bid/offered rates around the US dollar deposit rates quoted by the Federal Reserve. Their forward rate is consequently based on a 3-month bid rate of 5.16% and a 6-month offered rate of 3.95%. The 6-month period has 182 days and the initial 3-month period has 92 days. The rate for the FRA that is offered to the company, using the formula in the previous section, is as follows:

$$\text{FRA Rate} = \frac{(182 \times 3.95) - (92 \times 5.16)}{(182 - 92)\left(1 + \dfrac{92 \times 5.16}{100 \times 360}\right)}$$

$$= \frac{718.90 - 474.72}{90\left(1 + \dfrac{474.72}{36000}\right)}$$

$$= \frac{244.18}{90(1 + 0.0131867)}$$

$$= \frac{244.18}{90(1.0131867)}$$

$$= \frac{244.18}{91.186803}$$

$$= 2.68\%$$

Quite obviously, the deal is a very good one for the company under present financial conditions. The company's 3-month borrowing rate can now effectively be locked in, or hedged, at an annual interest rate of 2.68%, at least on a loan that is taken out in 3 months time.

❐   THE FRA DEAL

The company thus buys a 3 × 6 FRA from BT Bank for a contract amount of $3,000,000. The settlement rate is agreed to be the bank's 3-month US dollar deposit bid rate. It is also agreed that settlement of all amounts due in terms of the FRA will be made on settlement date rather on maturity date. When the fixing date arrives, the 3-month US dollar deposit rate is 4.5% and the bank's bid rate is 5.0%.

❒ OUTCOME OF THE HEDGE

Since the settlement rate is higher than the contract rate, the bank must settle with Luthor homes. In order to determine what the bank must pay, the contract rate must be subtracted from the settlement rate, resulting in a difference of 2.32% (5% − 2.68%). Of course, this is an annual rate and the notional loan was only going to be for a period of 90 days. The annual rate must thus be converted by dividing it by 360 days, giving the daily rate, which is then multiplied by the 90 days of the notional loan. The 2.32% is divided by 100, since it is a percentage, and thus:

$$\text{Rate} = \frac{0.0232}{360} \times 90$$

$$= 0.580\%$$

The bank must thus pay Luthor Homes an amount of $17,400 ($3,000,000 × 0.0058). However, since the bank will settle the amount at the start of the period, rather than at the end, the amount must be discounted for early settlement. The net present value of the $17,400, discounted at the rate at which the loan would now have been extended must be calculated. The discount rate must obviously be the current rate for a 3-month loan, which is also the settlement rate of 5%. However, the discount rate must be converted again to reflect the 90-day early settlement. This is calculated by:

$$\text{Discount Rate} = 1 + \frac{5.00 \times 90}{100 \times 360}$$

$$= 1 + \frac{450}{36000}$$

$$= 1 + 0.0125$$

$$= 1.0125$$

Since the rate calculated above is a discount rate, the amount to be discounted must be divided by it. The correct amount that the bank must pay to the company on the settlement date of the FRA is thus $17,185.19 ($17,400/1.0125).

❒ DISCUSSION

The construction company in the case study has not taken out a loan yet. All it has done is to secure itself against a rise in interest rates. The company is now free to negotiate a loan for $3,000,000, or for any other amount, from a bank or institution of its choice. It means that the company could in fact do better than paying an effective annual interest of 2.68%. If it found another bank, charging a lower rate than BT Bank at that point in time, the company could take a loan with that bank. It would then borrow at a lower rate and use the FRA settlement amount to defray part of the interest costs.

In fact, the company need take out no loan at all. It can just keep the money paid to it in settlement of the FRA. Should it still require the loan though, it has a $17,185.19 nest egg against the interest charges it will incur.

Had interest rates moved against the company, it would, of course, still have been obliged to pay the difference to the bank. Thus if the bank's lending rate had gone below 2.32% per annum, the company would have had to pay in on the deal. Given the low forward rate, such a scenario would have been most unlikely and the company was well served by the hedge.

As is apparent from the above discussion, the company cannot escape the consequences of the movement in interest rates although it is not obliged to take out a loan. It always remains bound to honour the terms of the FRA agreement. This is an important point of difference compared to an interest rate option. As is discussed in Chapter 6, they would allow the company to walk away from the deal if interest rates moved against it. However, a premium is due on an option, which is not the case with an FRA.

It is important to note that although the case study concerns a situation where it was anticipated that a loan would be required in the future, this is not a prerequisite for using FRAs. Nothing prevents a company from using an FRA to protect itself from interest rate rises on an existing loan.

Assume a company has an existing 1-year loan, requiring quarterly interest payments of 3-month US dollar Libor. The company could negotiate a 3×6, plus a 6×9 as well as another 9×12 FRA to hedge all the forward interest payments on the loan. That said, however, it would be more usual to hedge such a series of cash flows with an interest rate swap, as will appear more fully in Chapter 5.

Another important element to note is that an FRA obviously need not be taken out before or at the start of a loan. A business can allow itself to keep an eye on the interest rate markets, depending on the company's risk aversion. If, at the start of a loan, interest rate movements seem favourable, no action need be taken. However, action can be taken to protect the remaining interest rate payments, should it appear during the course of the loan that interest rates are moving, or might move adversely.

The same principles discussed in the case study are applicable to an interest bearing investment. The bank, in that case, was hedging itself against a fall in interest rates. Banks do not only sell FRAs to their customers, they also buy them from their customers. There is thus nothing to prevent a commercial company from approaching a bank with a view to selling them an FRA with a view to hedging a comparable cash, interest bearing investment.

CHECKLIST FOR THE REVIEW OF CHAPTER 3

General overview: the overall control objectives of the material dealt with in this chapter are to acquaint the business with the fundamental operational features of the spot interest rate market and FRAs.

	Key Issues	Illustrative Scope or Approach
3.1	What considerations are applied by the business when buying FRAs?	A forward rate agreement acts to secure an interest rate on a notional loan The notional loan will be for a notional principal over a period consisting of quarterly periods or any multiple thereof FRAs can be used to lock in the interest rate for future borrowings FRAs can be used to hedge the floating interest rate of existing borrowings An FRA is not an agreement to enter into a loan in the future FRAs are cash settled instruments, that will require payment at the end of the period, whether a loan is then entered into or not
3.2	When might FRAs be considered to manage interest rate risk?	When the company definitely anticipates obtaining future finance and: • The start date of the future finance is known and certain; and • The period for which the loan will be taken out is known and certain; and • The principal amount of the borrowing is known and certain; and • The company is concerned that future interest rates might rise When the company has an existing loan with a number of future interest rate payments still outstanding and: • The loan is subject to a floating interest rate • The company is concerned that the interest rate on the loan might rise in the future
3.3	What interest rate will be used in an FRA?	The interest rate that will be used in an FRA, is the forward-forward rate The forward-forward rate is an interest based on the current or spot interest rate, calculated forward mathematically on the basis of the current interest rate yield curve
3.4	What are the important market conventions of FRAs that the company should be aware of?	FRAs are said to be 'bought' and 'sold' The buyer of an FRA is the borrower in the notional future loan The seller of an FRA is the notional lender of the notional future loan The periods for which FRAs are dealt in always consist of 3-monthly periods or multiples thereof.

continued

Key Issues	Illustrative Scope or Approach
	An FRA would therefore not be available for a period less than 3 months forward from the present time, and would extend for a further period equal to 3 months or multiples thereof, such as 6, 9 and 12 months Quoting conventions require that the period forward is first stated, followed by the period to the end of the instrument, both periods are calculated from the present time. Thus, a 3×6 FRA does not indicate an FRA starting in 3 months time with a life of 6 months. It denotes an FRA starting in 3 months time with a life of 3 months

four

interest rate futures contracts

INTRODUCTION TO INTEREST RATE FUTURES

The exchange traded futures contract that we know today was originally developed from the forward contract in the agricultural market. It is therefore to be expected that futures contracts will resemble FRAs in the essentials, but differ in the detail. Forwards, futures and swaps are all variations of the same idea. The idea is the fixing of the terms and conditions through an agreement now, of a trade that will be done at an agreed future date.

A futures contract is thus primarily a standardised forward contract. This is also true of interest rate futures. A futures contract is essentially a standardised FRA. The contract is standardised in order to make it tradable on a public exchange.

reasons for futures contracts

During the nineteenth century, a number of developments took place, which led to the creation of futures contracts. One of the reasons why a need was felt that forward contracting left something to be desired, was that price discovery in forward contracting was not open and competitive. As in all OTC transactions, the forward contract price is agreed upon between two contracting parties in private. Neither party can be sure exactly how the price it is paying or receiving relates to the market price at the moment the deal is concluded. The weaker of the two parties is thus usually the one most at risk of getting a bad deal.

Another extremely important reason was the credit risk associated with forward contracting. This was especially the experience of the agricultural sector in the American Mid-West during the latter half of the nineteenth century. Both farmers and users of agricultural produce often experienced counterparty default, especially when market prices moved adversely for the defaulting party. The suspicion is always that the defaulting party defaults on purpose to get out of a bad deal, or at least to be able to negotiate a better deal.

Trading in forward contracts was also not continuous throughout the year. Very little produce was on the market between harvests, resulting in high prices. At harvest time, every farmer was trying to sell his crop, so that the market was flooded with produce, resulting in low prices to no prices. This state of affairs was obviously not in anybody's interest.

The Chicago Board of Trade (CBOT), which had already existed as a central market-place for grain since 1848, thus took a bold step in 1865. It then formalised grain trading by developing standardised forward agreements called 'futures contracts'. The CBOT® also began requiring performance bonds called 'margin' to be posted by buyers and sellers in its grain markets.

Others soon followed this development and the Chicago Butter and Egg Board, today named the Chicago Mercantile Exchange (CME) was established along with the Kansas City Board of Trade (KCBT) and many others. Futures exchanges currently proliferate throughout the world and it is estimated that at least one new exchange opens its doors somewhere in the world each year. So successful was the concept of an exchange traded forward contract that the underlying products of the contracts soon developed far beyond agriculture. Today agricultural products are in the minority of listed futures contracts that are available world-wide. The modern financial scene would be unimaginable without futures markets.

Because of one particular innovation particular to futures contracts, futures markets almost instantaneously became proper financial markets rather than pure commodity markets. That innovation is known as offsetting. Offsetting is a facility that allows any futures position to be exited by any party unilaterally, i.e. without the knowledge or consent of the counterparty. This was possible because of the function fulfilled by the clearinghouse of the exchange, which stands between the parties. Offsetting as it applies to interest rate futures contracts, is explained hereafter.

AN EXCHANGE TRADED FORWARD RATE AGREEMENT

Because interest rate futures contracts are principally and substantially equivalent to forward rate agreements, one would expect the futures price for a particular period forward to be equal to the FRA price. Indeed, the two prices will approximate each other quite closely. The futures price does however, have to be adjusted for convexity before it will equal the FRA price exactly. Convexity is a result of the fact that futures contracts are traded independently on a different market from interest rates. Although futures rates are derived from and related to rates in the money market, they do not move in lockstep with them. This difference in the actual change in prices is referred to as convexity.

Interest rate futures contracts are also much like FRAs in that delivery of the face value of the contract never takes place. The face value of a futures contract serves the same purpose and is equivalent to the notional principal of an FRA. Futures contracts are cash-settled upon expiration, like FRAs.

Some of the differences between FRAs and futures are significant. Futures contracts are 'marked to market' (for an explanation, see below) on a daily basis. FRAs on the other hand are cash settled only at the end of the period. The only other factor that does make a difference to the futures price is the element of trading costs that are present in futures trading and is absent from FRAs.

Interest rate futures contracts are a comparatively new development in the futures markets. The CME first listed financial futures contracts in 1972. They started by trading foreign exchange futures contracts. Interest related futures contracts were later introduced on the CME.

US Treasury Bill futures contracts were introduced by the International Monetary Market (IMM) in Chicago in 1976. They were in fact the first interest related futures contract. Since then interest rate futures contracts have been introduced on many futures exchanges. Apart from the IMM, interest rate futures contracts are also traded, *inter alia*, on the CBOT, the London International Financial Futures Exchange (LIFFE), the Marche a Terme Internationale Federation in Paris (MATIF), the Hong Kong Futures Exchange, the Singapore International Monetary Exchange (SIMEX) in Singapore, the Bolsa de Mercadorias & Futuros in Sao Paulo and the South African Futures Exchange (SAFEX) in Johannesburg. The list is by no means exhaustive.

In order for a contract to be traded in an auction on the floor of a public exchange, all the terms and conditions thereof must be agreed to beforehand, except for the price. In the case of a futures contract, all the terms and conditions are prescribed by the exchange before the contract is listed for trading. There is thus no question of the parties specifically agreeing to all the terms and conditions of the contract at any time. Each party individually accepts all the prescribed terms and conditions of the contract as listed by the exchange. A party implicitly accepts all the terms and conditions of the contract as listed, by trading it on the exchange.

One of the advantages of an exchange-traded contract as opposed to an OTC contract, is the previously mentioned question of price discovery. The price of the underlying is discovered in an open market in full view of and in competition with all interested parties. This engenders confidence in the prices achieved at any particular time.

counterparty credit risk in interest rate futures

Secondly, an OTC transaction always involves counterparty credit risk; also called counterparty risk. One party is always beholden to the other's willingness and ability to perform his obligations in terms of the contract. Futures exchanges have arranged matters in such a manner that the exchange is linked to a financially sound clearinghouse. The clearinghouse acts as a buyer to all sellers and as a seller to all buyers. It actually interposes itself between the parties who executed a trade on the floor so that neither party is even interested in the identity of the counterparty.

In addition to the interposition of the clearinghouse, all futures trading is done against margin account. A person must put up a prescribed amount of margin before a futures trade can be entered into. The margin that is put up is determined by the exchange based on the value of the contract, taking into account the historical and present price-volatility. Margin usually represents only a small percentage of the total value of the contract. It will often be less than 10% of the contract value.

Margin works in such a way that all accounts are 'marked to market' at the end of every trading day. That means that a party's futures positions are valued at their market value as determined by the closing prices at the end of every trading day. It means in effect that at the end of every trading day, each party's futures positions are compared to those same positions on the previous day. If the market moved in a party's favour, the margin account is credited with the amount by which the market moved favourably. When the market has moved unfavourably for a party, its margin account is debited with the amount of the unfavourable movement. If there are insufficient funds in the margin account to cover the debit, the debited party must then top up the account to the level originally required before the start of the next trading day.

This system ensures that there is no cognisable credit risk when dealing with established futures exchanges. In addition to strict self-regulation by the futures industry, there is also a great deal of government control and regulation. For example, in the 100-year history of the CME and its predecessor, there has never been a failure by a clearing member to meet any of its financial obligations.

offsetting futures positions

One of the most important features introduced by exchange traded futures contracts is their on-saleability. In any contractual relationship, the contracting parties are normally bound to one another and no substitution of parties can take place without the consent, agreement and co-operation of the other parties to the agreement. Because of the already explained role of the clearinghouse on a futures exchange, any party can get rid of the contractual obligations by substituting another party. The substituting party is found in the ordinary way, by means of the auction on the floor of the exchange.

Before this element is more fully explained by means of an illustration, keep in mind that on a futures exchange, because future events are being dealt with, you can sell what you do not yet have. In other words, you can initiate a position in futures contracts either by buying contracts or by selling them. You do not have to buy a contract first before being able to sell one. However, if you starts by selling a futures contract, there will be a legal obligation to buy one later, or to give delivery of the underlying asset. In the case of a futures contract on interest rates there is no delivery of the underlying. The short, or seller of the futures, has the same, albeit inverse obligation to the long, or buyer, of the futures contracts. The short must namely pay the difference between the price it sold for and the price on the day of expiration, if the latter price is lower than the former. This matter will become clearer as the discussion progresses in due course.

To illustrate the point of offsetting somewhat more clearly, consider the case of a risk manager in London whose company decides in August to take out a 3-month Eurodollar loan on September 1. She decides to go long five December Eurodollar futures contracts on the CME. During the last week of November, she decides that it is the opportune time for her to exit her futures positions. She merely goes back to the company's futures broker and puts in an order to sell five December CME Eurodollar futures contracts. When that order is filled, her company is in the position of being both a buyer and a seller of the identical asset for delivery at the identical time. The one position thus cancels out the other. Obviously, the company is now out of the market and holds no futures position.

If you are both the buyer and the seller on the same contract, you have contracted with yourself and there can obviously be no contract. What has in fact happened is that, whoever bought the five contracts now holds the same futures positions that were previously held by the company: the new buyer has thus been substituted for the previous buyer.

Exactly the same situation holds for the seller. A trader who initiated his futures position by, for example, selling five December CME Eurodollar futures, can offset that position at any time by putting in an order to buy five identical futures contracts. When the latter order is filled, the trader is both seller and buyer on the same contract and has eliminated himself from the market. In order to offset his position he bought the futures. Thus, it follows that the trader's counterparty must have sold the futures. The new seller, who sold the five futures contracts to the trader, has effectively taken his place on those contracts as seller. The trader is out of the market.

This feature of offsetting immediately gave rise to the development of futures markets as financial markets rather than as markets where goods and produce were sold. The futures markets thus became simple risk-management tools and they are used primarily for hedging and speculating. People kept on buying and selling the physical goods and commodities on the spot market. It is reported by the CBOT that less than 2% of all futures contracts traded are settled by physical delivery. This small element of physical settlement is probably explained by arbitrage trading.

A STANDARDISED CONTRACT – THE MINIMUM CONDITIONS

introduction

As previously explained, a futures contract must be a standardised contract in order to be tradable on a public exchange. It will thus be instructive to survey the basic requirements of a standardised contract and then to examine the salient terms and conditions of an actual interest rate futures contract.

Since all the terms must be standardised except the price, it follows that the prescribed contract might be quite extensive. However, certain minimum terms and conditions have to be included in order to make the system workable. It is not necessary for the purposes hereof to go beyond the necessary minima.

the underlying asset

The first and obvious standardised term of an interest rate futures contract is the financial instrument whence the futures contract derives its value. Like all derivatives, an interest rate futures contract has an underlying asset. In the case of interest rate futures, the underlying asset will be a financial instrument with a face value, denominated in a particular currency. For example, on the CME the major futures contract is the Eurodollar futures contract. Its underlying instrument is 'a Eurodollar time deposit having a principal value of $1,000,000 with a 3-month maturity'. Another example is afforded by the 30 year US Treasury bond futures contract that trades on the CBOT. The underlying asset is 'one US Treasury bond having a face value at maturity of $100,000 or a multiple thereof'.

In the case of all interest rate related contracts, the value of the underlying instrument will obviously change as the applicable interest rate changes. In the case of the Eurodollar contract, the applicable interest rate is 3-month Libor. At expiry, the contract will settle at the price of the British Banker's Association Interest Settlement Rate (BBAISR) at 11:00 A.M. London time, on the contracts last trading day. The futures contract thus settles in exactly the same way as an FRA settles, except that the futures contract settles at its expiry in the contract delivery month, while FRAs usually settle on their fixing for settlement value date. However, the difference is more perceived than real. The expiry date of a futures contract is set so that it equates to the settlement date of an FRA. It merely lacks a fixing date. In other words, the expiry date of a futures contract is the notional commencement date of the time deposit underlying the contract.

the contract size

The second standardised element of a futures contract is the quantity of the underlying. In the case of an interest rate contract, it is the face value of the underlying instrument. The previously mentioned Eurodollar contract's time deposit has a face value of $1,000,000. This value does not equate exactly to the notional principal of an FRA although it serves the same purpose. The face value of the underlying time deposit reflects the total cash flow at the maturity of the deposit. It thus reflects a payment of capital and interest.

The standard contract size has important implications. On a futures exchange one can only deal in multiples of contracts. For example, one cannot trade a portion of a contract such as a Eurodollar term deposit with a face value of $375,500. This means that a company's quantitative exposure to a particular interest rate may not be equal to any multiple of futures contracts listed for that interest rate. Thus, if a company needed to hedge an exposure to 3-month Libor on a principal amount of $4,375,000, it would have to choose between using four futures contracts or five. The business would thus be obliged to deal in a portion of a contract more or less than it required. The implications of this will be made clear when some examples of hedging interest rate risk with futures are discussed.

the price quote convention

The price quote in interest rate futures contracts is rather special. While all other interest rate derivatives are quoted in annual interest rates, futures contracts are quoted in points. A futures contract is arbitrarily given a value of 100. This actually means that it is worth 100% of its face value. In most futures contracts, pricing is based on a point system. Although the nominal value of the contract is 100, the price is given in points.

Obviously, being a futures contract, it cannot be worth 100% of its face value in the present. Its face value will only be paid in the future, on maturity of the notional underlying deposit. The face value thus has to be discounted at the current underlying interest rate term structure to its net present value at the time of the start of the notional deposit. Thus, the discount rate of a futures contract will approximate the forward-forward rate, because exactly the same considerations apply.

The futures settlement price is established by subtracting the applicable BBAISR from 100. Accordingly, a futures settlement price of 94.46 thus implies a settlement rate of 5.54% (100–94.46).

the minimum price movement or tick size

The concomitant of prescribing the quantity of the underlying and the form of the price quote is that the exchange must necessarily establish some unit in which bids and offers can be made. Keep in mind that a futures exchange operates like an auction. It would be most confusing if floor traders were obliged to shout out actual prices over the floor and if those prices could be structured in any manner whatsoever. The exchange therefore prescribes a bid/offer unit, which is referred to as a 'tick'. This means that any bid or offer must be in multiples of one tick. It also means that any bid or offer must be higher or lower than a previous one by at least one tick. It further follows that any price that emanates from the floor of a futures exchange will be an exact multiple of the ticks prescribed by the exchange for that contract.

In order to make the system workable, ticks must be small enough to accommodate small changes in interest rates and yet simple enough to make multiplication straightforward. Taking the example of the CME's Libor futures contract, one tick equals half a point, expressed as 0.005. The half point equals US$12.50, as will be shown in the following explanation.

The contract size is a 3,000,000-Eurodollar time deposit of 1-month maturity. An annual interest rate of 1% equals a monthly interest rate of 0.08333% (0.0008333), which in turn equals $2,500 on the contract ($3,000,000 × 0.0008333). Since one point is given as 0.01, its value must be $25 ($2,500/100). The value of half a point is consequently $12.50.

Bids and offers on the exchange are made in ticks, which in this case would amount to value adjustments of $12.50 per contract.

contract delivery months

The next important term of a futures contract is the month of expiration or delivery. It is also called the contract month. What it actually refers to is the month in which the notional deposit is due to take place. The contract month is thus the month during which the parties undertake to perform their contractual obligations: to make and take the notional deposit of $1,000,000 per contract, in the case of the CME Eurodollar.

The futures contract months of expiration are essential to the working of the system. Not all months into the future are necessarily available. The exchanges list only certain months as contract expiration months. The Libor futures contract on the CME lists the first 12 consecutive calendar months, including the current or spot month. Other contracts are not so consecutively listed. The 13-week Treasury Bill futures contract on the same exchange lists four months in the March quarterly cycle. This means that every third calendar month is a contract month starting with March every year, but the next four quarterly months are always listed. In addition, two serial months are listed. The two serial months are months that do not fall into the March quarterly cycle, such as April and May, for example.

Thus, if a business requires managing an interest rate exposure that starts in a month that is not available, the company will select either a nearer or a deferred futures expiry month. Although this may seem to represent a limitation on the use of futures, it is not. Futures contracts are not mechanisms through which the principal sums of money actually changes hands. The compromise on contract months that may be required by a business does not necessarily impact too harshly on a futures hedge if it is properly constructed. This element will become a lot clearer during the examination of how futures contracts are used in the management of interest rate risk, which follows later.

the asset delivery mechanism

Normally, in a futures contract it is possible to deliver the underlying asset. Although less than 2% of futures contracts are actually settled by delivery of the underlying, it is an important mechanism. It is the possibility of delivery that links the futures market with the spot market. It thus ensures that the correct relationship between prices on the futures markets and the cash markets are maintained, since mispricings will lead to arbitrage. Arbitrage will keep prices in the two markets related.

Two delivery mechanisms are found in interest rate futures contracts. Some contracts are settled by delivery and acceptance of the underlying financial instrument, while others are cash settled. An example of the first type of delivery mechanism is that of the 30-year US Treasury bonds futures contract that is listed by the CBOT, some of the details of which will be discussed presently.

When any asset is deliverable against a contract of purchase and sale, the particular asset must be described properly and correctly. Such details often give rise to protracted negotiations in contracts where large quantities of a class of goods are involved. Thus, it is not surprising to find that the prescribed terms and conditions for deliverable grades of the underlying asset can become very detailed. In the case of US Treasury bonds, it is apparent that not any US Treasury bond could be deliverable. The price of the futures contract could never be established properly if neither the buyer nor the seller knew what range of bonds were being traded. How would the futures price then relate to bond prices in the cash market?

Thus, the following description is given by the CBOT regarding deliverable grades in terms of its US Treasury bond futures contract:

> US Treasury bonds that, if callable, are not callable for at least 15 years from the first day of the (futures) delivery month or, if not callable, have a maturity of at least 15 years from the first day of the delivery month. The invoice price equals the futures settlement price times a conversion factor plus accrued interest. The conversion factor is the price of the delivered bond ($1 par value) to yield 6%.

By comparison, the cash settled contracts are extremely simple. The Eurodollar contract settles like a 3-month FRA, the buyer pays the seller if prices fall and *vice versa*. The paying party pays the value of the increase or decrease in rates in cash to the clearinghouse and the clearinghouse pays the receiving party.

the last trading day

In addition to the contract months, last trading days are also prescribed. As discussed already, every contract has a specified contract month, i.e. the month in which it expires, but there is also a last day on which the contract can be traded on the exchange.

Anybody who holds a position in a futures contract beyond the last trading day, will be contractually obliged to deliver the underlying financial instrument, or to accept delivery, whichever is applicable. In a cash settled contract, the holder of a futures position beyond the last trading day will be obliged to pay or accept payment of the cash settlement amount as determined by the procedures prescribed by the exchange.

For the risk manager it is thus imperative not to maintain a futures position beyond the last trading day of the contract. It is not desirable because physical dealing with the underlying financial instruments on the futures market is neither intended nor recommended for the purposes of risk management.

conclusion

The above points are the highlights of the minimum standardised terms of an interest rate futures contract. There are, as has been said, numerous other terms and conditions, especially those that relate to the specifics of delivery and acceptance of the underlying that do not concern us here. In addition, the contract specifies the times that the contracts will trade on the floor of the exchange, which are termed the regular trading hours (RTH) of the contracts. Most contracts usually trade after hours as well, but then trading is done on internationally linked electronic trading systems.

An examination of the terms and conditions of an actual listed interest rate futures contract may better illustrate this discussion. The 3-month Eurodollar contract listed on the CME has often been used as an example in this book. The reason is that it is claimed to be the most liquid of all exchange-traded contracts in the world, when measured in terms of open interest.

There are many other interest-rate related contracts traded on different exchanges all over the world, which makes it impossible to discuss all of them in detail. The differences between them are often inconsequential so that, if the basic principles are known, most of these contracts will become accessible to the reader. However, in the next section it is proposed to give a broad overview of the most important interest rate contracts that are available.

MAJOR INTEREST RATE FUTURES CONTRACTS

introduction

It is not possible to deal with all the exchanges that offer interest rate futures contracts. Nevertheless, a short foray into the major markets might be advantageous to a reader in order to gain some insight into the vast array and variations offered in the main markets. This will serve as an indication of how useful and flexible these markets are in managing the multiplicity of interest rate risk found in businesses throughout the world. The contracts offered on the main markets will thus be investigated. The main futures markets are to be found in Chicago and London. Some references to other important markets will also be made during the course of the discussion.

For the sake of convenience, the futures contracts will be discussed under two headings, namely those futures contracts that pertain to interest rates in the Euromarkets and those that pertain to national interest rates. In this mix of contracts, the reader will be able to gain a reasonably comprehensive view of the futures markets, even if not all countries and currencies are dealt with.

the euromarket

◻ EURODOLLARS

As already mentioned, the major interest rate contract related to Euromarket rates is the Eurodollar contract on the CME. The contract is designed to reflect changes in 3-month US dollar Libor. The ticker symbol for this contract is ED. The underlying asset of the contracts is a $1,000,000 time deposit with a 3-month maturity and the price quote reflects a discount rate implying a 3-month annual interest rate.

The CME also lists a contract that is analogous to the Eurodollar contract, but its underlying asset is a Eurodollar time deposit having a principal value of $3,000,000, with a 1-month maturity. The benchmark interest rate is thus 1-month US dollar Libor and the contract is simply known as 'LIBOR FUTURES'. It is priced and settled in a similar manner to the Eurodollar futures contract.

◻ EUROYEN

The CME also lists two Euroyen contracts as part of its interest rate products. The underlying asset, in both cases, is an Euroyen time deposit with a principal value of ¥100,000,000 and a 3-month maturity. The first contract is known as the Euroyen Libor futures, while the second is simply termed the Euroyen futures.

The benchmark rate for the first contact is 3-month Japanese yen Libor and it settles on BBAISR. The second contract trades on the benchmark 3-month Tokyo Interbank Offered Rate (TIBOR). The Euroyen contract's final settlement price is thus not BBAISR, but is based on the interest rate for 3-month yen deposits offered to prime banks in Tokyo. The contract is wholly compatible with the same contract listed by the SIMEX. Through the two exchange's mutual offset system, futures positions in the Euroyen contract can be initiated on either one of the two exchanges and offset on the other exchange. Like the SIMEX, the CME list 12 contracts in the quarterly cycle at all times, thus covering a period of 3 years forward.

Two more Euroyen contracts are listed by LIFFE. The first contract is termed the 'Three Month Euroyen (Tibor) Interest Rate Future', while the second is called the 'Three Month Euroyen (Libor) Interest Rate Future'. Both contracts have ¥100,000,000 3-month Euroyen time deposits as their underlying values and they are both priced as 100 minus the applicable rate of interest. The difference lies in the manner of their settlement.

The Euroyen (Libor) contract's settlement procedure demonstrates some unique features, although they apply to all the short-term interest rate contracts listed by the LIFFE. The settlement price is based on BBA LIBOR for 3-month yen deposits at 11:00 A.M. on the last trading day of the contract. The settlement price of the contract is calculated by rounding the applicable Libor to three decimal places and deducting it from 100. Then it is further rounded to the nearest 0.005.

The Euroyen (Tibor) contract is designed to comply with the Euroyen contract listed by the Tokyo International Financial Futures Exchange (TIFFE). Thus, the futures position will normally be transferred to the TIFFE for settlement there. Subject to certain conditions, the LIFFE contract thus settles subject to TIFFE rules. The TIFFE uses Zenginkyo determined Tibor, as at the last trading day of the TIFFE contract, to settle its contract. The interesting condition of the LIFFE is, that if the futures position is for some reason not transferred to the TIFFE, the LIFFE contract will settle at the TIFFE settlement price. However, if that should not be available, it will be cash settled at the LIFFE's exchange delivery settlement price.

◻ THE EURO

The introduction of the euro presented new opportunities, but also new challenges to the international financial system. Before its introduction, there were various national interest reference rates, such as Paris Interbank Offered Rate (PIBOR), while the euro could best be traded if there was a single reference rate. The International Swaps and Derivatives Association (ISDA) created a multilateral European Monetary Union (EMU) protocol that dealt with a number of issues relating to the euro. One of its main accomplishments was to replace the multitude of European national reference rates with the euro interbank offered rate (EURIBOR).

The LIFFE offers a 3-month Euribor interest rate futures contract. The underlying is a €1,000,000 3-month time deposit and it is quoted at 100 minus the rate of interest. The contract is cash settled, based on the Exchange Delivery Settlement Price (EDSP). The EDSP is based on the European Bankers Federation's Euribor (EBF Euribor) at 11:00 A.M. Brussels time on the last trading day of the contract.

In addition, LIFFE also lists a 3-month euro Libor interest rate future. The contract is based on an asset of a €1,000,000 time deposit with a 3-month maturity. It is identical to the Euribor contract, except that it settles at BBAISR at 11:00 A.M. London time on the last trading day of the contract.

◻ EUROSWISS

A futures contract based on a deposit of Swiss francs outside Switzerland is offered by the LIFFE. It is termed the 'Three Month Euro Swiss Franc (Euroswiss) Interest Rate Future'. It is based on an asset of a SFr1,000,000 3-month time deposit and is quoted at 100 minus 3-month Swiss Libor. It is cash settled at EDSP, which is BBA LIBOR for 3-month Euroswiss franc deposits at 11:00 A.M. London time, on the last trading day of the contract.

national interest rate futures

◻ US INTEREST RATE FUTURES

There is virtually an unrestricted choice of interest rate futures contracts. One can hardly imagine any type of interest rate exposure that cannot be managed by means futures contracts. There are in fact so many that one can do no better than to deal with only some of them superficially.

The CBOT interest rate contracts cover long-term interest rates by listing futures contracts with several US government and semi-government debt issues as their underlying instruments. Thirty-year US Treasury bonds, 10-year, 5-year and 2-year US Treasury notes as well as 10-year and 5-year Agency notes (notes issued by Federal Government Agencies). These contracts all have specifically described bonds and notes that are deliverable against the futures contracts.

Two very useful futures contracts, also listed by the CBOT, are the contracts on municipal bonds and mortgage rates. The former has a number of municipal bonds that are deliverable against the contract. The contract trades against 'The Bond Buyer™ 40 Index' and it is quoted at a price of $1,000 times the index, for a par value of $100,000. Thus, an index price of 85-00 indicates a futures price of $85,000. Individual municipal bonds can be related to the index and the futures contract via certain conversion factors supplied by the exchange.

The futures contract on mortgage rates is an extremely useful one. It trades against the current mortgage price index and the contract is priced at $1,000, times the value of the index. The basis of the index is the conventional 30-year, mortgage-backed security, issued by either the Federal National Mortgage Association or the Federal Home Loan Mortgage Corporation.

The CME lists long-term interest rate futures contracts through 10-year and 5-year Agency futures, each with a $100,000 face value of 10-year or 5-year Fannie Mae benchmark notes or Freddie Mac reference notes.

Apart from long-term interest rates, the CBOT also caters for short-term interest rates. It does so in the form of a contract on 30-day Federal Reserve funds. The CME also caters for the short-term market with its 13-week Treasury Bill futures. The underlying instrument is a 1-month (13-week) US Treasury Bill with a face value at maturity of $1,000,000. The contract is priced in half points, giving a value of $12.50 per half point. It is cash settled. In addition, the CME lists a 'Fed Funds Turn Futures', with an underlying overnight Federal Reserve funds deposit of $45,000,000.

☐ OTHER COUNTRIES

Countries outside the US are not as well served with interest rate related futures contracts, although there is no real shortage. In the UK, the LIFFE offers short-term interest rate futures contracts on short sterling interest rates. The underlying instrument is a 3-month sterling deposit and the underlying value is 3-month sterling Libor. The contract is cash settled on BBA LIBOR for 3-month sterling deposits.

Long-term interest risk management is catered for through the 'Long Gilt Future'. This contract has a £100,000 nominal value gilt with 7% coupon as its underlying. The gilt's time to maturity cannot be less than 8.75 years and not more than 13 years, calculated from the first day of the futures delivery month. Actual gilts that may be delivered in any delivery month are published by the exchange in a List of Deliverable Gilts. The contract EDSP is the LIFFE market price at 11:00 A.M. London time on the second business day prior to settlement day. The invoicing amount in respect of any particular gilt is calculated by a price factor system.

Between the CME, the CBOT and the LIFFE, futures contracts are available on a large variety of foreign government bonds. Some examples of these contracts are Japanese government bonds, German government bonds, Argentinean, Brazilian and Mexican government and Brady Bonds.

FUTURES MARKET TERMINOLOGY

All markets tend to develop their own peculiar terminology and ways of expression. It really constitutes a type of shorthand to speed up effective communication and to avoid misunderstanding. However, this type of market usage often serves only to make them less accessible to those of us who do not participate in them on a regular basis.

The terminology discussed in this section is not particularly strange and many readers will no doubt be entirely familiar with the usage described. However, to avoid later difficulties, the subject of long and short positions might as well be broached at this stage. They are not terms that are particular to either the interest rate or even the futures markets, but are used in all markets that deal with transactions that look to future execution.

'long'

The term 'long' is used to describe the situation where any *merx* is owned or possessed by a person, company or firm. A *merx* is any corporeal or incorporeal 'thing' that has commercial value. It thus includes not only physical moveable or immovable property, but also rights to and in such property. It also includes money and rights in and to money.

There are so many variations to how the word 'long' is used in this context, but basically, when a person owns or possesses something he is said to be 'long' that something. For example, if one has at one's disposal, in one way or another, $100,000, one will be said to be long $100,000. It is not even a requirement that the amount be stipulated as in the example. If US dollars are owned in any amount the owner's position will be termed 'long' US dollars, in respect of that particular holding. One is in fact 'long' whatever assets one may own or hold or has bought.

'short'

The term 'short' does not necessarily indicate the opposite of 'long'. The mere fact that one does not in any way own or possess any French francs or Russian roubles now, does not mean that one is short these currencies. One will only be short a currency, or an asset when one undertakes to pay that currency or deliver that asset on some future date, while one does not hold that currency or dispose over that asset. For example, if one, as a foreigner, should import goods from France, undertaking to pay in French francs upon receipt of delivery, one will be short French francs on the transaction.

'long' and 'short' in the marketplace

Market usage must be taken into consideration. In the interest rate markets, the terms 'long' and 'short' usually indicate long-term interest rates and short-term interest rates. Nevertheless, a position held in the futures market will still be termed long or short. Thus, if one bought three 30-year Treasury bond futures with March delivery, one would be said to hold a futures position of 'long three March T-Bond futures'. Conversely, if one sold the same contract, one would be said to hold a futures position of 'short three March T-Bond futures'.

A final comment on the manner in which the terms long and short are used in the futures markets will complete this part of the discussion on terminology. A person who is long an asset is also said to 'hold' a long 'position' in the asset. In a trading situation, the person holding a long position will often be referred to as 'the long'. Similarly, a person who is short an asset is said to have a short position in that asset and might be referred to as 'a short', or 'the short' in a trading situation.

For all of these purposes, futures contracts and options thereon are quite rightly also regarded as assets. Thus buying futures contracts is said to be 'going long the futures', while selling a futures contract will be termed 'shorting the futures'. Similarly, buying an option or holding an option entails being 'long the option' while selling an option is termed 'shorting' an option. When options are dealt with, however, it will be pointed out again that selling or shorting an option is mostly referred to as 'writing an option'.

'buying' and 'selling' futures contracts

The final terms that often cause confusion when dealing with futures contracts are the terms 'buying' and 'selling'. From the discussion thus far, it must be clear that the futures contract as such is not bought or sold. A futures contract, unlike an option, costs nothing. The term buying or 'going long' a futures contract really means that one is taking upon oneself the obligations of a buyer in a contract for future delivery of the underlying asset. Similarly, when one 'sells' or 'shorts' a futures contract, one is assuming the obligations of a seller of the underlying asset of the futures contract concerned. That is why one can 'buy' the futures while not paying anything and you can sell futures contracts, without receiving any money.

The legal obligations to pay and to deliver in terms of the contract refer to the underlying asset and lie in the future. As was discussed earlier, if a long futures position is held beyond the last trading day, the obligation to take delivery of and pay for the underlying asset becomes a reality. Also, if a short position is held beyond the last trading day, the party will be obliged to deliver the underlying asset and then payment will be received. The exceptions to this are of course the contracts that are cash settled.

A frequently asked question, arising from that explanation is whether one can 'buy' a futures contract, putting down only margin, and then receive all the profit on a rise in price, as if one had actually owned the underlying asset. In addition, by offsetting the futures position, one never actually pays for the asset, but one collects the profit on a price rise, or pays the loss on a price decline that occurred during the tenancy. The short answer to the question is yes. By buying a futures contract, one is placed in virtually the same position as an owner of the underlying asset, for as long as one holds that futures contract. That is why there are so many speculators on the futures markets.

Speculators never have to deal in the underlying physical assets. Dealing in the underlying assets would require large sums of capital and perhaps some other expenditure as well. To trade futures contracts, they only require a margin deposit, thereby obtaining all the benefits of possessing the underlying asset, without committing the capital represented by the futures contract and without moving out of the office. Speculators actually perform a vital function in the markets, because they provide much-needed liquidity, without which the markets would be much more volatile.

THE ROLE OF BASIS IN INTEREST RATE FUTURES

introduction

Reference has previously been made to the inevitable difference between spot interest rates and forward interest rates. It has been demonstrated that the difference between the two exchange rates is based on a calculation derived from the yield curve for similar or comparable instruments. As was demonstrated in the previous chapter, the time function underlies the yield curve and consequently the calculation of the forward-forward interest rate. It follows that the shorter the period to the expiration of an interest rate futures contract, the closer the futures price and the spot interest rates approach each other. This narrowing of the gap between the two prices continues until it is reduced to zero, at least theoretically.

The gap will be zero at the time when the futures expiration month is the spot month. This is necessarily so because its price will then no longer reflect a forward-forward rate, but a rate for a deposit made now. That is by definition a spot rate and arbitrage will ensure that the cash rate and the futures price in the spot month coincide. This gap between the two prices is known as the basis, or as the price basis. It represents one of the two factors that together make up what is referred to as the hedge basis.

price basis

The basis is described as being either positive or negative. It is always calculated as the spot price less the futures price, never the other way around. The basis is thus positive when the spot price is greater than the futures price and similarly, it is negative when the spot price is less than the futures price. Additionally, a positive basis is referred to as a technically strong basis, while a negative basis is regarded as a technically weak basis. The terms 'weak' and 'strong' in this context do not carry any implication that the risk manager should take any notice of. Whether the futures basis is positive or negative is another matter, as will appear from the further discussion.

changes in the basis

The result of a futures hedge will be influenced positively or negatively by the move in the basis during the time that the futures position is held. This statement contains probably one of the most important facts about futures trading. It is a fact that must seriously be kept in mind when using futures contracts for risk management purposes.

What the spot interest rate will be in the future is an unknown, but fortunately, what the basis will be when the futures expiry month arrives is known: it will be zero. Consequently, if it is known what the basis is when the futures contracts are bought or sold, then it is also known how the basis will move between that time and the time when the futures contracts expire. The two rates will converge. Since the basis will be zero at that future time when the futures contracts expire, it is accordingly known at the outset that the basis will narrow as time passes. If the basis starts as a positive one, it will change negatively until it reaches zero. If the basis starts as a negative one, it will change positively until it equals zero. The rule is thus that the basis will narrow and tend to zero in the futures expiry month.

quantitative basis

There is also another form of basis. Basis in this second sense refers to the difference in the quantity of the underlying traded in the spot market and the quantity of the underlying hedged in the futures markets. This type of basis will be referred to as quantitative basis. It must also be pointed out that quantitative basis is additional price basis. It comes on top of the basis formed by the price differential in the two markets. The total hedge basis established by a futures hedge thus consists of both price basis and quantitative basis. Since basis causes risk, it follows that adding quantitative basis to price basis increases the inherent risk faced by the futures hedger.

As has already been shown, futures contracts inevitably trade only in whole lots. You cannot buy or sell a portion of a futures contract. Thus, it might happen that a company has to manage a certain interest rate exposure, based on the principal amount involved, which is not matched by the amount of notional principal underlying any one or more listed futures contracts.

Quantitative basis does not change since it is a fixed and given quantitative difference established at the start of the hedge. The question arises as to what is the influence of quantitative basis on the result of the hedge. The answer to that question depends on whether the hedger under-hedges or over-hedges. By under-hedging is meant that the hedger uses less futures contracts than is required to equal his quantitative exposure in the cash market. Over-hedging indicates that the total quantity of the underlying principal represented by the number of futures contracts used in the hedge exceeds the quantity of the underlying principal being hedged.

In an under-hedged position, a portion of the hedger's cash market exposure is not hedged. The hedger still faces naked price risk on that portion of the principal. If the interest rates move adversely during the currency of the hedge, the unhedged portion of the underlying will suffer the full impact of the loss. The hedged portion will only be influenced by the move to zero of the price basis. The net result is that the hedger will only be partially protected against an adverse change in interest rates. However, should there be an advantageous change in the interest rate, the hedge will not cancel out the profit made on the unhedged portion of the exposure. The net result will thus be a more profitable hedge.

In an over-hedged situation, the opposite applies. In an adverse change in interest rates, the hedge will 'more than protect' the hedger, thus resulting in a profit on the hedge. Should there be an advantageous change in the exchange rate, the hedge will over-compensate and thus result in a loss on the hedge.

Both over-hedged and under-hedged situations have no limit to the loss or the profit that can be made. The limits are only circumscribed by how far the price of the under-lying can move adversely for the hedger during the period concerned. Nevertheless, the fact that futures contracts are for reasonably small lots also plays a role in limiting the potential loss or profit on changes in the quantitative basis. A hedged position should only be over-hedged or under-hedged by a portion of one contract. The 'naked' portion of the futures exposure, or over-protection, should therefore not apply to a great deal of money.

There are two fundamental rules relating to the movement of the hedge basis and its influence on the outcome of the hedge. The first rule applies to long futures hedges and the second applies to short futures hedges. These two fundamental rules will best be illustrated and formulated in the light of the case studies that follow.

THE FUTURES HEDGE RATIO

The final theoretical issue that needs to be mentioned before proceeding to case studies, is the hedge ratio. The hedge ratio in a way relates to the question of over-hedging and under-hedging that was discussed above. It is usually assumed that interest rate risk exposure is equal to the nominal amount of the borrowing or investment. A hedge of the exposure is thus expected to be hedged at a ratio of 1:1. This means that for every dollar nominally borrowed or invested, one dollar should be exposed to the opposite risk in the futures market. The fact that this is not always practically possible has already been mentioned.

Since the purpose of hedging is to minimise risk in the business and not to try to profit from speculation on the yield curve, it is imperative to optimise the number of futures contracts used. There are two ways of going about that. The first way is to compare the nominal amount of the borrowing or investment against the notional principal amount of the applicable futures contracts.

There may sometimes be an exact fit, but when that is not possible, the percentage over-hedge or under-hedge can be calculated. A further calculation can then be done. If the nominal amount of the exposure is reduced to today's present value, the new principal might give a better fit with a listed futures contract. The percentage over- or under-hedge can then be calculated and compared to the first iteration. The best fit can then be selected. Hedging the present value of a borrowing, rather than the nominal amount is usually done when large amounts of principal are involved. It is called 'tailing the hedge'.

All of the discussions so far can now be brought together in order to investigate what happens when futures contracts are actually used in a interest rate risk management situation. The importance of each element in determining what happens can best be explained by means of an analysis of two case studies. The important point demonstrated by the case studies is the effect that the basis change has on a futures hedge. It is a consistent element of all futures hedges and must be clearly understood.

case study 2: hedging a borrowing rate with eurodollar futures

◻ SCENARIO

In July, a company anticipates that it will require a loan of $2,750,000 for 1 year, starting in November. The treasurer knows that the loan will be linked to 3-month Libor. There had been a number of decreases in US dollar interest rates over the past few months and the treasurer is concerned that interest rates might start rising again towards the end of that year. She thus decides to hedge the borrowing rate.

◻ FINANCIAL INFORMATION

At the time that the decision to lock in the borrowing rate is taken, spot 3-month, US dollar Libor is quoted at 3.76000. At the same time, the November Eurodollar futures contract on the CME is trading at 96.16, implying an interest rate of 3.84% (100.00 − 96.16). The 3-month US dollar Libor yield curve is important in anticipating the basis move and so the treasurer calculates it from the quotes she obtains on the Eurodollar futures contracts.

The yield curve depicted in Figure 4-1 is quite normal and is known as a 'spoon curve' because of its resemblance to the shape of that article. The curve shows an expected decline in interest rates and then a steeply rising rate from September onward.

☐   THE HEDGE

The treasurer goes ahead with the hedge. Three contracts are the nearest rounded number of contracts that cover the company's exposure. The treasurer thus puts in an order to sell three November CME Eurodollar contracts and receives a fill at 96.15, implying an annual interest rate of 3.85%. Since the company is exposed to a rise in interest rates, i.e. it will lose money should rates rise, it must establish a hedging position that will profit when interest rates rise. The profit and loss on the hedging position must thus be the exact opposite of the profit and loss on the cash market situation.

There is now a negative quantitative basis. It is negative because the cumulative face value of the futures contracts is greater than the cash market principal. Thus, the cash market principal less the total of the face value of the futures contracts is negative.

The hedged position of the company is now as indicated in Table 4-1. Because of the way the price of the futures contract is structured, namely 100 minus the interest rate, it follows that the futures 'price' will decline as interest rates rise and *vice versa*. Therefore, since initiating a hedge by selling futures contracts will result in a profit when the futures price declines, it means that the position will appreciate as interest rates rise.

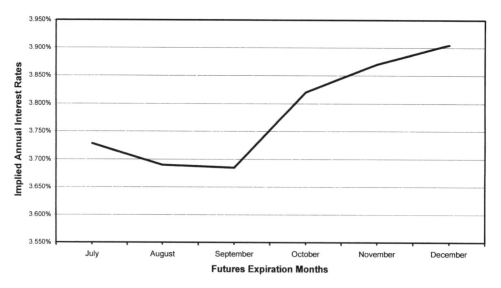

Figure 4-1   Three-month US dollar Libor yield curve based on the closing prices of the CME Eurodollar futures contract.

Table 4-1. Hedging anticipated borrowings with a CME Eurodollar futures contract

Date	Cash Market		Futures Market		Basis
	Position	Rate	Position	Rate	
July-01	$2,750,000 anticipated loan	3.760%	Short three × CME Nov. Eurodollar futures	3.850%	−0.090%

☐ OUTCOME I: INTEREST RATES RISE

Assume that interest rates rise, as the company feared. When the company takes up the $2,750,000 loan from the bank in November, 3-month USD Libor is quoted at 4.85%. Since the November futures month is now the spot month, the futures and spot prices are virtually equal.

The treasurer instructs the company's futures broker to exit the company's futures positions by buying three identical futures contracts, thereby offsetting the three existing short futures positions. She receives a fill at 95.14, implying an interest rate of 4.86%. The result of the hedge is indicated in Table 4-2.

As Table 4-2 indicates, the hedge is not a perfect one. The loss in the cash market, i.e. the difference between the interest rate the company tried to lock in (3.76%) and the rate it actually borrowed at, is not totally cancelled out by the profit realised on the futures market. Nevertheless, the loss in the cash market was severely curtailed and limited to a net loss of 0.07 percentage points. It will be noticed that the net loss is exactly equal to the positive change in the basis.

Table 4-2 indicates only the change in the price basis and ignores the effect of the quantitative basis for the moment. It is a given that the change in the price basis of a futures hedge has a direct influence on the outcome of the hedge. The outcome of the basis move is always known in principle from the start. Thus, whenever a company uses futures contracts to hedge an exposure, it must take into account the known influence of the price basis move. This matter will receive further attention at a later stage in this chapter.

Table 4-2. Result of a short futures hedge locking in a borrowing rate, using Eurodollar futures, after a rate rise

Date	Cash Market		Futures Market		Basis
	Position	Rate	Position	Rate	
July-01	$2,750,000 anticipated loan	3.760%	Short three × CME Nov. Eurodollar futures	3.840%	−0.080%
Nov.-01	$2,750,000 loan taken up @	4.850%	Long three × CME Nov. Eurodollar futures	4.860%	−0.010%
	Loss:	−1.090%	Profit:	1.020%	Change:
	Loss on Hedge:	−0.0700%			0.070%

In order to appreciate the effect of the quantitative basis on the result of the hedge, the actual dollar amounts involved require our attention. When the company anticipated the loan in July, they expected to pay an annual percentage rate of 3.76% on a principal of $2,750,000. Thus, the actual interest cost that they wanted to lock in amounted to $25,850 for the first quarter ($2,750,000 × 3.76%/4). At the rate of interest they ended up paying when they took out the loan in November, the cost had increased to $33,343.75, representing a 'loss' of $7,493.75.

Against this 'loss' of $7,493.75, there had been a gain on the futures market. However, the gain on the futures market must be calculated on a principal of $3,000,000 (three contracts), not the $2,750,000 exposure in the cash market. The 1.02% futures profit thus translates into a monetary value of $7,650, which is just adequate to cancel out the 'loss' in the cash market with small change of $156.25. If it were possible to buy futures with a face value exactly equal to the principal sum in the cash market, the profit in the futures would have been only $7,012.50, leaving a paltry, but net loss of $481.25. In this instance, the negative quantitative basis thus resulted in a small profit where there would otherwise have been a small loss.

❏   OUTCOME 2: INTEREST RATES DECLINE

The second possible outcome is that interest rates actually change favourably for the company. By November when the loan is taken up, the interest rate it has to pay is based on a 3-month Libor of 3.24%. When the loan is take up, the treasurer instructs the company's broker to offset the company's three short futures contracts. She receives a fill of 96.75, which implies an annual percentage rate of 96.5%.

The outcome of the hedge is illustrated in Table 4-3.

As appears from Table 4-3, the net result of the hedge is identical to the previous result. Again, the net result is that the net loss on the hedge is equal to the change in the basis. This demonstrates also that once a hedge with futures has been established the outcome is not affected by either a rise or a decline in the value of the underlying risk being hedged. Only the change in the hedge basis impacts on its outcome, and that is a known element. A hedge is thus a fixing of the outcome of an unknown event. The downside is also that a hedge not only eliminates the chance of loss, but also eliminates the opportunity for profit. The loss of the latter is the price of the former. Whether the price is worth it,

Table 4-3. Result of a short futures hedge, locking in a borrowing rate, using Eurodollar futures after a rate decline

Date	Cash Market		Futures Market		Basis
	Position	Rate	Position	Rate	
July-01	$2,750,000 anticipated loan	3.760%	Short three × CME Nov. Eurodollar futures	3.840%	−0.080%
Nov.-01	$2,750,000 loan taken up @	3.240%	Long three × CME Nov. Eurodollar futures	3.250%	−0.010%
	Profit:	0.520%	Loss:	−0.590%	Change:
	Loss on Hedge	−00700%			0.070%

depends on how much the company will be hurt by the adverse change against which it seeks protection. Another consideration that many companies take into account is that speculating on interest rates is not their business. They do not need to take risks that fall outside the normal scope of their business.

The influence of the quantitative mismatch in this outcome also deserves attention. On the favourable change in interest rates, the company improved its interest cost relative to its anticipated cost by $3,575. However, the loss on the futures market negated this profit. If the face value of the futures contract were equal to the principal, the loss would have amounted to $481.25, which is (not incidentally) the same as the loss would have been in the previous iteration under those same circumstances. Due to the quantitative mismatch however, the net loss has escalated to $850. Thus, when interest rates moved favourably for the hedger's cash market position, the negative quantitative basis exacerbated the loss on the hedge, which, in the first instance, resulted from the move in price basis.

The second case study will illustrate a hedge of the opposite cash market position. The rules regarding the influence of basis will be fully discussed thereafter.

case study 3: hedging an investment rate with eurodollar futures

☐ SCENARIO

In July, a company anticipates that the sale of a fixed property will be finalised in December. The company wishes to purchase another property with the money, but will have to invest it until it is required to pay for the new acquisition. It therefore decides to invest the money on deposit for 12 months with quarterly interest and notice. The company is given an investment interest rate based on 3-month dollar Libor.

☐ FINANCIAL INFORMATION

The company expects an amount of $3,750,000 to become available for the investment. At the time this is anticipated in July, December Eurodollar futures on the CME are trading at 96.09, implying an interest rate of 3.91%. Assume for the purposes of this case study that all the other financial information is identical to that which applied to the first case study.

☐ THE HEDGE

Interest rates have come down sharply during the last year and the company is concerned that they may decline even further. Because the face value of each futures contract is $1,000,000, the company's treasurer decides to use four futures contracts to hedge the $3,750,000 exposure in the cash market. Her order to buy four December Eurodollar futures contracts is filled at a futures price of 96.16, implying an annual interest rate of 3.84%. As in the previous case study, the quantitative basis is negative due to the over-hedge.

The hedged position of the company is illustrated in Table 4-4.

Table 4-4. Hedging an anticipated interest bearing investment using CME Eurodollar futures

Date	Cash Market		Futures Market		Basis
	Position	Rate	Position	Rate	
July-01	$3,750,000 anticipated investment	3.760%	Long four × CME Dec. Eurodollar futures	3.840%	−0.080%

❑   OUTCOME I: INTEREST RATES DECLINE

Assume that interest rates decline further to December and when the company is ready to invest the money, 3-month Libor is 3.15%. The treasurer instructs the company's futures broker to lift the hedge at the same time that the investment is made. The resulting sell-order is filled at a futures price of 96.98, with an implied annual interest percentage of 3.020%. The result of the hedge is shown in Table 4-5.

As indicated in Table 4-5, the trade in the futures market resulted in a profit. Although the calculation in the Table might look wrong, it is correct. The reason is that the futures price went from a low of 96.16 to a high of 96.98 when the hedge was lifted. Since the company had a long futures position as a hedge, the position gained 0.82 contract points during the term of the hedge. The sale of the futures contracts thus took place at a substantially higher price than their purchase price – still the only certain way of showing a profit.

The 'loss' in the cash market is obviously not a real loss. It is merely the difference between the anticipated investment rate and the realised one. In the circumstances, it is nevertheless an adverse change for the investing company. The rate that the company wished to lock in for itself was the higher, anticipated rate.

It is notable that the eventual net profit on the hedge is exactly equal to the positive change in the basis. As in the first case study, this is not happenstance. It was pointed out then also that once a hedge has been established, it is only influenced by the change in the price basis and not by any change in price.

Table 4-5. Result of a long futures hedge with CME Eurodollar futures contracts

Date	Cash Market		Futures Market		Basis
	Position	Rate	Position	Rate	
July-01	$3,750,000 anticipated investment	3.760%	Long four × CME Dec. Eurodollar futures	3.840%	−0.080%
Nov-01	$3,750,000 investment @	3.015%	Short four × CME Dec. Eurodollar futures	3.020%	−0.005%
	Loss:	−0.745%	Profit:	0.820%	Change:
	Profit on Hedge:	0.0750%			0.075%

The influence of the negative quantitative basis remains to be investigated. The interest yield for the first quarter at the anticipated rate would have amounted to $35,250. The amount that was in fact realised was $28,265.63, representing a shortfall of $6,984.38. The profit realised on the futures market equals $8,200, which results in an overall profit of $1215.63. This profit is greater than the profit indicated by the change in the basis. Table 4-6 indicates a profit of 0.075%, which, calculated on a principal amount of $3,750,000, equals $703.121/2. The over-hedge thus accounts for the additional profit of $512.501/2. It follows without analysis that a positive quantitative basis would always have the opposite effect to that of a negative basis.

☐ OUTCOME 2: INTEREST RATES RISE

In this iteration, a rise in interest rates will be assumed. When the company invests the $3,750,000 proceeds from the sale of its property, interest rates have risen and an annual rate based on 3-month Libor of 4.85% is achieved. The treasurer lifts the hedge and the four futures contracts are sold at a price of 95.135, implying a rate of 4.865%. The result of the hedge is shown in Table 4-6.

Unsurprisingly, Table 4-6 again demonstrates that the positive change in the basis resulted in an exactly equal profit on the hedge. In this case, the quantitative basis has the effect of cancelling out the profit, leaving a negligible loss of $31.25. The result is obtained by calculating from the information in Table 4-6.

The investment income for the first quarter that the company wanted to lock in was $35,250 ($3,750,00 × 3.76%). The actual income realised would now be $45,468.75 ($3,750,000 × 4.85%), representing a profit of $10,218.75. However, the profit is slightly more than cancelled out by the loss realised on the hedging futures contracts. Based on the $4,000,000 face value of the futures, the interest amount represented by the original long futures positions comes to $38,400.00. When these positions were exited, their interest value had risen to $48,650, resulting in an overall loss of $10,250 on the futures ($48,650 − $38,400). Keep in mind that the rise in interest value represents a loss to the long hedger, because it implies a reduction in the points value of the contract. When the loss is offset against the profit, an insignificant loss of $31.25 remains.

Table 4-6. Result of a long futures hedge of an anticipated investment rate using CME Eurodollar futures contracts

Date	Cash Market		Futures Market		Basis
	Position	Rate	Position	Rate	
July-01	$3,750,000 anticipated investment	3.760%	Long four × CME Dec. Eurodollar futures	3.840%	−0.080%
Nov.-01	$3,750,000 investment @	4.850%	Short four × CME Dec. Eurodollar futures	4.865%	−0.015%
	Profit:	1.090%	Loss:	−1.025%	Change:
	Profit on Hedge:	0.0650%			0.065%

Had there been parity between the principal in the cash market and the face value of the futures contracts, the hedge would have resulted in a small profit of $609.37. The negative quantitative basis thus had the effect of reducing the profit on the hedge to a minor negative amount. The rules relating to price and quantitative basis on the result of a hedge will be set out in the discussion of the two case studies.

DISCUSSION OF THE CASE STUDIES

The two case studies show how futures contracts can be effectively used to manage interest rate risk. The feature that most strongly distinguishes futures hedges from hedges with all other derivatives, is the effect that a movement in the price basis has on the result of the hedge. Another element that must be kept in mind is the effect of quantitative basis. Quantitative basis is an element that is always present when dealing with exchange traded derivatives that are by their nature available in predetermined lot sizes.

When using futures contracts to hedge interest rate risk, it must be kept in mind that the contracts are structured so that the interest rate moves that are being hedged change inversely to the value of those contracts. This seems to change the rules of the effect of basis movement on hedges with futures. The change is more apparent than real, but if one is perhaps used to hedging commodities and currencies with futures contracts, the formulation of the rules appear inverse, or opposite, to what one might be used to.

As far as moves in the price basis are concerned, when the interest rate yield curve is positive (an ascending price), a hedge with short interest rate futures contracts will always result in a loss on the hedge. The loss will not be more than the initial negative basis, as long as the yield curve remains positive. In other words, the result is not affected by any change in interest rates, but its outcome is solely determined by the fact that the price of futures contracts will approach the price of spot until they are virtually equal. The latter happens when the futures expiration is the spot month. Thus, when a short interest rate futures hedge is taken when a positive yield curve is in place, the risk manager must know that there will be a loss on the hedge. Although it is not known exactly how great the loss will be, it is known that it will approximate the initial basis to a very narrow margin.

Conversely, when the interest rate yield curve is positive, a long hedge with interest rate futures contracts will always result in a profit on the hedge. The profit will not be greater than the initial negative basis that was established when the hedge was taken. The profit is a result of the narrowing of the basis that occurs as the futures month approaches and then becomes the spot month. Thus, when a long futures hedge is established under positive yield curve circumstances, the hedger knows beforehand that there will be a profit on the hedge. Although it is not known exactly how big the profit will be, it is known that it will be nearly equivalent to the initial price basis.

The hedger therefore knows from the very beginning what the basis move and its effect on the hedge will be. Provision can therefore be made for its effect when calculating the advantages or disadvantages of the hedge beforehand. Its effect can also be taken into account when calculating the best hedge ratio. For example, if it is known that there will be a profit on the hedge, the hedge ratio might be adjusted to give a better result on an adverse move.

The influence of quantitative basis is additional to the effect of price basis. Quantitative basis does not change and consequently remains stable throughout the period of the hedge. In an over-hedged situation, the total face value of the futures contracts is greater than the principal amount being hedged while in an under-hedged situation the opposite holds. An over-hedged situation will increase both the profit and the loss on the futures leg of a hedge, depending on whether an adverse or a favourable move in interest rates occurs. An under-hedge has exactly the opposite result. The actual profit or loss resulting from either situation will be directly related to the size of the change in interest rates. This is not known at the time the hedge is entered, but the broad parameters of any possible change over the period of the hedge might well be known.

Consequently, if it is known that there will be a profit on the hedge, it might be wise to consider an under-hedge rather than an over-hedge. The under-hedge will diminish the profit on an adverse move, while slightly enhancing the profit on a favourable change in interest rates. An over-hedge on the other hand, can be used in a situation where it is known that there will be a loss on the hedge. The quantitative basis can be employed to decrease or neutralise the loss on an adverse change in rates, but it will exacerbate the loss in case of a favourable change.

These are all matters that should be considered, but especially calculated out before a hedge with futures contracts is entered into.

CHECKLIST FOR THE REVIEW OF CHAPTER 4

General overview: the overall control objectives of the material dealt with in this chapter are to acquaint the business with the fundamental operational features of interest rate futures contracts and the exchanges that they trade on.

	Key Issues	Illustrative Scope or Approach
4.1	Does the business consider when it might be appropriate to make use of interest rate futures contracts?	When a future exposure to interest rates is anticipated When there exists a variable interest rate exposure that can impact adversely on the company's cash flow or bottom-line If the company is averse to exposing it to counterparty risk in the process of managing its interest rate risk If the company does not want to encroach on its credit facilities in the process of managing its interest rate risk When the company would benefit by using off-balance sheet instruments to manage on-balance sheet interest rate risk

continued

	Key Issues	Illustrative Scope or Approach
4.2	In an interest rate futures hedge, does the company consider the current interest rate yield curve?	A positive yield curve will result in a negative basis which will strengthen during the currency of the hedge and tend to zero when the futures expiration month becomes the spot month. A negative yield curve will result in a positive hedge basis which will weaken during the currency of the hedge and tend to zero when the futures expiration month becomes the spot month
4.3	Does the company consider the effect of a change in the basis on the outcome of the hedge?	A long interest rate futures hedge with a positive basis will result in a loss on the hedge, while a short futures hedge with a positive basis will result in a profit on the hedge. The maximum loss or profit will be equal to the original basis. A long interest rate futures hedge with a negative basis will result in a profit on the hedge, while a short futures hedge with a negative basis will result in a loss on the hedge. The maximum loss or profit will be equal to the original basis
4.4	When the company constructs an interest rate futures hedge, does it take into account the impact of an over-hedged position?	If the hedge ratio is greater than 1:1, the company's position is over-hedged. An over-hedged position will: • In a long futures hedge with a positive basis: • Decrease the loss on the hedge or result in a profit on the hedge, when the underlying exchange rate changes adversely for the hedger's cash position and increase the loss on the hedge when the underlying exchange rate changes in favour of the hedger's cash position • In a long futures hedge with a negative basis: • Increase the profit on the hedge when the underlying exchange rate changes adversely for the hedger's cash position and decrease the profit on the hedge or result in a loss on the hedge when the underlying exchange rate changes favourably for the hedger's cash position • In a short futures hedge with a positive basis: • Increase the profit on the hedge when the underlying exchange rate changes adversely for the hedger's cash position and decrease the profit on the hedge or result in a loss on the hedge when the underlying exchange rate changes favourably for the hedger's cash position

continued

Key Issues	Illustrative Scope or Approach
	• In a short futures hedge with a negative basis: • Decrease the loss on the hedge or result in a profit on the hedge, when the underlying exchange rate changes adversely for the hedger's cash position and increase the loss on the hedge when the underlying exchange rate changes in favour of the hedger's cash position
4.5 When the company constructs an interest rate futures hedge, does it take into account the impact of an under-hedged position?	If the hedge ratio is less than 1:1, the company's position is under-hedged. An under-hedged position will: • In a long futures hedge with a positive basis: • Increase the loss on the hedge when the underlying exchange rate changes adversely for the hedger's cash position and decrease the loss on the hedge or result in a profit on the hedge, when the underlying exchange rate changes in favour of the hedger's cash position • In a long futures hedge with a negative basis: • Decrease the profit on the hedge, or result in a loss on the hedge, when the underlying exchange rate changes adversely for the hedger's cash position and increase the profit on the hedge when the underlying exchange rate changes favourably for the hedger's cash position • In a short futures hedge with a positive basis: • Decrease the profit on the hedge, or result in a loss on the hedge, when the underlying exchange rate changes adversely for the hedger's cash position and increase the profit on the hedge when the underlying exchange rate changes favourably for the hedger's cash position • In a short futures hedge with a negative basis: • Increase the loss on the hedge when the underlying exchange rate changes adversely for the hedger's cash position and decrease the loss on the hedge or result in a profit on the hedge, when the underlying exchange rate changes in favour of the hedger's cash position

five

interest rate swaps

INTRODUCTION TO INTEREST RATE SWAPS

Single currency interest rate swaps have enjoyed exponential growth during the period from 1987 to 1997. The first swap instruments were interest rate swaps, which developed during the 1960s as an offshoot of parallel and back-to-back loans mainly used to circumvent the UK's then current currency exchange controls. Academicians do not regard interest rate swaps as proper derivative instruments because they require the exchange of principal. Proper derivative instruments are by definition instruments with only notional principal that is never traded. Nevertheless, in the market place interest rate swaps are regarded and treated as financial derivatives.

Interest rate swaps really came into their own during 1980–1981. Once the flexibility and usefulness of interest swaps came to be generally recognised, trading took off and today they are the most heavily traded and thus also the most liquid of all financial instruments. Banks, financial institutions and companies daily use interest rate swaps to manage their exposures and cash flows. The many uses of interest rate swaps will become apparent as the discussion progresses. Suffice it to mention at this stage that with swaps, virtually any cash flow can be swapped for any other. This means that any exposure to an interest based cash flow can be changed to a different cash flow, based on no interest rate, or on a different interest rate. It also offers flexibility by allowing access to markets that may be otherwise inaccessible. Financing costs can be lowered through a judicious use of swaps.

In this chapter, however, the concern is with the basic structure of interest rate swaps and how they are most commonly employed in managing interest rate risk. Once the basics are properly understood, all other uses will become clear.

The purpose of an interest rate swap is obviously to create interest rate risk. The risk created can be structured precisely and used to manage the interest rate risk that a company faces very effectively. It is important to note that due to the nature of these swaps they create risk that includes periodicity. In other words, they include some regular, periodic payments and receipts of cash flows. They are therefore especially useful in managing risks that are related to regular payments or receipts of interest.

Unlike exchange traded instruments like futures contracts, swaps involve counterparty credit risk. In the early years, there were concerns that such risks would put a damper on trading interest rate swaps. These fears have proved unfounded. Experience has shown that the default rates on interest rate swaps are substantially lower than traditional banking default rates.

PRINCIPLES OF INTEREST RATE SWAPS

In common with all other swaps, an interest rate swap is essentially an exchange of income and payment streams, denominated in a single currency. They are thus also described as single currency, interest rate swaps. Each party (the counterparties) to a swap has an incoming and an outgoing cash flow. Since the cash flows are based upon interest rates, it follows that there must be a principal amount on which interest is calculated. This is known as the notional principal of the swap.

definition

A reasonably satisfactory definition of an interest rate swap is probably the following:

> It is a binding agreement between two parties whereby one party nominally lends to the other a principal amount, which the latter party immediately reinvests with the first party for the same period as the loan. Each party undertakes to pay periodical interest to the other on the loan and the investment, respectively, each party's interest payment being based on a different interest rate regime.

Most modern commentators will agree that the nominal loan and reinvestment is a legal fiction that can profitably be dropped from the notion of an interest rate swap. An interest rate swap is then:

> An agreement to exchange, for a specified term, periodic payments against receipts of interest, both calculated on the same notional principal, but at two different interest rate regimes.

The term 'interest rate regimes' requires some explanation. Two parties would never swap interest payments that were merely based on two different rates of interest. There would clearly be an advantage for the party paying the lower rate and receiving the higher rate. However, the counterparty to such a deal would be a loser from day one, and deservedly so.

A swap can only be arranged if it were in both parties' interest to do so. The 'regimes' that are thus referred to in the above definitions are the regime of fixed interest rates and the number of floating interest regimes such as Libor, Euribor, US Treasury Bill rates, etc. All fixed interest rates fall under one regime, and therefore a swap cannot consist of two streams of fixed interest rates, even though the actual rates might differ. A basic interest rate swap consists of a fixed interest rate and a floating interest rate. A swap may also consist of two floating interest rates, where the two rates fall under different regimes and these are called basis swaps.

Interest rate swaps consequently resolve themselves into two broad categories, namely fixed-against-floating and floating-against-floating swaps. These categories and their variations will become clear during the course of this chapter.

interest rate fras, futures and swaps

It would be true to say that interest rate derivatives come in only two flavours: future-based and options. Three instruments, namely FRAs, interest rate futures contracts and interest rate swaps, form a trilogy of future-based derivatives. They are interchangeable in their functions and uses, but still, they each have their particular niche in the marketplace.

Whatever might be achieved using any one of these instruments can also be achieved by using any of the other two. The circumstance of each case must dictate which is the better instrument to use.

counterparty risk in interest rate swaps

As an OTC instrument, parties to an interest rate swap face counterparty risk. The counterparty risk in swaps does not differ substantially from the counterparty risk in FRAs. As is the case in FRAs, each party to a swap is dependent on the willingness and ability of the other to perform its side of the bargain. Using interest rate swaps will therefore affect a company's credit facilities. It might well diminish the total credit facilities available to the company for other business. Banks and financial institutions will assess the counterparty risk very thoroughly before agreeing to a swap.

USES OF INTEREST RATE SWAPS

All interest rate swaps are made up of two legs of cash flows. As previously mentioned, a basic interest rate swap consists of a stream of interest payments based on a fixed interest rate, against a stream of interest payments based on some floating rate of interest. This is the most popular form of interest rate swaps. This is indicated by a survey done in the US.

The Weiss Center for International Financial Research of the Wharton School of the University of Pennsylvania undertook two surveys, one in 1994 and the second in 1995. The purpose was to determine the usage and practice of financial derivatives by non-financial corporations in the US. The second of these two surveys, which was supported by CIBC Wood Gundy, found that 83% of corporations using derivatives to manage interest rate risk, used them to swap floating rate for fixed rate debt. Such a swap is nothing more than a hedge against adverse changes in the interest rate during the term of a loan. This will be clear from the first case study in this chapter.

It must be noted that the survey found that there was substantial use of swaps for other purposes as well. Seventy percent of companies used them to swap fixed rate for floating rate, while 58% used them to fix the spread on new debt issues. There was also substantial use of swaps to lock in borrowing rates in advance of a new debit issue. These results give some indication of how ubiquitous the fixed-against-floating swap really is in the non-financial sector.

STRUCTURING INTEREST RATE SWAPS

Swaps can be structured in various ways. The basic structure of two interest rate based cash flow streams over a term allows for a lot of flexibility. Notwithstanding everything that has been said up to this point, it is not uncommon for swaps to have only one set of cash flows. That is to say, the swap might only consist of one period that coincides with the term of the swap. At the end of the term of the swap, there is a single payment by each party to the other party, which will be netted. The result is that only one party pays the net amount owed to the other party at the end of the term. This structure is referred to as a bullet swap. Nevertheless, whether a swap consists of only one or multiple sets of cash flows, the general principles remain the same.

spot or deferred start swaps

The first issue that arises is the date on which the swap starts. Just like any other commercial deal, a swap might start virtually immediately, or it might start at some agreed deferred time. A swap for virtual immediate implementation would be a spot swap, but a swap that is scheduled to start at some deferred date is known as a forward swap.

For risk management purposes, a swap is scheduled to start and end synchronously with the risk being hedged. When it is a borrowing or lending rate being locked-in in advance of a debt issue, the swap will of course be slated to end at the start of the new debt issue. The start date of the swap must clearly influence its pricing. When a spot swap is priced, spot interest rates are used to determine the swap rate. However, when a forward swap is priced, the applicable forward rate is used to calculate the swap rate. A swap arrangement in terms of which the swap will start at an agreed date in the future is called a deferred swap.

swap reset dates

Notwithstanding single-period bullet swaps, the most common structure for a swap is to consist of multiple payment periods. The dates on which the periodic payments are to be made are known as 'reset dates'. For example, were a swap to be based on 3-month Libor, payments would be made every 3 months from the start of the term.

Since interest is fixed in advance and paid in arrears, it follows that the date on which a payment is made to the swap, is also the date on which the floating rate interest is determined for the next payment. Payment dates are therefore the dates on which the floating rate is reset every time during the term of the swap.

the notional principal

The second important question that arises is what the notional principal must be. Normally the notional principal of the swap will be equal to the principal sum of the exposure being hedged or managed. However, if the notional principal of the swap were to remain immutable throughout the period of the swap, it would preclude the use of interest rate swaps when the underlying exposure was systematically being diminished. In order to provide for this contingency, it is possible to structure an amortising swap. Mathematically it is as simple to solve the equation for an amortising swap as for a deferred swap.

the cash flows

The third important element of swaps is the structure of the interest rate legs. These are fundamental to the purpose of a swap and consequently have to receive closer examination. The floating interest leg of fixed-against-floating swaps is usually based on 6-month or 3-month Libor, but lately Euribor is used almost as often. In practice, swaps amount to instruments through which Libor (or Euribor) is traded for forward delivery. How the swap rate is determined is discussed separately in a following section.

The floating leg is also normally specified as interest 'fixed in advance, payable in arrears'. Assuming that 6-month Libor is being used, the interest rate for the floating leg will be fixed according to the 6-month Libor quote at the beginning of each 6-month period, but only paid at the end of the period. The party paying the floating leg of the swap thus knows in advance what its interest payment will be in 6-months time.

However, it is not uncommon to have interest fixed and payable in arrears. Such an arrangement would be advantageous to the party paying the floating leg if interest rates did not rise by as much as indicated by the interest rate yield curve. Conversely, it would benefit the receiving party if rates actually rose by more than indicated by the yield curve. Again, it is not necessary to agonise too much about this matter when constructing a swap. If speculating on interest rate yields is not your business, don't make it your business.

Although it is not essential, it is usual and advisable to have the payments from both parties made on the same date. This means that on any reset date, both parties will be obliged to make payment for its interest payment for the period since the previous reset date or the start of the term, as the case may be. The importance of this synchronicity will appear from the discussion that follows.

netting

Finally, a most important subject is the netting of payments. This refers to the practice of netting the interest payments due. Since each party must pay to the other party at each reset date, it makes sense rather to net the two payments. That means that only the party with the greater payment pays the difference to the other party. This practice is extremely important as it influences the credit risk to which each party is exposed. The credit risk weighting of a swap is much less when the parties are required to make simultaneous interest payments, which are required to be netted.

International Swaps and Derivatives Association (ISDA) swap agreements make provision for this practice as one of their standard clauses. It seems however, that there is not necessarily universal legal enforceability of such netting clauses. The international enforceability of netting clauses in swap agreements has received wide and intense study from the ISDA. The legal opinions they have sought on this matter on a world-wide basis are available from their offices.

Any reader who wishes to deal in swaps is advised to seek legal opinion on the enforceability of such clauses in their country or the countries of any counterparty they might wish to deal with. Without a legally enforceable netting agreement, the credit weighting of swap agreements becomes quite severe.

the risk

As with all other derivatives, the purpose of the creation of swaps concerns risk. The risk is created to profit the speculator, but to reduce the risk of those who seek protection from risks incurred during the course of their business. It is thus appropriate to examine the risk created by interest rate swaps.

It is important to note that swaps start at par. They are also called par swaps. This means that there is no comparative advantage to either party at the start and it is thus said that the swap has no value. This state of affairs is a necessary precondition, since there would otherwise be an obvious arbitrage opportunity. Parity is achieved by adjusting the interest rate based cash flows so that the net present values of both legs are equal at the start.

In a fixed-to-floating swap, the payer of the fixed rate consequently faces the risk that the floating rate, which it receives, will decline. The swap then acquires a negative value for the receiver of the floating rate and a positive value for the payer.

The payer of the floating rate faces the risk that the floating rate will increase and thus increase its payments. In that event, the swap will acquire a negative value for the payer of the floating rate and a positive value for the receiver.

penalties

Unlike IRGs and other options, there is no premium to be paid for swaps. The cost of a swap is included in the basis point spread of the dealer. However, the swap rates and the risks are calculated over the term of the swap. Thus, if the swap is terminated, there will be a penalty payable. The size of the penalty will obviously depend on the length of the outstanding term and the value that the swap has gained (if any) for the party against whom the cancellation is made.

When a swap is structured, a company must thus be sure that no circumstances are present that may require lifting the hedge before the completion of the term of the swap.

THE SWAP RATE

One of the most important aspects of an interest rate swap is the fixing of the swap rate. The swap rate is actually the interest rate of the fixed leg of a fixed-to-floating rate swap. The rate is influenced by a number of factors.

As was stated above, interest rate swaps start off at a par value. This means that the net present values of both expected cash flows are equal at the start. The first germane issue is thus the period of the swap. The rate of the fixed leg will obviously be influenced by the period of the swap as it involves forward interest to be received. Just as important, however, is the level of applicable interest rates. This will appear more fully from the discussion that follows.

swap quotes

Obviously, any swap rate quote that can be obtained in the market will be based on current interest rates (given the currency of the swap) for the period of the intended swap. The quote for a swap rate is thus a calculation based on the current interest rates for the period of the swap and includes a premium for the dealer. This latter premium is usually quoted as a basis point spread over the benchmark interest rate off which the swap rate is calculated.

In well-developed markets for interest rate swaps, it will thus always be evident how the swap rate is arrived at. In US dollar swaps, for example, the US Treasury bond rate that corresponds to the period of the swap is used as the benchmark. To the benchmark rate, the bid/offer spread of the dealer is added to arrive at the all-in swap rate.

In the UK, sterling interest rate swaps are priced off the appropriate UK gilts. In less well-developed swap markets, swap rates are usually merely quoted as an all-inn rate. This makes the pricing of swaps somewhat less of a transparent affair. It is thus evident that the pricing of swaps is a specialist function. It is equally apparent that swap rates will differ from dealer to dealer. Obtaining quotes from the market is consequently a basic essential.

transparent rates

End-users of OTC derivatives have always been at a disadvantage when it came to pricing deals. As mentioned above, the only certain way to get a truly accurate idea of the market has always been to call as many dealers as one can get hold of for quotes. This is a tedious task, considering the multitude of deals some companies regularly make.

In April 1998 however, the ISDA, Reuters and Intercapital Brokers joined forces to change all that. The trio launched a new par-rate screen service to provide mid-market swap rates and dollar spreads to users and dealers.

The service offers a par swap curve (i.e. the curve formed by plotting the swap rates for different periods) for cash-settled swap options. For transactions in US dollars, swap rates and spreads will be listed in maturities of 2, 3, 5, 7 and 10 years. Swap rates will also be provided for three other currencies, namely French francs, Deutsche marks and Japanese yen in maturities of 1–10 years.

The swap curve is derived from the daily quotes given by 23 top market makers. The rates quoted are the mean of the rates quoted by the selected dealers. The quotes are those that are given at 11:00 A.M. local time, in New York and London, and 10:00 A.M. and 3:00 P.M. in Japan. A half-hour later, the rates are displayed on the Reuters ISDAFIX pages. Reuters also offers secondary screens showing the rates and spreads reported by each quoting dealer. The ISDA archives these quotes for future reference.

According to ISDA, the new service is designed 'to establish authoritative values against which exercised swap options can be settled, as well as to serve other valuation needs' These valuation needs include the cash settling of interest rate swaps. In order to gain the greatest validity for the quoted rates, the dealers involved are the largest dealers in the respective currencies. The 12 dealers whose quotes are used to determine the rate for US dollar swaps are listed in Table 5-1.

An important consideration is that, for US dollar spreads, the quoting dealers are required to indicate the US Treasury issue against which their quoted spread is benchmarked.

Table 5-1. The swap dealers whose swap rates are used for the published swap rates

Bankers Trust	Credit Suisse	JP Morgan
Capital Markets	Financial Products	Merrill Lynch
Chase Manhattan	Fuji Bank	Morgan Stanley
Citibank, NA	Goldman Sachs	SBC Warburg

PRACTICAL INTEREST RATE SWAPS

Having dealt with the general outline of how interest rate swaps are structured and priced, a better understanding of their use might be gained from examining a case study. The following case study is intended only to illustrate the basic application of interest rate swaps in a real world situation. Earlier it was pointed out that an interest rate swap is only another version of an FRA. The case study therefore represents a set of facts concerning interest rate risks that might equally have been managed by an FRA or by interest rate futures contracts.

Nevertheless, there must be an underlying advantage to making use of an interest rate swap, otherwise there would be no point in using it rather than an FRA or an interest rate futures contract. The obvious advantage of swaps is that they are concerned with cash flows. Although the other interest rate derivatives can also be structured to hedge interest rate related cash flows, swaps are inherently best suited to hedge that type of risk. It must also be noted that swaps can also be used to hedge single cash flows, such as when they are used to lock in lending or investment rates in advance.

The case study that follows is intended only to demonstrate an exchange of fixed-against-floating rates and examine the result.

case study 4: hedging a term loan with an interest rate swap

❏   SCENARIO

Pharma Helvetica SA, a Swiss pharmaceutical company has negotiated a $34,365,000 loan with its bank to finance a research project. The loan is for a period of 5 years at a rate of 0.75% above 6-month USD Libor. It follows that interest payments will be made every 6 months, with the first payment due at the end of the first 6-month period.

❏   FINANCIAL INFORMATION

The risk that the company faces is obviously that Libor rates will increase over the period, thus increasing the costs of the research project. As such increases could be substantial, the resultant cost increases might affect the company's total cost and pricing structure. Since careful budgeting is a priority of this company, they would choose to remain within budget rather than to profit from windfall changes in interest rates. At the time the company considers its options, the spot yield curve for Libor is as depicted in Figure 5-1.

As indicated by the steeply rising yield curve, the market expects a substantial rise in interest rates. Resulting from this perception of market expectations, the length of the period of the loan and the cash flows involved, the company decides to approach dealers in the money market to structure an appropriate swap.

At the time of their approach to the market, 6-month Libor is quoted at 3.80375% per annum. This calculates to 1.901875% for 6 months (3.80375/2). Pharma Helvetica wishes to receive 6-month Libor while paying fixed interest on the notional principal of the swap.

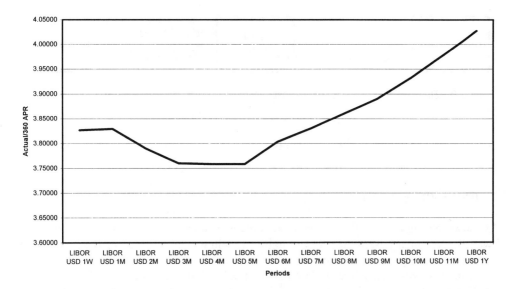

Figure 5-1   The spot Libor yield curve as reported by the British Bankers Association on a particular date.

☐   THE SWAP

The swap that is eventually agreed to between the company and an investment bank in Zurich starts and ends on the same day as the loan to the company from its own bank does. All periods in the loan and the swap therefore coincide. The actual pricing of the swap falls outside the scope of this book. There are however, many excellent texts on how they are priced. If the company is not itself a market maker in swaps, the swap will in any event be priced by the bank or other swap dealer. The company can at best shop around to determine the best deal it can find at that time.

The notional principal of the swap is $34,365,000. The cash flows of the swap arrangement are as depicted in Figure 5-2.

☐   THE HEDGE

Taken on its own, the swap arrangement as shown in Figure 5-2 exposes Pharma Helvetica to the risk that 6-month Libor will decline over the period of the swap. This risk is exactly opposite to the risk that the company faces on the loan from its own bank. Since the periods of the loan and swap are identical, as is the principal involved in each, the two

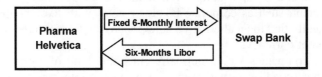

Figure 5-2   The cash flows of a fixed-to-floating swap agreement.

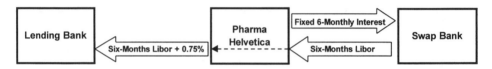

Figure 5-3 The cash flows of a hedge against a floating interest rate using a fixed-against-floating swap.

risks cancel one another out completely. The total situation as it applies to Pharma Helvetica is illustrated in Figure 5-3.

❐   DISCUSSION OF THE HEDGE

As shown by Figure 5-3, Pharma Helvetica receives a payment of 6-month Libor from Swap Bank, which passes directly through to Lending Bank. The company must add a further 0.75% interest to this payment in order to meet their obligation to the bank. The payment thus costs them a fixed 0.75% per annum. In addition, the company has to pay the fixed interest payment to Swap Bank. In effect, the company thus has total a fixed interest cost on the loan from Lending Bank amounting to the fixed interest payment plus 3/4%.

Whatever the changes in 6-month Libor might be over the next 5 years, the company will remain unaffected by it. The hedge is thus a perfect one. The company can keep its interest cost within budget and it does not face any further interest rate risk.

The company does however, face counterparty credit risk. The weight of this risk is determined by the credit standing of Swap Bank and may not be of serious concern to the company. The other downside of the deal is that the company has tied some of its credit facilities down through the swap arrangement.

The case study also illustrates a swap of fixed interest for floating interest. This is the position of Swap Bank. Swap Bank would be able to hedge its exposure to this swap, by arranging another swap, giving it an opposite risk exposure. For a non-financial company, however, such a swap would normally not be hedged, since it would be swapping a riskless payment of fixed interest for a risky payment of a floating rate. Nevertheless, it is a valid risk management tool and is usually employed under the circumstances illustrated in the second example discussed below.

ASSET SWAPS

An asset swap is virtually identical to a basic interest rate swap agreement inasmuch as it remains an agreement between two parties to exchange periodic interest payments over a term. However, an asset swap is unique in that one interest payment is tied to cash flows from an investment, such as corporate bonds or notes with fixed coupons. The other payment is typically tied to an alternative index, such as a floating rate or a rate denominated in a different currency.

Non-financial companies would normally enter this kind of swap as a speculative transaction, either based on a market view that interest rates are going to decline, or based on receiving a rate with which they are more comfortable dealing with.

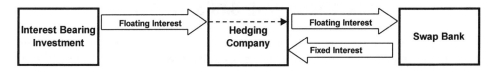

Figure 5-4   Hedging floating rate investment income, using an asset swap.

Should a non-financial company make an investment on which it receives a floating rate of interest, it could profitably enter into to such an arrangement as a hedge of its investment income. The cash flows would be as depicted in Figure 5-4.

It is evident from the figure that when the cash flows are arranged as above, the company with the interest bearing asset is left with receiving fixed interest from its investment after the swap. The floating interest cash flow, whatever its monetary value, merely passes through the company's hands to Swap Bank. This would regularly be the situation of a bank or other financial institution, but would probably not be very common in the non-financial sector. However, this example demonstrates that the company now faces no further interest rate risk on its investment income receipts. It has swapped a floating rate asset for an asset paying a fixed interest rate.

It can also benefit a non-financial company to use an asset swap to swap out of fixed interest from an asset to floating interest. Non-financial companies make cash investments from time to time. Their need to manage their investment income is exactly the same as the need of any investment company. They would therefore be as well served by an asset swap as any other investor. Asset swaps are commonly used by investors who seek to transform the cash flows of an asset or pool of assets without affecting the underlying investment position. What this implies is examined in the following case study.

For instance, suppose a US based corporate treasurer wanted to park cash from the company's European operations in a particular euro-denominated fixed rate bond issue. The bond pays a rate in euro, but the treasurer prefers to receive floating rate US dollar cash flows, since it has floating rate US dollar commitments.

The treasurer could purchase the bond and then enter into an asset swap to receive 6-month US Libor payments, plus or minus the applicable dealer spread, in return for paying the fixed rate coupon in euros. The swap would be adjusted to par such that the fixed payments on the swap match the fixed payments on the bond. This type of adjustment is explained in the Chapter 6 under off-market swaps. The cash flows are illustrated in Figure 5-5.

In effect, the treasurer has swapped a euro-based asset for a USD-based asset. The net result is that the corporation owns the desired asset, producing the desired cash flows.

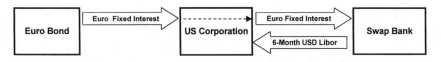

Figure 5-5   The cash flows of an asset swap out of fixed-to-floating

INTEREST RATE BASIS SWAPS

Interest rate basis swaps (IR basis swaps) are also known as single currency, basis swaps. This is to distinguish them from currency basis swaps where each of the two legs of the swap is denominated in a different currency. IR basis swaps create an interest rate spread that lies at the heart of this type of swap. Once such a swap position is taken in, the parties to the swap no longer face 'naked' interest rate risk. They are no longer affected by the appreciation or decline of any one of the two interest rates as such, but rather by the change in the interest rate spread created by the swap.

This swap structure is consequently very popular with banks and other financial institutions whose business it is to profit from interest rate differentials. Very often, they may use this structure to hedge themselves against the inverse spread, or interest rate gap, which might have come about as a result of their dealings with clients. It comes about because banks often fund themselves on a floating rate basis. They then lend out the funds at a different floating rate. This puts them at risk to a narrowing of the spread between the interest rate of their funding and the rate of their lending.

On the other hand, it is also a valid risk management tool for non-financial businesses. Depending on the view one takes of how the yield curve will change, one could swap normally calculated Libor against Libor in arrears, or swap 1-month Libor for 6-month Libor. The following case study is an example of a non-financial company using a basis swap more as a risk dampening strategy rather than as a total hedge.

case study 5: managing interest rate risk with a basis swap

❐   SCENARIO

US Trinket Imports Inc., an import/export company has obtained bridging finance over a 2-year term at an interest rate based on 3-month Libor. The company does not want to hedge the exposure, as it would like to remain able to benefit from favourable changes in interest rates. However, the view it takes of the market is that Libor has been traditionally more volatile than US Treasury rates. It would therefore prefer to pay a rate based on 3-month Treasury Bills rather than on 3-month Libor.

Obviously, the exercise does not involve changing the size of the actual interest payment. It concerns changing the underlying interest rate variable from 3-month Libor to the 3-month Treasury rate, which the company perceives as less volatile. Swaps are constructed at par, thus the net present values of the two legs of interest rate payments must always be equal at the start of the swap. The two base interest rates merely underlie the actual cash flows as the key variables.

❐   THE RISK

The risk the company faces as a result of the loan, is that 3-month Libor will rise and consequently increase their operating cost. It regards that as too risky a proposition and would prefer to be at risk of a rise in 3-month US Treasury Bill rate. However, nobody is prepared to lend it money at a rate based on US Treasury Bills. The company's cash flow position is shown in Figure 5-6.

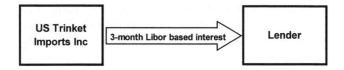

Figure 5-6   Unmanaged interest payments over a 2-year period.

The flow of principal is not indicated in the figure. It merely reflects the cash flow that is subject to the risk of an adverse change in the underlying variable rate.

❐   THE SWAP

The company enters a swap agreement with a swap dealer to give effect to its view of the interest rate market. The start and end date of the swap is identical to the dates applicable to the loan. The notional principal of the swap is also identical to the notional principal of the loan. The cash flows to which the company is now committed are reflected in Figure 5-7.

❐   DISCUSSION

US Trinket Imports now receive 3-month Libor from the swap, which merely passes through its hands to the lender in payment of the company's interest obligation. The company's net payment out is to Swap Bank and it is based on the 3-month US Treasury Bill rate. The company therefore has no further exposure to Libor, but only to the Treasury rate.

The company has now successfully arranged a loan based on US Treasury rates, which is not available in the market place. The company could as easily have arranged a fixed-against-floating swap, which would have hedged the loan rate. However, that is not what it intended. The case study not only demonstrates how a loan that is not otherwise available in the marketplace might be created, but also how any risk that is regarded as uncompetitive or inappropriate can be swapped for another.

❐   COUNTERPARTY RISK

Whatever the changes in 3-month Libor might be over the next 2 years, the company will remain unaffected by it. The swap arrangement has thus eliminated this risk, but has not eliminated the risk of adverse changes in the Treasury Bill rate.

The company does however, still face counterparty credit risk. The weight of this risk is determined by the credit standing of Swap Bank and may or may not be a serious consideration for the company. A further downside of the deal is that the company has

Figure 5-7   Risk reduced cash flows over a 2-year period.

tied some of its credit facilities down through the swap arrangement. It is one of the issues that a company must consider when it uses a swap for risk dampening or speculative trading. It must question whether the potential benefit of such a strategy is worth tying down some of its credit facilities.

CHECKLIST FOR THE REVIEW OF CHAPTER 5

General overview: the overall control objectives of the material dealt with in this chapter are to acquaint the business with the fundamental principles and operational features of interest rate swaps.

	Key Issues	Illustrative Scope or Approach
5.1	Does the business consider when it might be appropriate to make use of interest rate swaps?	Due to the length of the period involved, FRAs and futures are not readily available The interest rate risk faced by the company involves a cash flow of interest payments over the whole of the period. A swap might be the most effective instrument to hedge such an exposure The company does not wish to hedge the exposure, but rather to swap it for another risk variable, based on an interest rate The term of the exposure to be hedged is certain
5.2	How will changing interest rates affect the outcome of a hedge with a swap?	A properly structured swap is a perfect hedge and the outcome will not be affected by changes in interest rates during its term
5.3	What is the cost of an interest rate swap?	The cost of an interest rate swap consists of the basis points spread that the dealer quotes over the benchmark rate There will be a penalty for early termination
5.4	Will it benefit a company to shop around for quotes on swaps?	The interest rate bid/offered spread, which differs from institution to institution, will be a determinant of the cost of a swap Swap rates will differ from institution to institution
5.5	What interest rate risks can be hedged perfectly by means of an interest rate swap?	Interest rate cash flows based on floating rates that consist of either interest payable or receivable. The interest streams must be for an identical term as the swap The interest rate swap must be structured to mirror the interest rate payable or receivable that is being hedged

continued

	Key Issues	Illustrative Scope or Approach
5.6	Will interest rate swaps allow a company to speculate on its view of interest rates?	When a basis swap is arranged, a company can speculate on its view of the interest rate market by paying the leg that it believes will decline against receiving the leg that it believes will increase In a fixed-against-floating swap a company can speculate on its view of interest rates by swapping from a fixed rate into a floating rate that it believes will decline against the fixed rate.

SIX
interest rate options

INTRODUCTION

The concept of options is certainly well known to every businessperson. Yet, in order to gain a better understanding of how it is applied and used in the money markets, a more thorough analysis of the actual instruments is required.

Fundamentally, interest rate options, like all other financial options, are traded in two fora. The first and probably still the most common forum are the premises of banks, financial institutions and other money market dealers. There, interest rate options are created and tailored to suit a client's specifications. Such transactions are referred to as over the counter transactions and the resulting options are consequently called OTC options. The OTC appellation of options thus refers to the forum on which they are traded.

In addition to OTC options, there are also exchange-traded options. The only interest rate options presently traded on exchanges are options on interest rate futures. They trade on the same exchanges as the futures contracts that underlie them.

However, options are such flexible and complex instruments that it is insufficient merely to classify them by the forum that they trade on. There is a lot more to options than that they are either OTC or exchange-traded. Indeed, the topic of options is very wide and encompasses numerous specialised types of options that differ according to the underlying asset. There are also special option constructs such as caps and floors. They also vary depending on the requirements of the underlying asset. In the currency markets, these option constructs are built from normal interest rate options to suit particular needs. They will be examined in detail during the course of this discussion.

In the marketplace, the reader will discover an amazing and confusing array of choices of options. All sorts of interesting names are thought up for particular option constructs, add-inns and conglomerations. Very often, a different name does not translate into a different product. Banks fall over one another to service this lucrative market. They often give their products original and innovative names in order to create the impression of novelty or to differentiate their product from similar or identical products offered by others in the market.

Nevertheless, the fundamental principles of options are universal to all options, regardless of what they are called, where they are traded or what their underlying assets may be.

The only difference between the different categories of options is to be found in the changes in detail that only become apparent upon closer examination. The changes do not change the fundamentals, but many of the particular rules and structures vary, with different results.

In essence, an option is a limited risk instrument from a buyer's, or options taker's point of view. Unlike other interest rate derivatives, options are specifically designed to allow for a profit to the hedger upon a favourable move in the underlying exchange rate, while giving protection against an adverse move.

THE FUNDAMENTAL PRINCIPLES OF OPTIONS

An option is an agreement between two parties. One party grants the other party an option to do, or not to do something. The granter or giver of the option is, logically, known as the option giver or as the option writer. More importantly however, the granter of the option is also known as the option seller. Conversely, the person who is given the option is known as the option buyer. Prosaically of course, the option buyer is also known as the option taker and the option holder. The person taking the option, obviously 'holds' it, for as long as the option is valid.

In the financial markets, everything has a price. Options confer valuable rights; therefore, they have a value. That is the underlying reasons why options are not given, but are in fact bought and sold. Hence the terms option buyer and option seller.

Even in ordinary daily use, the term 'option' already says that the holder has a choice. That is to say, whatever the option may be about, the person holding it has a choice either to do something or not to do it. This then, is the second, very important element of an option. The buyer of an option is given the right to do something, but not the obligation to do it.

In order to explain the principle, an ordinary everyday example can be employed. Assume a person wishes to purchase a house. She finds a very attractive place at what she considers a fair price. However, she is unsure whether or not it is really such a fair price, because she does not really know the property market in that area all that well. She might, for example, want to investigate the town planning scheme to ensure that the other party isn't selling for some reason that she ought to know about. Planned future developments influence the value of the property adversely or favourably. She therefore requires some more time to investigate matters. On the other hand, while she is investigating and making up her mind, another buyer might just turn up and decide to buy the house ahead of her. Her best course of action would be to negotiate with the other party to give her an option to purchase the property at a price on which they both agree.

rights created by an option agreement – the call option

Consider the basic elements that are necessary to make an option deal, such as the one postulated above, a binding agreement. There are essentially four elements, but other elements are also added in order to make them commercially sound and acceptable. All the elements will be dealt with as the discussion progresses.

The first element that requires the agreement of the parties is what rights each party is giving to the other party in terms of the agreement. Still using the example of the option on fixed property, the right given by the owner of the property to the would-be purchaser is the right to purchase the property. An option conferring on the holder of the option a right to purchase is known as a call option in the financial markets. In terms of a call option, the holder has the right to call upon the option giver to perform his obligations. As previously stated, the holder of the option has a right to do something, which is to purchase the property in this case, but not the obligation to purchase it.

It follows without doubt that if there is a right to purchase, there must also be a purchase price. A right to purchase without a purchase price would be meaningless. There would in fact be no valid agreement in law. The purchase price is thus the second element that the parties need to agree upon and which must be included as part of the option agreement. In the financial markets, this price is called the 'strike price' of the option. It is the price at which the underlying deal is struck.

The third element is the agreement as to what the underlying asset of the option is. An option is a right that relates to something else. In the example, it is a right to purchase a property. The property is the subject matter, the rationale, but more properly, the underlier of the option. In the option agreement, the underlier must thus be a commercial asset that is properly identified.

The fourth element is time. Nobody would be prepared to grant an option for an indefinite period of time. The option granter virtually holds his property at the behest of the option holder. The option holder has rights, but has no obligations. The seller on the other hand, has no rights, only a potential obligation. That potential obligation will keep hanging over the option granter's head until the option is exercised, or expires. The period for which the option is valid and open for acceptance is thus an essential element of an option agreement. The last day of this period is known as the expiry day of the option, or alternatively, as the maturation date of the option.

It is also important to distinguish between the buyer and the seller of an option as opposed to the buyer and the seller of the underlying asset. The fixed property is the underlier in the example under discussion. The option thus gives the option holder the right to purchase the underlying. If she (the option holder) decides to take up, or exercise the option, that is, to exercise the right that it gives her, she will have brought about a binding agreement of purchase and sale of the property. In that resulting agreement of purchase and sale, the original seller of the option is also the seller of the property. On the other hand, she, being the buyer of the option, is also the buyer of the property. In this case therefore, the situation is that the seller of the option is also the seller of the underlier, while the buyer of the option is also the buyer of the underlier.

This explanation is valid only when applied to call options. The second type of option is known as a put option. A put option turns the situation around. The put option is an option where the buyer of the option obtains the right to sell the underlier to the seller of the option. The topic of put options will be discussed immediately hereunder. Nevertheless, the four elements mentioned and discussed so far are common to both option types.

All four elements of options can be combined to sum up the situation as far as call options are concerned. In call options, if the buyer decides to exercise the option before or at its maturation, the option seller will have the obligation to deliver the underlying asset to the option buyer against payment of the strike price. Simultaneously, the buyer must accept delivery of the underlier and pay the previously agreed price to the option seller. The element of price, i.e. the strike price of the option, is extremely important to the whole concept of options. It will be examined in greater detail after the topic of put options has been dealt with.

rights created by an option agreement – the put option

The four essential option elements that apply to all options have been mentioned and discussed in relation to call options. The call option was the point of departure, but as was stated above, these elements are found in all options.

A put option is in many ways the reverse of a call option. A put option confers on the option holder the right, but not the obligation, to sell the underlying asset to the option granter for the strike price of the option, during the period of the validity of the option.

As a consequence, when a put option is exercised, the seller of the option will be obliged to accept delivery of the underlier from the option holder and pay the previously agreed price therefor. The buyer of the option, on the other hand, will be obliged to deliver the underlier against receipt of payment from the option seller.

As an illustration of the principle of put options, consider the case of a certain Mr. Michael Cunningham. He acts as intermediary for a large property developing company that wishes to build a major shopping complex in the London Docklands area. He is trying to buy up suitable smaller properties in the area, which the company intends to consolidate and develop as a single unit. He approaches a certain Mr Patel who owns one such smaller property. Mr. Patel is not sure that he wants to sell. He is also not sure that the price is a suitable one. He wants to investigate the matter further.

On the other hand, Mr. Patel is aware of the fact that Mr. Cunningham can buy other properties instead of his (Mr. Patel's). They will serve Mr. Cunningham's purpose equally well. Mr. Patel would prefer not to miss a good deal. Thus, if the price offered proves to be a good one, he wants to accept it. The solution to his dilemma lies in negotiating an option with Mr. Cunningham. In this example, the opposite situation pertains to the one given in the first example.

Mr. Patel wants to be given the right, but not the obligation, to sell his property to Mr. Cunningham. If Mr. Cunningham were to grant such an option, he will be unable to complete his property purchases until Mr. Patel has exercised his option, or it (the option) has expired. This necessarily implies that both a strike price and a period of validity of the option must also be agreed on between them. Mr. Cunningham will also require a premium to be paid in return for the time that he has to spend holding his horses. That is a further matter for agreement between the parties.

The four elements of options mentioned previously are thus evident in this example. Essentially in a put option, there must be agreement on the right, but not the obligation, to sell the properly described underlying asset, the price to be paid for that asset and the period of the option. A closer examination of these elements follows.

summation

It is thus evident that whichever one of the two types of option is being dealt with, at its heart is a transaction of purchase and sale of some underlying asset. The two types of option therefore only differ insofar as, in the one case, the option holder is given the right to buy the asset, while in the other the holder is given the right to sell it. The following therefore constitute the fundamental elements of all options:

- an underlying asset;
- a strike price;
- a premium for the option;
- a period of validity.

the period of validity or maturity of an option

As mentioned previously, the fourth fundamental element of options is the period of its validity. It is a matter on which the parties will have to reach agreement before a proper option can come into existence. The parties will have to agree on from when and to when the option will be valid. The latter time is the time of expiry of the option. If the option is not exercised by its expiry date, it lapses and is of no force or effect. The expiry date is an important concept in financial options. It is not only a specified date, but also a specified time on that date. It is therefore the last day on which the option may be exercised, up to the stated time of that day, although that is often the close of business on the expiration date.

the option premium

Although it is not usual to have an option premium in residential property transactions as used in the example so far, it is not unknown in the higher end of the property market. Obviously, it is also quite conceivable to have an option without a premium being charged therefor. An option premium is consequently not an essential element of all options. Nevertheless, it is always an element in interest rate options, as it will be in other money market options. There will never be a free financial option, because the rights granted in an option are too valuable to be given away free. Thus, the final and perhaps most problematic element is the option premium.

Financial options were never viable until Messrs. Fisher Black and Myron Scholes devised the first option-pricing model in the 1970s. Consider the earlier example of purchasing a residential property. Due to the option agreement, the seller is required to give up his right to dispose of his property at the first available opportunity. In so doing, he may lose an opportunity to sell and the market might move against him while his waiting for the option holder to make up her mind. He would only place himself at this disadvantage if he were to gain something in the process.

The first thing the seller gains is the identification of a willing buyer. A bird in the hand, as it were. However, that is inadequate in terms of what he gives up. He will require value for value. The potential house buyer also gains an advantage. She will be able to reassure herself on the factors mentioned earlier in the example; that represents value. There must be proper compensation for value given and value received. Consequently, the parties must agree on the premium to be paid for the option. The premium is paid at the beginning. It is paid when the option is given and it is not returnable if the option is not exercised.

OPTION PRICING

The question now arises as to what the premium for a particular option ought to be. Option pricing has developed into a very sophisticated mathematical discipline. It is a complex, esoteric, but ultimately fascinating subject. There are extremely good textbooks and software available for the reader that is mathematically inclined.

The easy answer to the question postulated is of course that the market will determine the premium. While that is quite true, since the premium of any option is ultimately determined by market forces, the real question is – what factors will the market take into account in the process of pricing an option? The answer must indicate what the relative weight is of each factor. It is apparent that a number of factors will play a role in determining the price of an option.

This proved to be a difficult question to answer. In October 1970, Messrs. Fisher Black and Myron Scholes developed a mathematical model to predict option prices. Unfortunately, *The Journal of Political Economy*, published by Chicago University, rejected their article. Their explanation was that it contained too much finance and too little economics. There were some further false starts. However, after the intervention of two influential faculty members, *The Journal of Political Economy* eventually published the article in its May/June 1973 issue. It turned out to be one of the most influential articles ever published in the field of economics or finance.

Their work laid the foundation for options becoming the viable and popular instruments that they are today. The model has been a source of constant research and revision, yet it remains the basis of all modern option pricing models. It is also used to price many other derivatives. All good market analysis software packages include such an option-pricing model.

The value of an option will be reflected by its premium. The terms 'option value' and 'option premium' are used interchangeably. However, there are instances where the option premium may not accurately reflect the option value. The premium may be higher or lower than the 'true' value in terms of an option-pricing model. Like all other prices in the marketplace, options are miss-priced from time to time. However, for the purposes of this discussion the terms 'option value' and 'option price' will be used interchangeably.

The fact that a whole range of factors influences the premium of an option notwithstanding, the total value of an option consists of only two basic elements: intrinsic value and time value. However, before the difference between the intrinsic value and the time value of an option can be fully appreciated, the relationship between the strike price of an option and the price of the underlying asset must be discussed.

THE INTRINSIC VALUE OF AN OPTION

general observations

Since options are derivative instruments, they derive their value from the value of the underlying asset. The value of the underlying asset must thus be the most important element in the value of the option, although it is by no means the only one. Intrinsic value refers to that portion of the value of an option that is represented by the amount to which the option is 'in the money'. In order to clarify this issue, the terms 'in the money', 'at the money' and 'out of the money' will be discussed.

The strike price of an option is the price at which the option holder will, upon its exercise, be able to either buy or sell (depending on the type of option) the underlier. The three terms mentioned above, all describe the price of the underlying asset relative to the strike price of the option.

In order to illustrate the principle, reference can again be made to the first example of the lady wishing to purchase a house. In that example, the option holder obtained the option in order to gain time in which to investigate market conditions. Her investigation could only have revealed one of three possibilities. The first possibility is that she found that the strike price of the option was lower than the fair market value of the property. The second possibility is that she found it to be equal to the fair market value, and thirdly, she could have determined that it was higher than the fair market value.

The terms will now be examined individually in the light of the three possibilities.

an option in the money (itm)

If the investigation by the potential buyer revealed that the strike price of the option was much lower than the market value of the property, it would mean that she had a complete bargain on her hands. In that case, she could exercise the option and sell the house for an immediate profit.

This scenario illustrates the situation where the option would be said to be 'in the money' (ITM). It is an option to buy and the strike price of the option is lower than the price of the underlying asset. The value of the option will be high. In fact, the option's value must at least be equal to the potential profit. In other words, the value of the option must at least be equal to the amount by which the market value of the property exceeds the strike price of the option. That amount is also the amount by which the option is said to be ITM. The amount by which the option is ITM is also referred to as the intrinsic value of the option.

It follows that only an ITM option has intrinsic value. That is so because the intrinsic value of an option is by definition equal to the amount of money by which the option is ITM. All other options can therefore only have time value. As will become evident, the actual value of an ITM option will even be higher than its intrinsic value, because it also has time value.

an option at the money (atm)

If the strike price of the option were found equal to the fair market value of the property, the option would nevertheless have a value. The value of the option will then be based on those factors that influence the time value of an option. Its value would obviously be less than its value would have been, had it been ITM. Under the circumstances, market parlance would have it that the option was 'at the money' (ATM).

an option out of the money (otm)

However, if the investigation revealed the strike price to be greater than the market value of the property, its value will be even less than if it were at the money or in the money. It makes sense that nobody will exercise an option to purchase a property at a price greater than its fair market value. The strike price would be said to be 'out of the money' (OTM). Therefore the option has a low value, but it is not worthless. It is not worthless, because it has 'time value'. Over time, the price of the underlying might change so that the option moves into the money. That possibility gives the option time value. The more time there is available for that price change to happen, the greater the time value of an OTM option.

some terminology clarified

Before the time value of options can be discussed, there must be complete clarity on the terminology used. Options terminology is often confusing. Initiates know what is meant, although what is being said may in fact be technically incorrect. Thus, a brief explanation follows.

Although it is actually the *strike price* of the option that might be in, at, or out of the money, the convention is to refer to the *option* itself as being in, at, or out of the money. Notwithstanding the fact that the strike price of the option is fixed for the duration of its validity, it is also conventional to refer to the option as moving into or out of the money. Of course, it is not the option or its strike price that moves. Only the price of the under-lying asset 'moves', or changes by growing or declining.

THE TIME VALUE OF AN OPTION

general observations

An option has time value because, during the remaining period of validity of the option, the market value of the property may change. If it does, the strike price might yet become ATM or even ITM before the option expires. As long as there is a possibility of the spread between the market price of the underlier and the strike price of an OTM option narrow-ing, the option has value. Indeed, as the spread narrows, so the value of the option will increase.

As has already been mentioned, an option must have value even if it is OTM. Indeed, the reason is not merely that the period left to maturity may allow it to get into the money An option that is already ITM may go deeper into the money, or it may move OTM. Similarly, an option that is ATM may, over time, move into the money or OTM.

It has also been mentioned that an ITM option's total value will be greater than its intrinsic value. Thus, taking the total value of an ITM option, its time value can be calculated by simply subtracting its intrinsic value. The total value of an ITM option, less its intrinsic value, must equal its time value. Time value is the only other value that an option can have. Therefore, the surplus value of an ITM option over its intrinsic value must constitute time value. That time value will be subject to the same influences that affect the time value of ATM and ITM options.

The price and value movements of options take place over time. The possibilities of value changes exist within a time frame. Therefore, the markets can and will place a value on time. However, the time value of an option is not a constant. It is a very dynamic value that changes, often dramatically, over the period to the option's maturity. This is due to a number of factors that either give or remove the hope of profit. The hope or expectation of gain lies at the base of every factor in the market that influences value. The factors that influence the time value of an option will be examined hereunder.

price of the underlying

It might have been inferred from previous discussions that the price of the underlying asset of the option is the single most important factor that determines the value of an option. That inference would be correct. The closer the price of the underlier comes to the strike price of the option, the better the chances are that the option will move into the money. Thus, the option has a higher value. It also follows that an option that is ATM will have the greatest time value.

If the option is ATM and it moves further and further OTM, its value will decline. If it is OTM and moves closer and closer to the money, its value will increase. For reasons that will become clear later, when an option moves into the money, its total value will increase, but its time value will decrease. That is why it was stated earlier that ATM options have the greatest time value of all options of the same type, with the same underlier and the same expiry date.

time to maturity

The price of the underlier of an option changes over time. The greater the time left until the expiry date (maturity) of the option, the greater the chance that its value may improve, relative to the strike price of the option.

It follows that the more time to expiry, the greater the time value of the option. As its time runs out, so the time value shrinks. However, the time value does not shrink linearly in lockstep with time to maturity which decreases linearly. At the start of the life of an option its time value will diminish slowly, but the closer it gets to expiry, the faster its time value will approach zero. Zero is what the value will be at expiry time on expiry day.

This argument must not be taken too literally. It cannot be inferred from the above that the time value of an option will be at its greatest right at the start of its life, on the first day of its validity. This is not necessarily so.

The other factors that influence the time value of an option have such a major impact, that the single influence of time to maturity often becomes imperceptible. Not only does it become imperceptible, its effect often seems to be ignored, turned on its head, reversed and trivial. Yet, it is there. Undeterred and quietly it is gnawing away at the values of all options, exercising its subtle power. Moreover, in the end it wins. It wins because when the option expires, its existence is terminated and its value is zero.

market volatility

Clearly, the time value of an option is based on the probability of the option getting into a better position *vis-à-vis* the price of the underlier. Although the amount of time left will increase that probability, the volatility of the price of the underlier will also be a determinant of that probability.

In the markets' evaluation of an option, volatility is seen as opportunity. The greater the risk, the greater the opportunity. In other words, the greater the volatility in the underlier's market, the greater the chances are that its price will hit the strike price of the option and put the option ITM. Therefore, the higher the volatility in the market of the underlying, the greater the time value of the option.

The impact of the volatility phenomenon on option values is so great that it has given rise to speculators indulging in what is known as volatility trading. Many traders are of the opinion that it is easier to call the direction of market volatility, than to call the overall price movement of the market. When volatility rises, the premiums of all options increase. Conversely, when volatility falls, all option premiums decline. Volatility traders consequently buy options when volatility is low and sell when volatility is high.

Market volatility is a definite factor that should be considered when buying options. Option premiums that are inflated simply because of high volatility in the market should be avoided if possible. On the other hand, high volatility in the underlying market with its concomitant increased risk may be the reason why risk managing the exposure is essential. The higher price of a hedging option then becomes unavoidable. It must be accepted as the price of neutralising a high-risk situation. The price of not hedging might be even greater.

implied volatility

It is often difficult, but mostly impossible to measure current market volatility. Since volatility is measured by determining the standard deviation of prices, it can only be measured after the event. Thus, current market volatility is implied from current option prices. This would not have been possible without the option pricing models.

The volatility is implied from the prices of both OTC and exchange traded options. The implied daily volatilities are published in the financial press as well as in the market reports of banks and other financial reporting enterprises.

the 'risk-free' interest rate

The final factor that influences the value of an option is the price of money. Because time is such a valuable element of the value, it follows that the time value of money must also be factored into the premium. The 'risk free' interest rate during the period of the currency of an option is the rate that is used by most option pricing models. In the US this is usually one of the Treasury rates.

conclusion

A number of observations are relevant. As is evident from the discussion up to this point, the time value and thus the total value of options is constantly changing. The value of an option will consequently change up and down during the course of any trading day. As the price of the underlier moves, the premium of the option will also move.

A very important difference between the price moves of the option and its underlier is evident at this stage. As the next topic will explain, the value of an option does not move in a direct relationship with the price of the underlier. The price relationship between an option and its underlier is therefore not linear, but follows a curve described by a mathematical ratio, which will be discussed presently. It also follows that the value of an option is less volatile than the price of its underlier.

An important fact to be kept in mind is that an ITM option will have less time value than an ATM option. The reason for this phenomenon is to be found in the interaction between the non-linear relationship of the prices of the option and its underlying and the intrinsic value of an option. Consider an imaginary ATM call option with a value of $500. All its value is time value. Now the underlier appreciates by $100. The option value does not increase by $100. However, the option is now ITM. As will be explained in the next section, the delta of an ATM option dictates that the value of the option, after the price move of the underlying, will now be $550. Since the intrinsic value of the option is now $100, the time value of the option is now only $450 ($550 − $100).

Time value thus declines as an option moves deeper and deeper into the money, until it is so deep ITM that the price of the option and the price of the underlying start moving in lockstep. There will still be time value left in the option at that stage, but it represents the lowest percentage of time value of that an option can have.

The explanation of these observations can be found in the mathematical ratios known as the Greeks.

THE GREEKS

introduction

The great Homer said '*timeo Danaos et dona ferentes*' (I fear the gift-bearing Greeks). The gifts that these Greeks bring however are not to be feared. They do not bring hidden antagonists, but rather, they bring knowledge that can be used to advantage. That is why it is important to understand them, otherwise options might all be Greek to you.

It has already been mentioned that the value of an option does not change by one unit for every one unit that the price of the underlier changes. Yet, whenever the price of the underlier changes, the premium, or value of the option, changes with it. What is the relationship?

the mathematical relationship

A number of mathematical equations are built into option pricing models to describe the price relationship between options and their underliers. These equations are known as 'the Greeks', because they have (mostly) been given names of letters of the Greek alphabet. Only the most important ones will be discussed here. They are delta, gamma, theta and vega.

❏ THE OPTION DELTA

The major Greek that is of concern to a risk manager is delta. Delta is sometimes referred to as 'the hedge ratio'. A number of websites on the Internet give option prices on stocks and futures. They often include the option deltas as well. This information can be important in the construction of a hedge or in a 'place-holding' strategy.

Delta is a variable ratio that changes as the price of the underlier changes. Its value can be anything between zero and 1. An option that is deep ITM has a delta of 1. An option that is ATM will have a delta of 0.5, while an OTM option's delta will be close to zero. The delta value is often also expressed as a percentage. Thus, an option with a delta of 0.5 might also be said to have a delta of 50%. The reason is simply that the option delta indicates the percentage that the value of the option will change for every unit that the value of its underlier changes. The delta value of an option therefore means that an option with a delta of 0.5 will change in value by only half as much as the underlier does, from that point onwards. The value of an option with a delta of 1 will react one-on-one with the underlier; i.e. its change in value will be directly related to the change in value of the underlier.

As an example, consider the premium of a call option with a delta of 0.25. The value of the option will increase by only 25% of any price increase of its underlying asset. At the same time, while the value of the underlier increases, the option will be getting closer to the money. The closer it gets to the money, the higher its delta becomes. For these reasons, the delta value of an option describes an 'S' curve when it is plotted against the possible values of its underlier.

❏   OPTION GAMMA

Since the delta of an option changes as the price of the underlier changes, it is a valid concern what the rate of that change might be. This is exactly the function of gamma. Gamma is a measure of how much the delta of an option changes for every one unit of change in the underlier. In other words, it indicates how fast, and by how much the hedge ratio changes. ATM options that are close to expiry have the highest gamma.

It follows from the above that gamma is a very important ratio in hedging. It is extensively used in risk managing portfolios, but will probably not be of as much use to the business manager concerned with transactional currency risk.

❏   OPTION THETA

Theta is a ratio that measures the change in the premium of an option relative to its time to maturity. The generally accepted definition is that theta is a measure of the change in the premium of an option for a given change in the period to expiry. It usually refers to the passage of 1 day.

Theta thus describes how much time value of an option is lost from day to day, merely because of the passage of time. Time decay is slower at the start of the life of an option and then increases as maturation approaches. Thus, like gamma, theta is highest for ATM options that are close to expiry.

❏   OPTION VEGA

This ratio relates the change in the value of the option to another major option price element, namely volatility. Vega indicates the change in the option premium for a 1% change in volatility. Volatility and option premium are directly linked. The relationship is therefore linear.

As volatility increases, uncertainty increases. The premium increases because the high level of uncertainty gives the holder of a high volatility option a greater chance of profitable exercise. Thus, if the option premium were to be plotted against volatility, it would result in a straight line at a 45° angle to the x- and y-axis.

EXERCISING OPTIONS

It almost goes without saying that it is only the buyer of an option that can exercise it, precisely because it is only the buyer or holder that is given the choice. Exercising an option naturally brings the life of an option to an end.

In the financial derivative markets, only an option that is ITM can be exercised. This is different than, for example, options on stocks, indexes and certain exchange traded funds. Such options can be exercised whether they are in, out, or at the money. However, if you think about it, why would somebody want to exercise an option that gives him a worse price for the underlier than he can get by simply doing the transaction on the underlying market?

european and american style options

There are two styles of option – American and European. An American style option can be exercised at any time during its currency. Whenever the option is ITM, the holder can exercise it. By contrast, a European style option can only be exercised on its day of expiration, on condition that the option is ITM. Note again the difference regarding stock and index options. Whenever you buy or sell an option, make sure you know which style of option you are dealing with, because it does have an effect on the risk.

The seller of a European style option is at risk only on the expiration day of the option, while the seller of an American style option is at risk at all times during the life of the option. American style options are more popular and give much more flexibility. However, they are more expensive than European style options.

the result of exercising an option

When an option is exercised, or when an ITM option is automatically exercised at expiration, the holder is assigned a long or short position in the underlying asset. The position that is assigned will obviously depend on whether it was a call or a put that was held and exercised.

If an interest rate put option were exercised, a short position in the underlying instrument will be assigned. The option holder will be short the underlying instrument at the strike price of the option. This means that the erstwhile option holder will now be a seller of the underlying instrument, at the strike rate of the option. If the option holder does not already possess the underlying interest rate instrument, it will immediately have to be purchased at the current price. Since the option was by definition ITM, a profit will be realised by exercising the option.

When an interest rate call option is exercised, a long position in the underlying instrument will be assigned. The holder of the option will be long the underlying instrument at the strike interest rate of the option. This means that the option holder will be a buyer of the underlying instrument at the strike rate of the option. The option holder can avoid that situation by immediately selling the underlying instrument at its then current interest rate. Since the option was by definition ITM, a profit will be realised by exercising the option.

It must also be noted that it is very seldom to the benefit of an option holder to exercise an ITM option before its expiry. The reason is the time value that still forms part of the total value of the option prior to its expiry. The profit that can be realised upon the exercise of an option is only its intrinsic value, or at least that part of its intrinsic value that was gained while that particular option holder was holding it. All the time value is lost when the option is exercised. If an option holder therefore wishes to liquidate a long option position, it will always be preferable to sell the option, thereby realising a price greater than the mere intrinsic value.

Once one has exercised a call option and paid the price, one has the underlier at one's disposal. The show isn't over yet, because there is a choice. One can either hold on to the underlier in the hope that it may gain further in value, or one can sell it immediately to make a profit. If one holds on to it, it is, of course, at the risk that it may lose value again.

A further consideration, of which account should be taken before an ITM option is either exercised or sold, is whether it has gained sufficient value to cover the premium paid. When the option has appreciated by the same amount as the premium paid for it, it is said to be at breakeven. Obviously, a profit will only be realised once the option's price moves past breakeven. All other considerations apart, it does not make sense to exercise an option that is not at least at breakeven, unless it is very close to expiration and the market is moving away from the strike. At that time, the option might as well be exercised in order to mitigate some of the loss.

holding an option to maturity

There are risks involved in holding an option to expiry. Holding an option places no obligation on the option buyer. The holder can walk away from it. However, nobody should, or would want to walk away from an option that is ITM. A few basic factors should therefore be kept in mind when interest rate options are used in managing currency risk.

When options are bought, the old adage of *caveat emptor* (let the buyer beware) applies, albeit in a somewhat unusual context. When a currency option is held it is vital that its expiration date is well noted. Secondly, the value of an option should be monitored at all times. An ITM option should never be allowed to expire unless there is automatic exercise. Thus, make certain that an ITM option is exercised timeously. If it is not exercised timeously, the total advantage of having bought it will be lost. This is true of all OTC options. The danger is less with exchange traded options. Usually, they are automatically exercised when they expire ITM.

THE RISK OF THE PARTIES TO AN OPTION

generally

Since options are derivative instruments, it follows that they carry risk. They are created and modelled with the express purpose of creating specific, identifiable and quantifiable risk. They are modelled to mirror in some way, the financial risks that a commercial enterprise encounters in the normal course of its business activities.

A risk manager's concern is always financial risk to the company and the control of that risk. It is thus imperative to know how the risks inherent in options are structured so that realistic evaluations of their value under any circumstances can be done by a company. It is also necessary that realistic expectations be held regarding what options can and cannot accomplish for a business. A thorough understanding of the risks incurred when dealing in interest rate options is therefore required.

the buyer's risk

The first order of investigation is the risk incurred by the buyer of an option. When an OTC option is purchased, two types of risk are faced: market risk and counterparty risk. Since credit risk falls outside the scope of this book, only the market risk will be dealt with. The market risk involved in buying a call or a put option is the same, whether the option is OTC or exchange traded.

When an option is purchased, the premium is paid. The premium paid for the option represents the maximum amount that can be lost by the purchaser. The total premium will be lost only if the option is held until expiration and if it expires OTM.

However, it is not necessary for the buyer to lose the entire premium paid. Depending on all the circumstances and the terms of an OTC option, it can be sold back to the seller before its expiry. A sellback will at least recoup a portion of the premium paid. A particular advantage of OTC options is that they can be sold back in whole or in part. This provides a degree of flexibility that can be used in response to changing circumstances.

The timing of a sellback will obviously depend on the state of the underlying market at the time as well as the changes in the value of the option. Nevertheless, if it is clear that the option is OTM and will not come into the money before expiry, the option can be sold back to the seller for 'fair value'. It makes no difference what the reason for the sellback is. This facility of an option can be used whenever it suits the holder. Thus, the same holds true should the commercial transaction, giving rise to the purchase of the option, fall through. This would be the case when the option was bought to lock in an anticipated interest rate.

Exchange traded options, as will be seen later, are always freely on-sellable at current market value. The only limitation is obviously liquidity. There must be buyers in the market for that option at the price. However, the futures markets are so liquid that a buyer would quite readily be found.

Against the risk faced by the option buyer, the upside potential for gain is theoretically unlimited. It is only unlimited in theory because, theoretically, there is no limit to how high the price of the underlying asset can rise. As is well known, there is always a limit to the price of any asset in real life. There is also a theoretical limit to how much profit a buyer can make on a put option. Consider that a put allows the buyer to sell the underlier at a certain price – the strike price. The profit he can earn is determined by how much the market price declines below the strike price of the option. Since the market price cannot go below zero, the limit of a put option buyer's profit is equal to the difference between the strike price of the option and zero. Because there is zero chance of the underlier's price ever reaching zero when it concerns an interest rate, the actual profit limit is obviously less than that difference.

That having been said, there have been occasions when negative interest rates have prevailed. This happens when a currency is under severe pressure, either upward or downward. Nevertheless, these instances are so rare that they can be discounted for present purposes.

the seller's risk

The risk that the seller of an option faces is of a different order altogether. The seller irrevocably gains the premium and need never give it back. If the price of the underlier moves against him, he will lose the full value of that move, less the premium received.

The seller (or writer) of a call option will lose money the moment the price of the underlier begins to rise. Keep in mind what was said above on how the values of options change. The seller of a call will start losing money only when the price of the underlier exceeds the strike price of the option sold. The option will gain in value the moment the underlier's price moves upward. The seller of an option is always at risk that the option will gain in value after he has sold it. The loss is however, not realised unless the option expires ITM or is exercised whilst it is ITM.

A put option will gain in value if the price of the underlier starts moving down. This means that the underlier is becoming less expensive, while the seller of the put has undertaken to buy the underlier at a fixed, higher strike price. Once the price of the underlier has fallen through the strike price of the put option, the option is ITM. If the seller were now called upon to fulfil his part of the bargain, he would have to buy the underlier at the strike price, which would be higher than the market price.

If the option were thus exercised, the option seller would be saddled with the underlying instrument that he could get rid of at a loss only. That is, unless he were prepared to hang onto the underlier in the expectation that the price will rise, which would allow him to show a profit on the sale of the underlier.

OTC INTEREST RATE GUARANTEES

introduction

OTC interest rate options are extremely liquid instruments. In the commercial world of interest rates, the reader will most likely find that interest rate options are not known by that name. Usually, they are called interest rate guarantees (IRG's). Don't be misled by names. An IRG is just an option on an interest rate.

The borrower is offered a guarantee that the interest rate she pays will not exceed a certain agreed level. Such a guarantee is equivalent to a call option. The guaranteed rate is the strike price of the option. In order to obtain the guarantee, a price will have to be paid. That is the option premium. An investor again, will be offered a guarantee that the interest received will not be less than a specified minimum. That equates to a put option. The guaranteed rate is the strike price of the option and the price paid for the guarantee is the option premium. The person who gives the guarantee is the option writer.

Most commercial banks have established IRGs that they offer to clients. Minimum sizes for transactions will vary from bank to bank, but an extra premium may be charged if the amount involved is too small. Since there is plenty of competition when it comes to interest rates, there is as much competition when it comes to interest rate guarantees. It will be to a company's advantage to shop around for the best premium on any particular guarantee it may require. It is not necessary to get the guarantee from the same bank or dealer that grants the loan.

pricing interest rate guarantees

Interest rate guarantees are priced on the previously mentioned Black–Scholes model. As is the case with FRAs, the interest is payable at a discount on settlement date.

The option expiration date is referred to as the settlement date of the guarantee. It is the date on which the underlying rate of the guarantee will be compared to the strike rate. If the guarantee is ITM, the difference is paid. This will become clear from the case study hereunder.

From this payment structure, it is evident that an interest rate guarantee is primarily a mechanism for locking in a rate of interest in anticipation of a later transaction. Its use is by no means limited to this, but it lends itself ideally for use in this type of situation.

fair value

One of the previously mentioned advantages of using options is that, under appropriate circumstances, they can be sold back to the bank or other writing institution for fair value. Whereas exchange-traded options can be sold on the floor of the exchange, OTC options have to be sold back to the option writer.

''Fair value' is a value of an option determined by means of an option-pricing model. It is equal to the present value of the payoff expected at option expiry. The expected payoff is 'expected' under particular market conditions of the underlier. It is always 'expected' that the market price of the underlying asset will change in accordance with a 'risk neutral' random walk. The 'expectation' is accordingly concerned with an idealised market situation and not with the real one. The latter is obviously unknown. In the result, the value that is obtained approximates the value of the option, with a certain, known error.

Two major algorithms are used to do the calculation, namely the Euler method and the Milstein method. The Milstein method provides a better approximation and thus a smaller margin of error. These mathematical algorithms need not detain this discussion much further as commercial enterprises will seldom be writers of OTC options.

However, in a later chapter some case studies will be examined in which the writing of OTC options are employed as part of a risk management strategy. Such a strategy would virtually always be undertaken in close co-operation with a bank or other financial institution. Nevertheless, for those readers who are interested in doing these calculations themselves, very good texts on the subjects are available, such as *Derivatives– The Theory and Practice of Financial Engineering,*by Paul Wilmott and published by John Wiley & Sons.

case study 6: locking in a borrowing rate with an IRG

❒   THE SCENARIO

An UK based company discovers in April that its cash flow projections indicate that a short-term loan of some £2,520,000 will be required in August. It is anticipated that the loan will be required for a period of 3 months.

UK interest rates have remained stable recently, but the company fears that an interest rate rise may be imminent due to some inflation fears. The company will be able to obtain a loan that is based on 3-month sterling Libor. The company decides to lock in the present Libor rate until it is required at the beginning of August.

❐ FINANCIAL INFORMATION

On the day that the company approaches the market for an indication rate, sterling Libor is quoted as 5.24500%. The company wishes to protect itself against an interest rate higher than the present rate and thus seeks a guarantee with a strike ATM. The premium for such a guarantee will obviously be greater than for a strike at a higher rate.

❐ THE IRG

The guarantee that the company obtains has a strike of 5.24500% per annum. This calculates to a quarterly rate on sterling Libor of 1.32580% (5.34500 × 91). The guarantee is a call option because it guarantees a rate 'not greater than' the strike price. The notional principal of the guarantee is £2,520,000. The option settlement date is the August 6 and the exercise style is European.

The guarantee thus locks in the cost of the anticipated loan at £33,410.65, plus the premium paid on the option.

❐ STERLING LIBOR RISES

On option settlement day, 3-month sterling Libor has risen to 7.56%, as the company had feared it might. When the company thus takes up its loan from its bank, it obtains the loan for 3 months at an annual rate of 7.56%.

The writer of the guarantee has to pay the company the difference between the strike rate of the guarantee and actual 3-month Libor, being 2.215% (7.56 − 5.245). Calculating the actual amount due is straight forward, but all the required elements must be kept in mind.

$$\text{IRG Settlement} = \frac{7.56 - 5.245}{100} \times £2,520,000.00 \times \frac{91}{360}$$

$$= 0.02315 \times £2,520,000.00 \times 0.2528$$

$$= £14,746.55$$

The 3-month loan that the company took out on August 6 will actually cost them £48,157.20. Calculated against that is the settlement figure of the IRG, which leaves them with a net cost after the hedge of £33,410.65, which is the exact interest cost that was locked in. However, the premium paid for the option must still be added to this total.

❐ STERLING LIBOR DECLINES

It follows from the above example that if sterling Libor had declined by August 6, the company would have been able to negotiate its loan at a lower, more favourable rate. The option would then merely have been left to expire without value. The company would thus have achieved a saving of the difference between the locked-in rate and the lower rate of interest at which it eventually took up the loan. However, the saving would be mitigated by the premium cost of the option.

☐ DISCUSSION

The case study provides an illustration of the most basic use of an IRG in managing interest rate risk. Nevertheless, it is the way most often required and employed in the non-financial sector. It is evident from the study that an IRG acts like a contract of insurance. As in insurance, there is a period of cover and there is a non-returnable premium paid for the cover.

The IRG equivalent of a put option would give exactly the same protection against a downward move in interest rates. In this case the guarantee would be to an investor, guaranteeing a rate of interest 'not less than' the strike rate. It would also be a perfect hedge at the strike rate.

Many companies believe that options are expensive. They realise that options are much like insurance and they know insurance is expensive. They therefore believe options must be expensive too. This is not so. The basis of the pricing of financial options is quite different from the way insurance premiums are priced. Insurance companies price their products based on their claims experience. They expect disasters. The Black–Scholes model is based on entirely different premises. Its result is wholly unrelated to insurance premiums. An option must actually be priced before a company can evaluate whether, under each particular circumstance, the option is expensive or not.

The point of the case study is to show that an IRG will hedge an exposure just as effectively as any other interest rate derivative. It establishes a 'perfect' hedge, because, when held to expiration, the option locks in the interest rate indicated by the strike price. The major advantage of an option is however, that it allows a profit to be made if the price change of the underlying is favourable to the hedger. This is not possible in a hedge with other derivatives, unless the hedge is adjusted during the term. Adjusting for price changes presents its own dangers. A hedge with options thus allows a clear advantage, except for the cost of the premium.

OTC OPTION VARIANTS

There are innumerable variations on the basic structure of interest rate options. Since it is such a fiercely contested market, a lot of innovation has been engendered by the competitive spirit. The are variations on option structures to suit every occasion and requirement.

The most important of these are probably caps and floors. A cap is really a series of IRG calls covering multiple expiration periods, while a floor is a series of put options with the same effect. In the next chapter attention will be given to the strategies that are available when employing such option variants.

OPTIONS ON INTEREST RATE FUTURES

general observations

Options on futures contracts are a comparatively recent development. Since interest rate futures contracts are themselves a recent development, options on interest rate futures were introduced concurrently with the listing of futures contracts.

Armed with the dual instruments of interest rate futures and options on interest rate futures, the risk manager is empowered through a wide range of alternatives. Not only does it provide flexibility and increased safety, but it also allows smaller amounts to be hedged. One of the major drawbacks of the OTC instruments has always been that they are usually available only for larger amounts of notional principal. When the required notional principal becomes too small, OTC derivatives might be illiquid or unavailable. Futures and options on futures largely redress this problem.

The discussion hereunder does not in anyway derogate from what was said about options generally, earlier in this chapter. It makes sense that certain changes would be required in order to make an option exchange tradable. Ordinarily, options can be tailor-made to suit the requirements of the parties. When a standardised agreement, such as a futures contract becomes the underlying asset and when in addition, the option itself is intended to be traded on a public exchange, substantial amendments and adjustments are inevitable. The major adjustments are discussed under the headings of option standardi-sation and of option classification.

OPTION STANDARDISATION

As has been stated before, on a public exchange there is no room for negotiation on anything other than price. The rest must be a given. Once the exact nature of the article being auctioned is a known fact, the only remaining question is what the market is prepared to offer and bid for that article in monetary terms. It therefore follows that in order to make interest rate options exchange tradable, all their elements have to be standardised, except for the premium. The option premium is consequently the sole subject matter of the auction on the floor of a public exchange.

the underlying futures contract

Futures exchanges offer options on the interest rate futures contracts that trade on that exchange. In other words, one cannot buy an option on the Chicago Board of Trade (CBOT) on a contract that trades on the London Interest and Financial Futures Exchange (LIFFE). This situation is fluid and may change.

The recent co-operative agreement between the CBOT and the Eurex in Frankfurt is a case in point. Such agreements will have the result that the products of one exchange will become tradable on another. The principle remains firm, however. Each exchange offers and takes responsibility for its own contracts. The co-operative agreements only facilitate trading of futures and options on futures through one exchange to another.

In an open outcry exchange, options usually trade physically on the floor of an exchange in a pit next to the pit where the underlying contract is traded. In the result, one can only trade options offered by an exchange on its contracts. Exchanges do not necessarily offer options on all available contracts. In addition, the ranges of options that are available also differ from contract to contract.

the option expiration date

The next element that is standardised is the option expiration date. A futures contract, say on 90-day Euroyen, is offered by an exchange for say the standard delivery months of March, May, July, September and December. Options on the contract may however be offered with expirations that do not coincide with these delivery months. For example, options might be offered that expire on the third Friday of every calendar month. If such were the case, one would find that an option with expiry on the third Friday of January would probably have the March futures contract as underlier. The same would apply to the February options. However, the March options would have July futures as underlier. In the futures market the convention is to say that March options exercise into July futures. It means that the July futures contract is the underlying asset of the March options contract.

A moment's reflection will confirm that an option with a futures contract as underlier must expire before the underlier does. If this were not so, there would in fact be no underlier. Keep in mind that if an option expires ITM, the holder is assigned a position in the futures contract that underlies the option. In the case of a call option, the holder will be assigned a long futures position, while in the case of a put, a short futures position will be assigned.

For all practical purposes, futures contracts' lives end on the first delivery day or the last trading day, whichever comes first in any particular case. Open futures contracts are then being executed. If the option expiry date were to coincide or even to post-date the first delivery day of the underlying futures, the option holder would not really have any opportunity to offset the assigned futures position. The person may be called upon to take or give delivery of the physical asset the moment the option expires ITM. This would negate the whole purpose of having options with futures contracts as underlier. Due to these considerations, option expiration dates will always predate the delivery month and the last trading day of the underlying futures contract.

option strike prices

Options are listed with fixed strike prices. You cannot negotiate the strike of an option on futures. The exchange always specifies the strike intervals as part of the listed option contract. How it is specified will depend on the price quote of the underlying futures and the size of the contract.

A typical example is offered by options on the 1-month Libor futures contract listed on the CME. The underlying asset of the option is one IMM 1-month Libor futures contract. The price quote of the futures is in points and this is mirrored by the option. The prescribed strike price intervals are every 0.125 points for all expirations. Thus, strikes of options will be at 92.125, 92.25, 92.375 and so on.

Another example is Eurodollar options that also trade on the CME. They too are priced in points and have strikes at intervals of 0.25 points. You will thus find strikes on 95.00 and 95.25. However, near month expirations, additional strikes are added every 0.125 points.

Other than in the case of OTC options, options on futures contracts are not ITM, ATM, or OTM relative to the spot interest rates. The options are regarded as ITM, ATM, or OTM in relation to the price of its underlying futures contract. The price of the relevant futures contract is therefore the most important factor in determining the premium of the option.

It is evident that the fact that option strike prices are prescribed rather than negotiable is not really a great disadvantage. The strikes are spaced very close together. As a result, this feature of exchange traded options, which some perceive as a limitation, is in fact rather academic.

conclusion

With the standardised elements that have been discussed so far, options became exchange tradable. The standardised features of options have not proved to be a limiting factor in their popularity. Options on futures still allow for a variety of alternatives. As options on interest rate futures became increasingly popular, the exchanges initiated many permutations of their option structures and rules. On many popular contracts, options are available with weekly expirations as well as with monthly expirations. Additionally, the usual options with expirations closer to the contract delivery months are also available.

As the popularity of options trading on the futures exchanges increases, these options are also gaining in liquidity further into the future. The welcome result of this trend is to make longer-term positions in options on futures increasingly feasible.

The standardised features allow options to be classified and therefore easily identified. Our next step is consequently, to investigate the classification of options on futures.

OPTION CLASSIFICATION

The next step in making options exchange tradable, was to classify the standardised options on futures. Options have to be easily identifiable in order to avoid confusion regarding the precise option that is being dealt with at a particular time. With classification, it becomes possible to do exactly that. Through option classification it is possible to identify exactly which option is being offered and which option is being bid in the controlled confusion of the options trading pit.

The first level of classification is into option types. As already discussed, there are only two types of option, namely calls and puts. The second level of classification is into option classes. A class of option consists of one of the two option types regarded with its underlier. For example, a reference to Eurodollar call options is a reference to a whole class of options. However, within that class of options, there are still options with a great variety of strike prices and expiration dates.

It follows that in order to specify a particular option more information on the option would be required. For that reason, a third level of classification divides options into series. An option series consists of all options of the same class with identical strike prices and expiration dates. Thus, the full series description of a particular option on the Eurodollar futures contract might be described as a 'CME Eurodollar March 2001, 92.50 call'. Another example of an option series is 'CME 13-week Treasury Bill April 2001, 92.75 put'.

When orders are placed on futures exchanges for the purchase or sale of options, the full series description must be used. It is the only description that will be accepted. Although the name of the exchange does not technically form part of the description of the option series, it is safer to include it as well. This is due to the many similar futures contacts trading on different exchanges and its inclusion will obviate unnecessary confusion.

SELLING OPTIONS ON FUTURES

A special word is required regarding the selling of options on futures exchanges. Just as in the case of futures contracts, one does not have to be the holder of an option in order to sell one. Putting it differently, you can short an option without being long that option. Obviously, you can short either a put or a call. No restrictions exist on the selling of options on futures exchanges.

The market also uses the term 'writing an option' interchangeably with 'selling an option'. Actually, an option is written when an options position is initiated by selling it short. The seller of the option is then referred to as the option writer. When an option is written without the writer holding a deliverable long futures contract against the option if it were exercised, the person is said to write naked options. Alternatively, it is said that the option is not covered. Writing uncovered or naked options exposes the writer to serious risk of loss.

writing naked options

To illustrate this, consider a trader who writes a call option that then moves deep into the money. If it were exercised by the holder, then he would receive a long futures position. The writer, or seller of the option, would be assigned a short futures position at a price equal to the strike of the option. The price of the underlying futures contract must have risen substantially for the call option to come into the money so deeply that the holder considered it advantageous to exercise.

The writer of the option, who now has a short futures position, will already have lost a lot of money, albeit an unrealised loss, when the option is exercised. When the short futures position is assigned, the futures price at which a futures contract to liquidate his position could be bought, is now much greater than the price at which the futures were shorted. The writer's short futures position will keep on losing money while the price of the underlying rises, or stays at the higher level.

Being short futures in a rising market is clearly an unenviable position. Everybody would wish to avoid that at all cost. Keep in mind the earlier discussion when the risk profile of a short option was examined. Then it was stated that the writer of an option had limited profit potential, but unlimited risk. The writer of a call option, as in the present example, would face unlimited risk on a rise in the price of the underlying, against a maximum profit of the receipt of the premium.

Writing naked calls is not a strategy for risk managers. It is a speculative trade and it is indulged in by those who intend to profit from changes in currency markets. Banks and financial institutions are the most prolific writers of OTC options. From the nature of their business, they have to be. They also write options in the futures markets, but then usually only to hedge currency risks that they assumed in other instruments.

Writing an option as a hedge is usually not considered a naked write. The reason for this view is that there must exist some countervailing risk, making the option write more of the nature of a covered write. This means that the short option is covered by another, opposite risk. Strictly speaking though, a covered write in the futures markets refers only to an option that is written while a futures contract is held that can be delivered against the short option.

case study 7: hedging an interest bearing investment using options on futures

❑ SCENARIO

Pentabouw, a property development firm in Amsterdam has invested $1,750,000 in Euro-dollars in anticipation of a development they are planning in Miami. The investment was made at 3-month USD Libor. At the company's board meeting in July 2001, it is decided to protect that investment from reductions in US dollar interest rates. The company anticipates further decreases in US dollar interest rates before the investment rollover date in September.

Because the company does not want to tie up any of its credit facilities, it decides to hedge in the futures market. In addition, because the company wishes to maintain the possibility of increasing its income should interest rates actually rise against their expectation, they want to hedge with options.

❑ THE OPTION CONTRACT

The treasurer of the company decides to use the Eurodollar contract on the CME. The underlying asset of the contract is a 3-month time deposit with a face value of $1,000,000. Option strikes occur at intervals of 0.25. The company is interested in the September contract. In July, the September contract options have strike intervals of 0.125.

The September option contract expires on September 17. It is thus the appropriate option to handle the company's investment rollover, which occurs on September 14.

❑ FINANCIAL INFORMATION

Three-month USD Libor is quoted at 3.69625 on the day that the company's treasurer investigates the financial markets to determine the entry point of the hedge. September Eurodollar futures are trading at 96.435, implying an annual interest rate of 3.565%. Fortuitously, the September futures contract is in contango compared to spot and the August contract, but the further deferred months are all trading in backwardation.

Keeping in mind that the points value of futures contracts trade inversely to interest rates, it means that there is a positive yield curve for 3-month Libor beyond September.

From June to September the curve slopes downward because interest rates are progressively lower, but after September, interest rates grow progressively higher.

The underlying asset of the option is one Eurodollar futures contract. Since the notional value of a Eurodollar futures contract is $1,000,000, the treasurer decides to use two options to hedge the company's exposure. This represents an over-hedge, the implications of which will be examined later.

Pentabouw seeks protection against a drop in interest rates. A drop in interest rates means a rise in the points value of the Eurodollar futures contract. It therefore seeks protection against a rise in the points value of the Eurodollar contract. Consequently, the company must buy call options.

❏ SELECTING THE STRIKE

The first order of business for the treasurer is to select the best strike for the option. The treasurer must select the call ATM in order to obtain the best hedge. Two strikes are in contention: the first being the call at strike 96.50 and the other at strike 96.38.

The call option at strike 96.50 is slightly OTM, while the call at 96.38 is slightly ITM. For all practical purposes, the two strikes are both ATM. Assume for the purposes of this case study that the treasurer selects the call at 96.38. The call will be more expensive, but it will afford protection against an adverse move from a slightly higher rate of interest.

❏ THE HEDGE

The premium of the option is priced at 10.5 points. Since the value of one point is $25.00, the option premium is $262.50. The company thus purchases two 96.38 September Eurodollar calls at a total cost of $525.00. The notional principal of the hedge is $2,000,000. The hedged position is shown in Table 6-1.

Both possible outcomes of the options hedge will be examined.

❏ LIBOR DECLINES

Assume that when the investment rollover date of September 14 arrives, 3-month USD Libor has declined further, as expected. The spot rate is now 2.9325% and the September contract, now being the spot month, is trading at 97.1075 points. The futures price implies an interest rate of 2.8925%.

The investment is rolled over at a rate of 2.9325 annual percentage rate, yielding an amount of $12,972.24 investment at the end of the 3-month term. The call options are ITM since the price of the underlying futures contract has risen. The two options thus

Table 6-1. A hedge of interest on an investment with options on futures

Action Date	Spot	CME	Basis
		Premium	
July-01	Long two × 96.38 Eurodollar call options @	$525.00	
July-01	Expectation −3.69625%: $16,350.77		

expire ITM and two long futures positions are automatically assigned at a price of 96.38. The treasurer instructs the company's futures broker short two September Eurodollar Futures contracts, which is filled at a price of 97.1075. The result of the hedge is shown in Table 6-2.

The figure is based on a calculation of the monetary values of the principal and interest rates concerned over the 3-month period. Note that the basis change is exactly equal to the net profit on the hedge. It is a feature of hedging with options on futures, that the change in basis will determine the result of the hedge, as it does with a hedge using futures contracts. For a full discussion on changes in basis and their influence on the outcome of a hedge, see the Chapter 4.

☐   DISCUSSION

The net profit on the hedge is due to the use of a long futures hedge in an interest rate contract. The profit is enhanced by the fact that the notional principal of the option contracts is greater than the company's exposure in the spot interest rate market. The enhancement results from the fact that the profit in the futures market is made on a greater amount of principal than the loss in the spot market.

Against this net profit, account must be taken of the premium that was paid for the two options. Thus, the net cost of the hedge after accounting for the premium is an amount of $225.62 net ($299.38 profit − $525.00 premium). The actual amount of interest received from the investment of $12,972.24 is increased by the profit on the futures market of $3,677.92, less the gross cost. The result after premium is thus that the company realises a net income on its investment of $16,125.16. This result is practically identical to the result that was expected at the start of the hedge.

☐   LIBOR RISES

Assume that when the roll-over date arrives, USD Libor has increased. The company achieves an investment rate of 4.35% and the September Eurodollar futures contract is trading at 95.72. The implied annual interest rate of the futures contract is 4.28%.

The call options are OTM and they expire without value. The company has thus spent an amount of $525 on premiums to cover themselves against an eventuality that never

Table 6-2. Result of hedge with options on futures of investment income after a decline in interest rates

Action Date	Spot	CME		Basis
			Premium	
July-01	Long two × 96.38 Eurodollar call options @		$525.00	
July-01	Expectation −3.69625%: $16,350.77	Assigned two long futures $18,301.11		−$1,950.34
Sept.-01	Roll-over rate − 2.93250% $12,972.24	Short two futures $14,623.19		−$1,650.95
Sept.-01	Loss: −$3,378.53	Profit: $3,677.38		Change:
	Net profit on hedge:			$299.38

materialised. This small sum curtails the profit shown in respect of the improved rate they obtained on the roll-over date.

❐   DISCUSSION

Since the premium paid for the options were so low, it was always going to be worth the company's while to hedge with options. Had they used any other derivative, they would not have been able to take any advantage of the favourable increase in interest rates. Since there was no loss on the options other than the premiums, the fact that their notional principal was greater than the exposure in the spot market played only a marginal role in the result of the hedge. The only effect that the higher notional value of the options actually had on the result of the hedge was that it increased the total premium paid. Since the premium was so low, that effect was negligible.

In the result, the over-hedge was a good thing, as it usually would be when hedging with options on futures. On condition that the option premiums are not expensive, the over-hedge will always allow increased protection on an adverse move in the value of the underlying, while having minimal effect in the case of a favourable move.

CHECKLIST FOR THE REVIEW OF CHAPTER 6

General overview: the overall control objectives of the material dealt with in this chapter are to acquaint the business with the fundamental principles and operational features of OTC interest rate options as well as exchange traded interest rate options.

	Key Issues	Illustrative Scope or Approach
6.1	What type of OTC option will protect the company against a rise in the underlying interest rate?	An IRG call will appreciate as its underlying interest rate appreciates. If the company would suffer a loss, or be disadvantaged when an interest rate rises, an IRG guaranteeing a rate 'not greater than' the strike rate will provide the necessary protection
6.2	What type of option will protect the company against a drop in the underlying interest rate?	A put IRG will appreciate when the option's underlying interest rate drops. If the company would suffer a loss, or be disadvantaged when an interest rate drops, an IRG guaranteeing an interest rate 'not lower than' the strike rate will provide the necessary protection
6.3	What obligations are incurred by the buyers of interest rate calls and puts, respectively?	The only obligation ever incurred by the buyer of an option, is the obligation to pay the premium
6.4	Does the company consider the use of European style options?	European style options can only be exercised on their expiry date

continued

Key Issues	Illustrative Scope or Approach
	They are cheaper than American style options They are appropriate when there is complete certainty when the underlying interest rate exposure will commence or end
6.5 Does the company consider the use of American style options? They are appropriate when flexibility is required as to when the interest rate exposure will commence or end	American style options can be exercised on any business day during their currency They are more expensive than European style options
6.6 What factors determine the value of an option?	Option values are determined by: • The time value of money – the higher general interest rates, the higher the value of options. The relationship is not linear • The time to maturity of the option – time decay will cause options to lose value. The relationship is not linear. Time decay accelerates towards maturity • The interest rate relative to the strike of the option – the closer the rate of interest is to the strike of the option, the higher the value of the option. The relationship is not linear, but is indicated by the delta of the option at any particular time. • The volatility of the market – the higher the volatility of the market, the higher the premiums of options. The relationship is linear
6.7 Does the company consider the relative advantages of OTC interest rate options?	OTC options will not establish a quantitative basis, because they are tailored to the quantity of the underlying currency required by the company The strike price of the option can be negotiated to suit the circumstances and preferences of the company The expiry date of the option can be negotiated with the option writer to suit the circumstances of the company The company will be able to exercise the exercise style of the option – American or European

continued

Key Issues	Illustrative Scope or Approach
	There is no obligation to make an investment or to take out a loan
	The company does not utilise any of its credit facilities when it buys an IRG
6.8 Does the company consider the relative disadvantages of OTC options?	Although most premium determinants are matters of public record, interest rate dealers give different quotes on options, primarily because different volatilities are experienced by different dealers. Obtaining the 'best' premium for a particular option may be difficult, if not impossible and will require a lot of shopping around
	The company incurs counterparty risk
	OTC options can only be sold back to the option writer and nobody else. They can be sold back for 'fair value', which is a calculated price according to an option pricing model. For the reasons given above, 'fair value', as calculated by a particular dealer, therefore does not necessarily represent the best price available in the market
6.9 What benchmark is used to determine whether OTC interest rate options are ITM, ATM, or OTM?	The benchmark is the spot interest rate
6.10 What type of option on futures will protect the company against a rise in the underlying interest rate?	A put option on a futures contract that has a price based on points will protect against a rise in the underlying interest rate
	Because of the points structure of a futures contract on interest rates, the contract points will increase when the underlying interest rate drops and increase when the underlying interest rate increases
	A put option will gain in value when the price of the underlying futures contract falls in response to a rise in the underlying interest rate
6.11 What type of option on futures will protect the company against a drop in the underlying interest rate?	A call option on a futures contract that has a price based on points will protect against a drop in the underlying interest rate

continued

Key Issues	Illustrative Scope or Approach
	Because of the points structure of a futures contract on interest rates, the contract points will increase when the underlying interest rate drops and increase when the underlying interest rate increases
	A call option will gain in value when the price of the underlying futures contract rises in response to a fall-off in the underlying interest rate
6.12 Does the company consider the relative advantages of options on interest rate futures?	They are bought and sold on public exchanges with visible price discovery and therefore represent fair market value
	They can be freely sold back on the open market at the ruling market price for that strike
	They are available for smaller amounts of notional principal
	No counterparty risk is incurred
	Trading costs and commissions are typically less than a dealer's bid/offered spread
6.13 Does the company consider the relative disadvantages of options on interest rate futures?	All their terms and conditions are predetermined by the exchange on which they trade. Only the premium is determined by market participants
	The company may incur basis risk because of a quantitative mismatch. A change in the hedge basis during the life of an option may result in a profit or a loss on the hedge
6.14 What benchmark is used to determine whether options on interest rate futures are ITM, ATM, or OTM?	The benchmark is always the current price of the underlying futures contract

seven

strategies with interest rate swaps, swaps based derivatives and swaps mimics

INTRODUCTION

Hedging is the basic risk management strategy with all financial derivatives. The technique of hedging is quite simple, as was demonstrated in the preceding chapters. It was also evidenced that every derivative instrument has its particular strengths and weaknesses. Innumerable strategies have evolved to make greater use of the strengths of some derivatives and to neutralise the weaknesses of others. Derivatives have been combined with each other, structurally amended and varied to suit every possible need demanded by business.

In this chapter, some of the major risk management strategies and variations of swaps structures will be examined. The variations in structures were developed to allow different strategies to be adopted. It is impossible to deal with these exhaustively, because there are limitless permutations of strategies and structures. However, once the major structures and strategies are known, it becomes reasonably easy to understand and use others that may be encountered in the marketplace.

In this context, it is worth noting some of the findings of the previously mentioned research done by the Weiss Center for International Financial Research of the Wharton School of the University of Pennsylvania. As was mentioned in an earlier chapter, the study found interest rate swaps to be the most popular derivative among companies in the non-financial sector.

The implications are thus clear. Interest rate swaps are regarded as the 'standard' derivative instrument for managing interest rate risk and they are seen as relatively inexpensive. It also appears that the use of interest rate derivatives is associated mostly with the financing activities of the companies in the survey. These factors have been taken into account in selecting strategies and structures for discussion in this chapter.

In the first part of this chapter, some specific uses of swaps will be investigated. Some combinations of swaps with other derivatives will also be discussed, including an examination of the usefulness of these variations.

Developments in futures contracts, especially with regard to the introduction of futures contracts on swaps, the trading of futures 'strips' and the resultant pre-packaged 'bundles' and 'packs' also require attention. Consequently, those developments and their uses will be given due consideration.

During the course of these discussions, some of the more important variants of other derivative instruments will also be discussed. Variant forms of other derivatives that approach and mimic some of the features of swaps cater for specific business situations and as such, they lend themselves to a multiplicity of purposes and strategies.

STRATEGIES WITH STANDARD INTEREST RATE SWAPS

In Chapter 5, it was demonstrated how swaps are used to hedge exposures resulting from loans and investments. It was also noted that since cash flows are the most basic risk element of a swap, they are best suited to hedge exposures that consist of streams of floating interest rate based payments. When the opposite strategy is followed, namely swapping out a fixed interest rate exposure into a floating rate, it does not constitute a hedge but is usually based on the view the company takes of the interest rate market.

arbitrage

Apart from a straight hedge, the most common use of an interest rate swap is to arbitrage in different interest rate instruments. The arbitrage opportunity arises as a result of the weight each market sector places on the credit risk of borrowers. It is possible to arbitrage the cash flows received from a swap against the actual or implied cash flows received from a strip of interest rate futures, interest rate caps and interest rate floors.

If financial markets were truly efficient, as is assumed in financial theory, arbitrage should not be possible. The impossibility arises from the assumption that the same price information is available to all at the same time and can be absorbed and adjusted at the same rate. It follows that the net interest payments made by two similar derivatives should be identical. In practice this is often not so. Price discrepancies do occur and give rise to arbitrage opportunities.

In the following discussion, an arbitrage between a bond and a bank loan will be examined.

case study 8: a debt market arbitrage

Consider the position of two companies, the one rated AAA by Standard and Poor and the other BBB. Because of the difference in their credit ratings, the two companies will not be able to raise finance at the same rate. The two companies do not represent the same credit risk and thus the interest rates at which they can raise finance will be higher for the company with the higher risk.

Suppose each of these two companies wished to raise $50,000,000 on a 5-year term loan. If they approached their banks, the company rated AAA might typically be able to raise a 5-year loan at Libor plus 1/2%. The BBB company would most likely be able to do no better than Libor plus 1%. In the bank credit sector of the debt market, the interest rate differential between the two companies is thus 1/2%.

If the two companies were to issue bonds, the AAA company could raise finance at a fixed 71/2% over 5 years, but the BBB rated company would have to pay 9%. The bond market thus weights the credit risk difference at 11/2%. The possibility of arbitrage now arises because of the difference in credit weightings between the bank credit sector and bond sector of the debt market. Advantage of the arbitrage opportunity is taken by means of an interest rate swap between the two companies.

❐ THE SWAP

The AAA rated company starts off by issuing 5-year bonds with a value of $50,000,000 and a 7.5% coupon. Simultaneously it arranges a swap between itself and the lower rated BBB company. The notional principal of the swap is $50,000,000. BBB pays 7.5% and receives LIBOR. AAA receives 7.5% against paying Libor. The cash flows of this swap are illustrated in Figure 7-1.

❐ DISCUSSION OF THE STRATEGY

It is apparent that both parties benefit from the swap arrangement. The AAA company is receiving the same fixed interest through the swap that it is paying out to the bond issue. The cost to it on that leg is thus nil. The net interest rate cost to the company is the Libor it pays to the swap. The net effect is thus that it is paying 1/2% less than it would have had to pay on a bank loan. Should it wish to peg the Libor rate, in order to avoid the risks involved in paying a floating interest rate, there would be innumerable ways of achieving that. Libor could be hedged using other derivatives, or by a swap where the company received Libor while paying a fixed rate of interest to the swap.

The BBB company also benefits greatly. It receives Libor through the swap and pays Libor plus 1% to the bank. The net cost on that leg is thus 1% interest. In addition, it pays 7.5% to the swap. Its total interest cost is consequently 8.5%. This is 1/2% better than the 9% it would have had to pay on a bond issue.

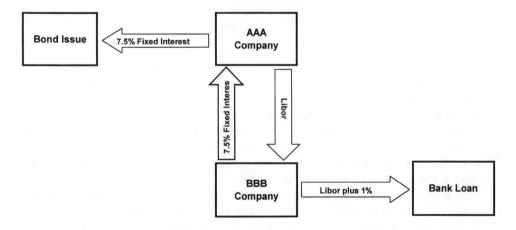

Figure 7-1 The cash flows in a debt market arbitrage

In the premises, both companies gain 1/2% advantage through making use of the swap. Of course, exactly the same arbitrage arrangement is often used where the lower rated company may not be able to access the bond market at all. The above swap structure thus gives the lower credit rated company indirect access to the bond market, while it reduces the borrowing cost of the higher rated company.

❐ MANAGING 'OFF-MARKET' CASH FLOWS WITH SWAPS

In Chapter 5, emphasis was placed on the calculation of the fixed rate interest leg of the swap. As was then explained, the swap rate is determined from the Treasury rate for US dollar swaps, or from the applicable gilt rate for sterling interest rate swaps. Consequently, the fixed rate leg of a fixed-to-floating swap is usually a calculated rate. The rate of the fixed leg is derived from a market rate; in addition, the dealer's spread over the relevant treasury or gilt rate is included to calculate the all-in swap rate.

However, it is not always convenient to have the calculated swap rate for the fixed rate in a particular situation. It might happen in a particular instance, that a business requires a specific fixed rate rather than the swap rate. The business might, for example, require this particular fixed rate because it is locked into a fixed rate instrument paying an historic interest rate. Whatever the prime cause might be, such mismatches with market related rates often arise for one reason or another. Such mismatched, or historic rates are called 'off-market'.

The off-market rate may be higher or lower than the market swap rate. Market practice thus makes provision for swaps where the fixed rate to be paid or received is not the swap rate. Such swaps are usually referred to as 'off-market swaps'.

case study 9: arranging an off-market swap

Assume that the swap rate is 5.407% for a 5-year US dollar swap, while 6-month USD Libor is quoted at 3.66%. Assume further that a company wished to receive 6% fixed rate from a swap, paying 6-month Libor to the swap. There are two ways of inducing a counterparty to agree to such an arrangement.

Firstly, the company wishing to receive the higher off-market rate could offer an up-front cash payment to the counterparty. The cash payment would serve the purpose of compensating the counterparty for paying a higher interest rate than the market is prepared to pay at that time. Consequently, the cash payment must equal the net present value of the difference between the fixed interest to be paid to the swap and the interest that would have been paid at the swap rate. The net present value is found by discounting the difference between the future cash flows at the swap rate.

The alternative would be for the company that wishes to receive the higher than market fixed interest rate, to add a margin to the floating interest that it will pay to the swap. Thus, the counterparty will be compensated for paying more than the market rate by receiving a floating rate greater than the market rate.

The opposite situation is often also encountered. It may well be that a company wishes to receive a fixed interest rate below the current market rate. In this case, it will seek a counterparty that is willing to compensate it for receiving a lower rate. The compensation may take either of the two forms mentioned above.

SWAPS STRATEGIES WITH SPECIAL TERMS

In many cases, recurring business situations have required the amendment of the standard terms of swaps to meet market requirements. The adaptability of the basic swaps structure allows its use in many situations. In many cases, it was found that some small amendments to the basic terms of swaps would render them especially useful and suited to particular circumstances. In this section, several of the more common special term swaps will be discussed.

early termination swap

The versatility of swaps is such that virtually any need in the market can be accommodated. Early termination of a swap can add to its cost, because there will be a penalty. This means that when swaps are used to hedge an exposure to interest rates, the risk manager must be sure of the term of that exposure. If there is any doubt that the term of the exposure being hedged might be shorter than anticipated, a swap might be too costly to use as a hedge.

The market can however, accommodate this need through an amendment to the standard terms. Swaps that provide for early termination are usually referred to as callable swaps.

case study 10: structuring a callable fixed rate swap

Assume a company wishes to finance a particular project and it has access only to floating rate funds. Its projections indicate that it will take a maximum of 5 years to completion of the project and a minimum of 3 years. It will require the financing only for as long as it takes to complete the project. During this term, it wishes to hedge the interest rate exposure, but does not wish to incur penalties if the project is completed earlier.

The company could enter a 5-year callable fixed rate swap. This type of swap provides for a specified lockout period. The lockout period relates to the period during which the swap may not be cancelled. In terms of the swap arrangement, on a given 'call date', one of the parties has the one-time right to cancel the swap. No penalties will be incurred even if interest rates had moved against the cancelling party and in favour of the other party.

Given the facts of the above assumption, the company would arrange a swap for a term of 5 years with a lockout period of 3 years. It would retain the right to cancel on the call date at the end of the 18-month period. In return for this right to cancel, the counterparty would charge a premium on the spread used in a regular fixed rate swap.

There would obviously be a penalty if the company were to cancel the swap during the lockout period. However, the penalty would be less because it would be calculated only on the outstanding period of the lockout and not on the outstanding portion of the term of the swap.

It gets even better. If, at the call date, interest rates have moved in favour of the cancelling party (declined in the case of this case study), the existing swap can be terminated and reset at the lower market rate. The company thus gets two bites at the cherry, albeit at a slight premium compared to the cost of a regular swap.

◻   RETAINING THE ADVANTAGE OF FAVOURABLE MOVES

In Chapter 5, it was mentioned that swaps provide a perfect hedge. Unfortunately, the downside of a perfect hedge is that while it protects perfectly from adverse changes in interest rates, it is also a perfect shield against favourable ones.

Traditionally, a hedger seeking to hedge against unfavourable rate changes while retaining at least some potential of profit from favourable changes would buy options as their derivative of choice. Nevertheless, swaps are the derivative of choice in the case of interest rates to such an extent that adaptations have been made to also accommodate businesses that wish to have it both ways, using interest rate swaps. Such swaps are normally referred to as adjustable fixed rate swaps, which, as far as can be determined, is an unintended oxymoron.

case study 11: hedging a borrowing rate with an adjustable fixed rate swap

◻   THE SCENARIO

Armatech, Inc., a manufacturer of speciality armoured vehicles for defence and policing purposes has just closed a 7-year term loan to finance its acquisition of Industrial Transmissions plc. The $17 million loan facility is priced on LIBOR plus an applicable grid-based margin. The term loan amortises in equal monthly instalments over a 10-year term. It is a condition of the financing that Armatech must hedge 100% of the facility for a minimum of 3 years.

Armatech's management takes a conservative view on interest rate risk. The company wants to minimise its exposure to interest rate risk. It would therefore prefer to hedge the exposure by swapping it out for a fixed rate. However, the company's revenues are vulnerable when the economy weakens. Therefore, management requires a strategy that provides some benefit when interest rates decline. Nevertheless, the company regards interest rate guarantees as too expensive.

◻   THE SWAP

As a solution, Armatech enters into a 7-year, 100% adjustable fixed rate swap. In terms of the swap arrangement, the company swaps from 1-month LIBOR, currently quoted at 6.50%, to a base fixed rate of 7.75%. The swap rate of such an adjustable fixed rate swap would be somewhat higher than for a comparable regular interest rate swap. Assume, for the purposes of this case study that it is 0.25% higher.

Like a regular swap, Armatech will be paid the difference if Libor rises above the fixed rate of 7.75%. They will be 'paid the difference' because of the standard netting of payments clause. If Libor is below the fixed rate at the start of any period of the swap, Armatech will have to pay the net difference between the two rates. This is standard swap procedure. The essential difference between this swap arrangement and a regular swap lies in what happens to the fixed rate when the floating 1-month Libor declines.

When Libor declines from its initial level of 6.50% to, say 6.25%, the fixed rate will automatically also drop by 0.25% to 7.50%. If Libor falls again to 6.00%, the fixed rate will adjust to 7.25%. The fixed rate will continue to decline one-on-one with Libor as it declines during the term of the swap. However, should Libor subsequently increase, the fixed rate will also increase in lockstep with Libor, but it will never exceed the original fixed rate of the swap, which is capped at 7.75%.

❐ DISCUSSION

Because a regular swap arrangement gives rise to a perfect hedge, interest rate changes during the term of the swap cannot affect the outcome. That is why hedging is often described as a technique of making uncertain outcomes certain. The swap arrangement described above amends this ground rule slightly.

If the company had made use of a regular swap arrangement, it would effectively have paid a fixed 7.75% interest on its loan, whatever happened to 1-month Libor in the interim. Of course, had 1-month Libor declined, the company would have had to forego the advantage of paying a lower rate of interest. This is usually accepted in the interest of certainty.

With the swap structure described in this case study, Armatech would have the advantage of any decline in 1-month Libor, for as long as Libor stayed lower than its original 6.5%. At the same time, the company would have been fully hedged against any increase in Libor to above the initial 6.5%.

There is no advantage without a price. In the example used, the price of certainty was an initial rate of 1.00% over 1-month Libor. That would have been the price of a standard swap. For the added advantage of being able to benefit from declining interest rates, the company pays an additional rate of 0.25% interest.

Whether the additional interest paid is worth the advantages is a decision each company will have to make for itself on each occasion that they face interest rate risk. There is no right or wrong answer. It depends on the total financial condition of the company and the economic conditions under which it operates at any particular time. Most of all, risk management issues are decided by management's aversion to different levels of risk at different times in the economic cycle.

SWAPS AS THE UNDERLYING ASSET OF OTHER DERIVATIVES

Since swaps are the most popular interest rate derivative, it is not surprising that the market has found occasion also to use it as the underlying asset of other derivatives. This is an interesting and growing development. Since a swap is itself a derivative, the structure wherein it becomes the underlying instrument of another derivative, must be a double derivative. Perhaps it should be called a 'derived derivative'.

Indeed, there are other instances of derived derivatives and they are not new. The first one that comes to mind is options on futures. Futures are derivatives and so are options. An option on a futures contract is therefore also a derived derivative. The first strategy that will be dealt with in this section is so new that it has not yet been launched on the market at the time of writing. The second is a well-known one, having been around for many years.

FUTURES ON SWAPS

On July 17, 2001, the Board of Directors of the Chicago Board of Trade (CBOT) approved a plan to launch a swaps complex which includes 10-year and 5-year interest rate swap futures and futures options. At the time of writing, they have not been launched yet. However, the CBOT expects the launch in the Autumn of 2001.

The purpose of launching futures contracts with interest rate swaps as underlying asset, is to furnish new, more effective risk management tools for swaps market participants. It is hoped that they will be of particular value to those market participants seeking alternative benchmarks to Treasury securities.

The new futures contracts will offer investors and other OTC market participants a vehicle for hedging credit and interest rate exposure. Moreover, compared with the OTC market, the trading of swaps futures will reduce administrative cost and eliminate counter-party risk. This, in turn, will enhance the overall swaps cash market.

These contracts will not replace swaps. They are rather valuable additions to the financial markets in their own right. Apart from providing the benefit of a possible alternative benchmark for the swaps markets, they present new arbitrage and hedging opportunities. If the contracts prove to be popular and successful, they might well be able to grant access to the swaps market for many smaller participants who were for reasons of size and credit rating unable to do so previously.

contract structure

The structure of the contract is interesting. Underlying the two futures contracts is a 10-year fixed-against-floating swap and a 5-year fixed-against-floating swap. The only difference between the two contracts is the terms of the respective underlying swaps. In each case, the notional principal of the swap is $100,000. The swap is standardised at a swap rate of 6% per annum, paid semi-annually, while the floating rate is 3-month Libor.

The trading unit of the contract will be the price of the fixed-rate side of the swap. In other words, what the traders of these contracts are really trading is the forward price (value) of the swap rate. The contract is cash settled and the final settlement price is determined according to a formula that incorporates the ISDA benchmark rate for a 5- or 10-year US dollar, 3-month Libor based swap.

The price basis of the futures contract will be points. Each point will represent a value of $1,000 and each point is broken down into fractions of one-quarter of one thirty-second of a point. As to why that should be so abstruse, only the those that design these things can answer for such travesties. Instead of the cumbersome one-quarter of one thirty-second of a point, the basic price decimal of the contract value is actually 0.0078125, which, it is surmised, starts with too many zeroes. One quarter of one thirty-second of a point consequently equates to a value of $7.8125 per contract.

discussion

The introduction of this contract presents the market with a number of new opportunities. The price of the fixed leg of the swap will vary with 3-month Libor. If Libor goes up, the price of the fixed leg will come down and *vice versa*. It must be mentioned that it is the exchange's expressed intention to launch options on this contract simultaneously with the futures contract itself.

It follows that the contract presents another way in which 3-month Libor can be hedged. If one is at risk of a rise in 3-month Libor, one can sell swap futures, while one would buy the futures if one were hedging a 3-month Libor based investment. Under perfect market conditions, this would give the same result as a hedge with Eurodollars. However, arbitrage opportunities may arise.

Arbitrage opportunities might also arise against the swap market. An important factor in determining the swap rate is credit rating. Since there is no counterparty credit risk in futures contracts, there may well be a disparity between the price of the swap futures and the price of the fixed leg of a particular swap.

A party who is long swap futures will gain if Libor falls. Thus, a long swap futures position equates to paying 3-month Libor against receiving fixed interest in a regular swap. Conversely, a short futures position would be equivalent to paying fixed interest against receiving 3-month Libor.

There is thus no doubt that there will be many occasions on which the quick and easy access to futures markets will be preferable to the process of arranging swaps. If it is considered that interest rate swaps are not generally available for notional amounts of less than $1,000,000, the opportunities created by the introduction of these contracts could be very beneficial to smaller businesses.

OPTIONS ON SWAPS

The following strategy is a well-known one that involves taking out an option on the swap rate. It is thus the option version of the previously discussed futures contract. Instead of buying or selling a futures contract on the swap rate, this allows for the trading of an option on the swap rate. Keep in mind that this option is different from buying or selling an option on the aforementioned futures contact.

This option strategy gave rise to a product that is called a swaption. Because an option is a derivative, like a swap, a swaption is another example of a derived derivative. A swaption is really a regular option with the fixed interest rate leg of a swap as its underlying variable.

interest rate swaptions

An interest rate swaption is an option-based agreement that provides protection against rising swap rates, i.e. the fixed rate leg of a fixed-against-floating swap. In exchange for a single up front premium, the purchaser owns the right, but not the obligation, to enter into a specified fixed rate swap transaction at some point in the future.

It is important to note that the full terms of the swap that will be entered are agreed at the start of the swaption. This is because the exact structure of the swap will influence the price of the swaption. When the option is exercised, the parties are obliged to enter into the swap. The option is thus not cash settled and the agreed upon swap is indeed the underlying deliverable instrument.

Because a swaption is an OTC instrument, it can be tailored to suit the needs of the client. Depending on the structure of the swaption, it may be exercised on a specific date in the future or at anytime during its life. In the first case, it will be termed a European style option, while in the second case it is known as an American style option. As is always the case with the two exercise styles of options, European style options will be cheaper than American style options.

A swaption can be structured to protect against a rise in swap rates or against a decline in swap rates. The first type would be a call option, but it is not so called. Since it would be the sort of option required by a party anticipating that it would pay the swap rate, it is known as a payer option. Similarly, a put swaption, guaranteeing a floor swap rate, would be of interest to a party that anticipates receiving that rate; it is thus termed a receiver swaption.

If market swap rates rise above the swaption strike price, the client may exercise the option, if it is an American style option. Otherwise, it will be exercisable on the expiry date. Upon its exercise, the swap will commence under its agreed and specified terms. The fixed interest rate of the swap will be at the rate of the strike price of the swaption.

If market swap rates have declined by the arrival of the expiration date of the swaption, it expires worthless and the client can enter into a swap at the then current lower market rates. In essence, a swaption is a cap on future swap rates. Swaptions are thus often used to hedge expected future borrowings.

case study 12: hedging the swap rate on future borrowings using a swaption

❒   THE SCENARIO

Assume Yellowstone Earthmoving Machines (YEM) is bidding on a $100 million deal to supply earthmoving equipment to an African country. If YEM wins the contract, it will finance the manufacture of the equipment with a 3-year syndicated bank facility, on a floating rate of interest.

The contract on the tender will not be allocated for 6 months. YEM wants the certainty of a fixed rate on its financing and they would therefore wish to hedge their financing with a fixed-against-floating interest rate swap. Further, they are concerned that swap rates might rise prior to the allocation of the tender, thus straining their cost projections on the deal.

The correct course of action puts them into somewhat of a quandary. They could enter into a forward swap, but that would be unwise, since they do not yet know whether they will be awarded the contract. They are thus reluctant to lock the company into a forward swap. Therefore, the company chooses to purchase a payer swaption.

❒   THE SWAPTION

The swaption that is agreed to with National Swap Bank (NSB), provides YEM with the right to enter into a fixed-against-floating interest rate swap at, say 7.00%, commencing in 6 months from the start date of the Swaption. Assume that the up front, swaption premium is the equivalent of 0.15% per annum.

Assume further that after 6 months, YEM is awarded the contract. It is now preparing to close its financing deal with the syndicate of banks. As was feared, the rate for 3-year fixed-against-floating swaps has risen to 7.50%. YEM could now exercise its 'ITM' option and enter into a fixed rate swap with NSB at 7.00%.

On the other hand, if fixed rates had fallen to, say 6.50%, YEM would let its option expire worthless and enter into a swap at the current swap rate of 6.50%.

☐   DISCUSSION

By purchasing a swaption, YEM had the benefit of knowing its maximum out-of-pocket expense. If YEM had lost the tender, or rates had fallen such that the swaption was OTM, the only cost to the company would have been the up front premium.

Of course, it must be taken into account that swap rates must rise by at least 0.15% for the company to break even on its hedge. The company's actual protection against rising swap rates thus actually start at 7.15% (swaption strike plus premium), rather than at the nominal 7.00% strike rate of the swaption.

STRATEGIES MIMICKING SWAPS

One of the major reasons for the popularity of interest rate swaps is that they are multi-period instruments. Both options and futures are by their nature single period instruments, since each instrument covers a single interest period. Since hedging interest rates is most popularly connected with financing and debt, which in turn, tends to include multiple interest rate periods, swaps are for that reason alone most suited as risk management instruments.

It is also not surprising that the ever-innovative marketers at banks, exchanges and other financial institutions would come up with multiple products to address this situation. In order to give a wider choice to their clients, strategies have been devised to mimic the multi-period interest rate element of swaps using futures and options of both the OTC and exchange-traded varieties. The only way the mimic can be achieved is to link a number of such single period instruments together in order to form a linked 'chain' of single interest rate periods. Taken together, these chains then form a single, multiple period interest rate instrument.

futures strips

The first such strategy mentioned here involves the use of futures contracts. A linked chain of futures contracts is known as a 'strip'. Such strips are often used to hedge the floating interest rate leg of a swap. To hedge between futures and swaps then, it is necessary to transact a strip, i.e. a co-ordinated purchase or sale of a series of futures contracts with successive expiration dates.

Unlike a swaption, which 'locks-in' the fixed interest rate of the fixed leg of a swap until it starts, a futures strip serves to hedge the floating rate leg during the currency of the swap. Thus, a company that finds itself on the floating rate side of a swap is allowed to hedge the floating rate without actually entering into another, counteracting fixed-against-floating rate swap. This feature is obviously both desirable and convenient since it eliminates further counterparty risk and an additional tying down of the company's credit facilities.

Furthermore, a strip of futures contracts allows a hedger to hedge multiple interest rate periods directly. Thus if a company borrows money that requires periodic payment of interest, it might not be necessary to arrange a swap. A strip of futures can be bought or sold, as the case may be, to hedge the interest payments. It thus effectively equals a swap, inasmuch as the hedger now pays a fixed rate of interest through the strip of futures contracts. The 'fixed' rate in this instance will be the implied rate at which the futures contracts are bought when the hedge is entered. The following case study illustrates the point.

case study 13: hedging a borrowing rate with a futures strip

❒   THE SCENARIO

Consider the case of an engineering firm that funds itself with 3-month Eurodollar time deposits at Libor. Assume the company has a customer who places an order for sub-assemblies to be manufactured and paid for upon delivery. The company costs out the project at $10 million, with a time to completion and delivery of 1 year. At the time that the order is placed firmly, the company raises 3-month funds at 3-month Libor plus 2% and it has to rollover this funding in three successive quarters. If they do not lock in the funding rate and interest rates rise, the project could go over budget and thus prove to be unprofitable.

❒   FINANCIAL BACKGROUND

The three quarterly re-funding dates of the company's loan fall shortly before the next three Eurodollar futures contract expirations in September, December and March. At the time the finance is obtained, 3-month Libor is fixed at an annual percentage of 3.5175. The prices of those three futures contracts are 96.525, 96.48, and 96.34, respectively. These prices correspond to annual yields of 3.475%, 3.52% and 3.66%, respectively. The company's initial borrowing rate is thus 5.753/4% and it could lock in the total cost of funds for the year by means of the three futures contracts, sold simultaneously as a 'strip'.

❒   THE HEDGE

The company is at risk of a rise in 3-month Libor. A rise in that rate would cause the price of the futures contracts to drop. In order to hedge the company's interest rate exposure, the company would sell futures contracts, thus ensuring a profit on a decline in their price. The company needs to sell ten contracts for each of the expiry months. This would make the nominal principal represented by the futures contracts equal to the company's $10 million exposure in the cash market.

Assuming that the company receives the fills for each of the contracts as was mentioned above, the question arises as to what the actual interest rate that the company has now locked in. The company has a different interest rate for each of the four quarters. If it kept in mind that the interest rate for each of the four quarters are now fixed, the calculation is quite straight forward. The actual rates for each quarter needs to be calculated, keeping in mind that these rates are all based on 360-day years. After multiplying those rates together, they can then be annualised to actual dates. The calculation is as follows:

$$\left[\left(1 + 0.0357175 \times \frac{91}{360}\right) \times \left(1 + 0.03475 \times \frac{91}{360}\right) \times \left(1 + 0.03520 \times \frac{91}{360}\right) \times \left(1 + 0.03660 \times \frac{91}{360}\right) - 1\right] \times \frac{360}{365}$$

$$= [1.008891458 \times 1.008784028 \times 1.008897778 \times 1.009251667 - 1] \times 0.9863$$

$$= 3.58\%$$

As the calculation shows, the Libor rate has been locked in at 3.58% for the year. The company has to pay a 2% premium and its interest rate cost will thus be locked in at 5.58%. The company can now use this rate as a basis for calculating its budgeted cost for the project.

❐ RESULT OF THE HEDGE

On the refinancing dates of the company's loan, the company would liquidate the appropriate hedging contracts by buying them back. With the September refunding, the September contracts would be liquidated; December contracts would be liquidated in December and the March contracts would be liquidated in the following March.

Assume that when the company refinances at the rollover dates, the rates the company has to pay are at 6.00%, 6.15% and 6.35% for the respective quarters. The corresponding futures are liquidated at 94.02 (5.98%), 93.88 (6.12%), and 93.66 (6.34%). The overall results of the hedge are shown in Table 7-1.

❐ DISCUSSION

The unhedged interest expense over the four quarters, amounting to $557,924.79 would have equalled an effective annual rate of 5.58% before adding the 2% premium the company pays over Libor. Had the company not hedged in this manner, its actual interest rate would thus have been 7.58%. This is substantially higher than the actual interest cost after the hedge.

Table 7-1. Result of a hedge against rising interest rates using a futures 'strip'

Date	Cash Market		Futures Market	
	Interest Cost Calculation	Amount	Profit/Loss on Futures	Amount
1st quarter	$10 million × 0.0357 × 91/360	$90,285.90		
2nd quarter	$10 million × 0.06 × 91/360	$151,666.67	Ten contracts × (9652.5 − 9402) × $25	$62,625.00
3rd quarter	$10 million × 0.0615 × 91/360	$155,458.33	Ten contracts × (9648 − 9388) × $25	$65,000.00
4th quarter	$10 million × 0.0635 × 91/360	$160,513.89	Ten contracts × (9634 − 9366) × $25	$67,000.00
	Total Libor Interest:	$557,924.79	Profit on Futures:	$194,625.00
	Net Interest Cost:	$363,299.79		

The net cost after taking into account the profit on the futures contracts represents an annual interest rate of 3.63%. When the company's 2% premium over Libor is added, its effective rate of interest amounts to 5.63%. This is slightly higher than the anticipated 5.58% rate the company originally intended to lock in. The reason for the disparity is the movement of the hedge basis. As can be learnt from Chapter 4, a short hedger in a futures contract can expect a loss on the hedge not greater than the amount of the hedge basis, established at its start.

Had interest rates moved lower over the life of the hedge, the company would have incurred an opportunity cost. The opportunity cost would be roughly equal to the difference between the effective (hedged) rate and the lower rate that could have been realised by foregoing the use of futures. This is because once a position is hedged with futures contracts, there is no longer any opportunity to profit from a favourable move in interest rates.

The minimal difference between the target rate and the effective funding rate can be attributed to the fact that the re-funding dates were quite close but not identical to the futures expiration dates. If the respective dates were further apart, the funding rates and the futures rates would not necessarily converge as closely as those used in the above example.

❏ PRE-PACKAGED FUTURES STRIPS

The strategy of using strips of futures contracts is so sound that exchanges have had to come up with solutions to the inherent problems involved in buying or selling such strips. The basic problem with buying strips of futures contracts is that the orders will not necessarily be executed simultaneously. The time delay between the execution of orders can allow substantial price moves to occur during the fills. This can lead to disparities in the hedge basis. In addition, it would be impossible to order a futures strip at one price. There would be a price for each individual contract in the strip.

To expedite the execution of strip trades the CME, for example, offers bundles and packs for Eurodollar and Euroyen futures. Bundles and packs are simply 'pre-packaged' series of contracts that facilitate the rapid execution of strip positions in a single transaction rather than constructing the same positions with individual contracts. They make it possible to trade the contracts required to hedge a multi-period interest rate exposure at a single price for the pack or bundle. Also, because the contracts are grouped together, it makes for lower trading costs. The purchase of a futures pack or bundle is charged as one trade per bundle, rather than one trade for each of the individual contracts. Thus, the trading costs will be less than those incurred when multiple futures contracts are traded.

When a bundle or pack trade is completed, positions in the individual futures contracts are established in the company's accounts in the conventional way, as if they had been traded individually. Bundles and packs are simply execution conventions on the trading floor of the exchange. From a risk manager's point of view there is no difference between futures positions established through trading a bundle or a pack and those established by executing futures contracts individually.

☐ FUTURES BUNDLES

On the CME, bundles are the simultaneous sale or purchase of one each of a consecutive series of Eurodollar or Euroyen contracts. Thus, if a company needed to hedge an exposure in the cash market of $10 million, it would trade ten bundles.

Being pre-packaged units, there are finite numbers of contracts in a bundle. The bundles are constructed to cover different periods into the future. Currently 1-, 2-, 3-, 5-, 7-, and 10-year Eurodollar bundles are available for trading. Only 1-, 2-, and 3-year bundles are available for Euroyen futures. It would therefore not be possible to trade futures strips covering, for example, 18-month, 21-month, or 27-month periods as a bundle. Obviously, a company could cover such odd, non-annual periods through a futures strip.

The first contract in any bundle is generally the first quarterly contract in the strip. Consequently, if it were now August, the first contract in a bundle would be the September contract, while if it were January or February, the first contract would be the March contract of that year. A 2-year bundle therefore consists of the first eight Eurodollar contracts in the quarterly cycle.

As is evidenced by this structure, bundles are primarily intended to cover periods that start in the immediate future. Fortunately, it is also possible to cover forward periods. However, here the choice is more limited. There is a 5-year 'forward' bundle available, which is composed of the 20 Eurodollar contracts from years 6–10.

☐ FUTURES PACKS

Packs are another simultaneous purchase or sale of an equally weighted, consecutive series of Eurodollar or Euroyen futures contracts. However, the number of contracts in a pack is fixed at four and consequently one pack covers only one period of 12 months. Packs are ideal to cover forward exposures, since they are not pre-packaged in the same way that bundles are.

They are designated by a colour code that corresponds to their position on the yield curve. For example, the white pack covers the first year while the red pack consists of the four contracts that constitute year 2 on the curve. Apart from the first year pack, there are generally nine Eurodollar packs (covering years 2–10) and two Euroyen packs (spanning years 2 and 3) available for trading at a given time.

☐ PRICING BUNDLES AND PACKS

It has been mentioned that one of the advantages of pre-packaging futures contracts is that all the contracts can be traded at a single price. Keep in mind that each futures contract further into the future has a different price from the earlier one. Exactly how one price for a bundle or a pack is achieved is quite ingenious.

Bundles and packs are both quoted on a 'net change' basis from the previous day's settlement prices. The price quotation reflects the average of the net price changes of the bundle's constituent contracts. For example, a trade might be executed in the 2-year Euroyen bundle at a price of -1.5. That represents an agreement between the buyer and the seller to exchange the first eight Euroyen contracts at prices which are one-and-a-half ticks lower than the previous day's settlement price for each contract involved. The price of − 1.5 that was used in the example is termed a fractional trade price.

There is also a difference between bundles and packs in the way they are price quoted. The smallest price increment for a bundle is 0.25 basis points. The smallest price increment for a pack is 0.50 basis points. What this means exactly will be cleared up during the discussion that follows.

❑   THE PRICING ALGORITHM

A CME pricing algorithm is used to assign whole-tick prices to each of the constituent contracts. It cannot be as simple as taking only the fractional trade price and deducting that from each of the contracts. That would unbalance the pricing structure of the futures contracts. Futures contracts can only change by one whole tick. A fractional trade price can therefore not be implemented. The function of the pricing algorithm is thus to assign a valid, whole-tick price to each of the constituent contracts to give a result that is consistent with the fractional trade price.

The algorithm is based upon the following principle: the necessary price adjustments begin with the most deferred contract in the bundle or pack, and are worked forward toward the nearest contract. Net changes are to be kept as uniform as possible.

This will be more clearly explained by means of an example. Assume that a trade is executed in the 2-year bundle at a price of −2.50. In this case, the first eight quarterly contracts are exchanged at an average price of 2.50 basis points (the fractional trade price) below the previous day's settlement prices.

The algorithm must now assign price adjustments to each of the eight contracts, beginning with the most deferred one in the bundle and working forward toward the nearest contract. In this example, the six most deferred contracts are exchanged at −3, and the first (nearest) two contracts are exchanged at a net change of −1, for an average price change of −2.50 for the bundle:

$$[(-3 \times 6) + (-1 \times 2)]/8 = -2.50$$

❑   INTEREST RATE CAPS AND FLOORS

An interest rate cap and an interest rate floor are just two sides of the same coin. Both are strategies designed to duplicate the multi-periodicity of swaps, using interest rate guarantees. It is one hedging strategy with two names to distinguish the two purposes served. They are usually grouped together for the purposes of discussion.

An interest rate cap puts an upper limit or maximum rate (the cap rate) on a given floating interest rate, such as Libor or Prime. It amounts to a multiple-period call option. The strategy here is exactly the same as was discussed previously on futures strips. In this case, interest rate call options, usually referred to as interest rate guarantees (IRGs), are linked together in a chain to cover multiple interest rate periods. IRGs making up the chain are often referred to as 'caplets' in this context.

An interest rate floor puts a lower limit or minimum rate (the floor rate) on a given floating interest rate, such as Libor or Prime. In this case, the construct amounts to a multiple period put option. Interest rate guarantees, guaranteeing a lower limit are linked together to form a chain covering multiple interest rate periods. The constituent IRGs are referred to as 'floorlets' in this case.

The effect of these IRG chains is to hedge a longer period of interest rate exposure, guaranteeing the upper or lower interest rate, as the case may be, at the start of each interest rate period. If the floating rate is above a cap level at any rollover or interest calculation date, the holder or owner of the interest rate cap is paid or credited for the difference. If the floating rate remains unchanged or declines, the holder of the cap enjoys the benefit of lower borrowing rates.

Similarly, if the floating rate is below the floor level at any rollover or interest calculation date, the holder of the interest rate floor is paid or credited with the difference. If the floating rate remains unchanged or increases, the holder of the floor enjoys the benefit of the same or higher investment rates.

A cap or floor is purchased with a one-time up front fee or premium. Once the premium is paid, there are no other costs or risks associated with the hedge.

An example of a cap will suffice to illustrate the discussion. Assume a borrower has a $15 million 3-year revolving credit facility tied to 1-month Libor. Core outstandings are $13.5 million. The company consequently uses 1-month Libor, currently at 3.58%, as its primary borrowing index. For planning purposes, the company has assumed that Libor will not rise above 4.00%. The company is comfortable with Libor to that level.

Without any hedge, the borrower is vulnerable to Libor rising above the 4.00% mark. In order to protect its projections, the company decides to purchase an interest rate cap on 1-month Libor at a strike of 4.00%. The contract will cover a notional principal of $13.5 million. The company pays an up front premium for 2 years of protection.

Assume that 1-month Libor rises above 4.00% to, say 5.50%. The company will incur higher interest expense on its borrowings. However, under the cap agreement, the company would be reimbursed for the difference between actual Libor (5.50%) and the cap level (4.00%) on the notional principal. Regardless of how high Libor rises, the company is fully protected above 4.00% on the contracted notional amount for the next 2 years.

CHECKLIST FOR THE REVIEW OF CHAPTER 7

General overview: the overall control objectives of the material dealt with in this chapter are to acquaint the business with some advanced strategies to manage interest rate risk, using swaps and related, multi-period interest rate derivative constructs.

	Key Issues	Illustrative Scope or Approach
7.1	Does the company ever consider the use of interest rate swaps to manage its interest rate cost?	Swaps can create access to the bond market where the company does not presently enjoy such access A disparity often exists between the interest rate charged by the banking sector and the debt markets for the same credit rating

continued

	Key Issues	Illustrative Scope or Approach
		Through a swaps arrangement companies with different credit ratings can make use of interest rate disparities, each to lower its interest rate cost on a particular exposure.
7.2	How can off-market cash flows be managed using interest rate swaps?	If the company wishes to receive or to pay an off-market fixed rate above the market: • Pay or receive an up front premium • Pay or receive a premium on the floating rate In both cases, the premium should be calculated to result in a par swap If the company wishes to receive or pay an off-market fixed rate below the market: • Receive or pay an up front premium • Receive or pay a premium on the floating rate In both cases, the premium should be calculated to result in a par swap
7.3	Does the company consider the use of swaps with special terms in order to meet its specific risk management needs?	Callable fixed rate swaps are routinely available that allow for early termination of the swap without a penalty, but subject to an initial lockout period Adjustable fixed rate swaps are routinely available, subject to a premium on the dealer's spread, that allow a profit to the company on a favourable move in interest rates
7.4	What are the main features of futures on swaps?	Futures on swaps will reflect the forward price of the swap rate against 3-month Libor They will provide a hedge to lock in the swap rate on a swap to be entered into in the future They will provide arbitrage opportunities with the swaps market They will be able to be used as a hedge against 3-month Libor The underlying variable is the swap rate of a standardised swap and the contract is cash settled

continued

	Key Issues	Illustrative Scope or Approach
7.5	Under what circumstances might the use of futures on swaps be appropriate?	When the company intends to arrange a fixed-against-floating swap based on 3-month Libor When the company is exposed to changes in the swap rate against 3-month Libor on intended future borrowings When the company perceives a mispricing between the swap rate it is offered on a swap and the swap rate implied by the futures price
7.6	What are the main features of a swaption?	A swaption is an OTC option on the swap rate It can be referenced to the swap rate against any floating interest rate It can be used to lock in the swap rate of any intended swap to be entered into in the future The underlying asset of the option is a specifically arranged swap Upon the exercise of a swaption, the parties enter into the underlying, pre-arranged swap
7.7	Under what circumstances might the use of swaptions be appropriate?	When the company intends to enter into a fixed-against-floating swap to manage the risk of an uncertain future borrowing or investment and it is concerned that the swap rate might rise or fall during the interval of uncertainty
7.8	What are futures strips?	Futures strips are series of consecutive expiration futures contracts linked together to form a synthetic multi-interest rate period futures instrument
7.9	What are the uses of futures strips?	Futures strips can be used to hedge the floating rate leg of a swap, effectively swapping it for a locked in interest rate A futures strip can replace a swap by directly hedging an exposure to a floating rate of interest, thus equating a fixed-against-floating swap Strips can be constructed to cover any period forward and any period of exposure

continued

	Key Issues	Illustrative Scope or Approach
7.10	What are futures bundles and packs?	Futures bundles and packs are pre-packaged futures strips
		Bundles and packs are merely the result of execution conventions recognised by an exchange and do not constitute a new derivative instrument
		Bundles consist of consecutive quarterly cycle futures contracts, covering 2 or more years at a single price, called the fractional trade price
		Packs consist of four futures contracts in the quarterly cycle, colour coded for convenience to indicate the period forward covered by each pack
7.11	What are interest rate caps and floors?	An interest rate cap is a linked chain of interest rate guarantees that together guarantee a maximum interest rate during a period consisting of shorter, multi-interest rate periods
		An interest rate floor is a linked chain of interest rate guarantees that together guarantee a minimum interest rate during a period consisting of shorter, multi-interest rate periods
		Both caps and floors are options that require a premium to be paid

eight

strategies with interest rate options and exotic interest rate options

INTRODUCTION

Although interest rate options are only the second most popular derivative for managing interest rate risk, they are nevertheless very adaptable instruments that enjoy considerable demand. In response to the varied situations that invariably recur in national and international business, strategies with options proliferate.

It is not only option strategies that proliferate. These flexible instruments are adapted, twisted, turned and skewered to meet the most exacting demands. These demands and strategies have spawned a whole shooting gallery of special term options, also called option variants. These are really options with special terms and conditions that allow a variety of needs to be fulfilled.

Many variants are decidedly biased to speculation rather than risk management. However, there is a continuing debate where the line between risk management and speculation should be drawn. It is not a debate that this author would like to be embroiled in. Thus, for the purposes of this book, a non-contentious strategy will be adopted: an option or option variant is speculative in nature when the author deems it so.

The first order is to take a closer look at option strategies that have in mind the reduction of the premium cost. This need has also inspired the creation of a number of special term options. This will be followed by a discussion of the class of options known as exotics. This is such an open-ended and wide class of options that only the most commonly encountered and generally useful ones will be dealt with.

COST REDUCTION STRATEGIES

It is evident from earlier discussions that the cost of hedging is extremely important in determining its relevance to the value that is added by the activity. As in all other business activities, it is always important to find the most cost-effective way of achieving a desired result. This requirement has lead to the development of a number of strategies with options that allow for a lower cost to the hedger.

Swaps and futures are not concerned in this discussion. As far as swaps are concerned, the only cost involved is the spread of the dealer. These form such an integral part of a swap's structure that they lend themselves to cost reduction strategies only in very limited ways.

Similarly, there is no cost to futures contracts, except for trading costs. That is because interest rate futures are really contracts for difference (CFDs). Consider for a moment the effect of buying a cash settled futures contract. The contract value is not payable. Only when the contract is sold, or when it expires, is payment made or received for the difference between the contract value at the start and at the end of the trading period.

Given the major benefits of options, it is remarkable that they are not more popular than swaps. The two major benefits are namely that options allow a profit on a favourable move in interest rates and that they do not impinge on a company's credit facilities.

As might be expected, reducing the premium cost of options can only be achieved by means of a compromise between an option's cost and its advantages. In other words, in order to reduce the cost of hedging with options, some of their advantages must be sacrificed. Since there is no free lunch, one cannot enjoy the full advantage of an option without paying the full price. Nevertheless, there may be a free snack, inasmuch as one may not have to give up all the advantages of using options in order to reduce the premium cost substantially – even down to zero

Some cost reduction strategies refer specifically to ways in which options, whether they are OTC options or options on futures, can be combined and traded simultaneously, resulting in an overall lower option premium. The simplest way of reducing the cost of an option is to accept part of the risk. A number of strategies will achieve this end.

degrees of risk acceptance – trading otm options

The first alternative that a company has in constructing a hedge with interest rate options is to accept some of the risk itself. How much of the risk it wishes to bear depends on the circumstances of the company and the particular circumstances of the interest rate risk faced by it. The first strategy is therefore to select an option that is not ATM (at the money), but is somewhat out of the money (OTM). The further OTM the option is, obviously, the lower the premium payable will be.

With OTC options, a very precise trade-off can be made between the additional risk and the premium payable. The reason is that the strike price of the option can be precisely selected. The OTC products that essentially have the same features are named differently and will be discussed separately.

Using options on futures cannot give such a precise result, but the same effect can be approximated, which will serve for illustrative purposes.

case study 14: locking in a borrowing rate with OTM options on futures

❏   THE SCENARIO

Consider the situation of a construction company that expects to borrow $12,725,000 for 3 years, paying 3-month Libor. It requires the loan in order to finance a large contract for which it has won the tender. The loan is scheduled to commence in December and it is now August. The company is thus exposed to the risk that USD Libor will rise before the loan commences in December. Such a rise would increase the project cost and impact negatively on the projected profits from the contract.

☐ FINANCIAL INFORMATION

Assume that in the beginning of August the financial information is as follows:

- Three-month USD Libor is quoted at 3.65625
- the October 2001 Eurodollar futures contract on the CME is trading at 96.32, implying a rate of 3.68%
- CME Eurodollar December put options are priced as per Table 8-1

☐ SELECTING THE HEDGE

The CME Eurodollar contract has an underlying asset of a 3-month time deposit of $1,000,000 and one point (0.01) is equal to $25.00 on the whole contract. Every option has one futures contract as its underlying and it is priced in exactly the same manner as the futures contract. Given the 3-month Libor quote on the day, the company expects to pay $116,314.45 in interest on the loan for the first quarter.

The structure of the CME futures contract is such that in order for the company to protect itself against a rise in Libor, it must purchase put options. A put option will gain value as the points value of the futures contract declines. The points value of the futures contract will decline as the interest rate increases. A Eurodollar put option will thus protect the company against an increase in 3-month Libor.

Option strike prices are 25 points (0.25) apart. The monetary value of that difference thus equals $625 ($25 × 25). It follows that for every one strike further OTM that the company uses, this represents an interest rate cost increase of $625 per option. In order to hedge exposure in this example, the company would require 13 options. Thus, on the total hedge each strike represents $8,125 unhedged risk carried by the company.

The company is well acquainted with its market. It knows that given its competitive position in the market and its profit margin, it could afford to allow for some flexibility in the actual interest cost of the project. The hedge under discussion will only lock in the interest cost of the first quarter, not the total interest cost for the whole year.

Options on futures are in, out or at the money relative to the price of the futures contract and not Libor. The put option at the 96.50 is the first option in the money

Table 8-1. Put option prices on December 2001 CME Eurodollar futures contract

Strike Price	Put Premium	
	Premium	Amount ($)
95.75	1.75	43.75
96.00	4.75	118.75
96.25	12.00	300.00
96.50	25.00	625.00

(ITM). The put at the 96.25 strike is the first strike OTM and its premium is less than half of that of the previous put. The next strike down is 96.00 and its premium is a further 50% + discount on the premium of the ATM option.

The company thus has a choice of three puts. As it will require 13 options to cover its exposure to the loan, the company has a choice. It can select either the first put ITM at a cost of $8,125, or the put at the first strike OTM at a cost of $3,900, or it can select the put at the last strike for a mere $1,543.75.

If it selects the first put OTM, it will guarantee for itself an interest rate not exceeding 3.75% per annum. This would involve it in an interest rate cost of no greater than $119,296,00. This represents an increase of $2,989.43 in the total cost of interest. Under the circumstances, this increase is minimal. Even if they were to select the next strike down, it would involve them in a maximum cost of $127,250, which represents an increase in cost amounting to $10,935. This type of cost/advantage trade-off is central to risk management with options.

Using OTC options, the trade-off can be tailor-made to provide a more exact fit, but the principle remains the same. At the heart of any hedge with interest rate options is the idea that in principle, the potential of a small, limited loss is accepted against the potential of unlimited gain, subject to a cost. With this strategy, the basic advantage of a hedge using interest rate options has been retained, but the size of the limited loss has been marginally increased against the advantage of a substantially smaller outlay in option premiums.

❐   INTEREST RATE COLLARS

The interest rate collar sets out to achieve almost the same as that achieved in the previous case study. The differences are that it is achieved through OTC options and is used to hedge a borrowing rate rather than locking it in. This is because an interest rate collar is a multi-period interest rate instrument.

An interest rate collar sets a maximum (cap) and minimum (floor) boundary on a given floating interest rate, such as Libor or Prime. Instead of combining a long call and a short put as was done in the case of options on futures, this strategy combines an interest rate cap and an interest rate floor. It may be said that the same can be achieved by buying a borrower's IRG and selling a lender's IRG. In that case, the hedge will be for a single period only.

Whether in single period or multi-period hedges, the principle remains the same. If the applicable interest rate rises above the strike level, the client is paid the difference at option expiry or at its exercise, whichever happens first. If the rate falls below the floor level at expiry or exercise, the client pays the difference.

It is important to note that this strategy is not limited to reducing costs. Some collars can be transacted at zero cost. The lower the cost, the closer together the strike prices of the cap and the floor will be. The client thus exposes itself to losses at a higher level.

If a collar is terminated prior to maturity, a collar may result in a gain or a loss for the cancelling party, since there will be a penalty if the rate had moved against the cancelling party.

case study 15: hedging borrowing rates with an interest rate collar

Suppose a company has just completed a mid-sized acquisition that will be financed with a syndicated bank credit facility. The facility is a $300 million, 5-year term loan, combined with a reducing revolving credit facility and with grid based Libor pricing. The financing includes a 50% hedge requirement for a minimum term of 3 years.

Management believes that 3-month Libor, currently quoted at 3.525%, is headed higher during the foreseeable future, although it may eventually reverse course. The company and the syndicated banks have agreed that the maximum Libor rate threshold to comfortably support the projected cash flows is 4.75%. The company wants to mini-mise the up front cost associated with an options hedge and wants to retain some room for profit if Libor declines.

The company enters into a $150 million, 3-year interest rate collar with a cap of 4.75% and a floor of 3.00%. The notional amount of the hedge is agreed to decline in conjunc-tion with the scheduled loan amortisation. This is the equivalent of buying call options with strikes of 4.75% and selling put options with strikes of 3.00%. Theoretically, the premium is reduced to the extent that the income generated by the sale of the puts is offset against the premium paid for the calls. The net payment is thus substantially smaller. The company will now be protected against rises of Libor higher than 4.75%, but it is at risk when Libor falls below 3.00%, since it will then have to pay the difference.

Every 3 months, the debt will be re-priced based on the prevailing Libor rate. Simul-taneously, any payments due under the collar will be determined. If LIBOR has risen above 4.75%, the borrower will be reimbursed for the difference. For instance, if Libor is at 5.50%, the company will be paid the 91-day value of 0.75 APR (5.50% − 4.75%). If Libor has declined below 3.00% to, say 2.5%, the company will owe 0.50% on the collar (3.00% − 2.50%). If Libor is between 4.75 and 3.00% on any of the 3-monthly re-pricing dates, no collar payments are due.

Over the next 3 years, the interest rate cost on 50% of the company's debt is secured at no more than 4.75% and no less than 3% per annum.

☐ VERTICAL OPTION SPREADS

Vertical option spreads are based on the same underlying idea that zero and reduced cost strategies are. The idea is that some of the advantages of a hedge with options are foregone in the interest lowering cost. This was also the idea in the previous strategy, but vertical spread strategies, like zero-cost strategies, rely on income from the sale of certain other options in order to offset or minimise the cost of the long, hedging options.

Vertical spreads are done with options of the same type. One can thus have a vertical spread with call options, or a vertical spread with put options. If calls and puts are mixed in a single position, the result is not a vertical spread. It might amount to some other synthetic derivative, which will be dealt with later.

The spread is called vertical because one option will be bought or sold at a strike higher than the other option. There are a number of possible permutations, but only two are relevant to the risk management or hedging: bull call spreads and bear put spreads.

❑   A BULL CALL SPREAD

The discussion that follows presupposes IRG structures. When options on futures are used, the reverse of the positions mentioned will give the result described. This will be pointed out as the discussion progresses.

A bull call spread is established by buying a call option at the strike required by the hedge, probably, but not necessarily ATM. Another call is then sold at a higher strike. The call at the higher strike will be OTM and will thus be cheaper than the lower call, but the premium income from its sale will mitigate the cost of the purchase of the first call.

The result of this strategy is that the hedger will be protected against an appreciation of the underlying interest rate, but only up to the strike of the short call. Beyond the strike of the short call, the loss on it will neutralise any further gain on the long call. The hedger has thus effectively reduced the insurance obtained against an adverse appreciation of the interest rate in return for a lower premium. In a hedge with options on futures, a bull call spread will protect the hedger against a decline in interest rates.

❑   A BEAR PUT SPREAD

A bear put spread is the mirror image of the bull call spread. The purpose and strategy is the same. A hedger seeking protection against the devaluation of an interest rate will purchase the required number of put options at the strike required. The hedger will then proceed to select a lower strike at which to sell an equal number of put options, thus mitigating the price of the long puts. The result will again be a hedge at a reduced cost. When options on futures are used for such a strategy, the hedger will be protected against a rise in interest rates, up to the rate implied by the point value of the short put with the lower strike.

❑   CONCLUSION ON VERTICAL SPREADS

There is more to the strategy of vertical option spreads than might appear at first. The illustrations given above only indicate a very basic manner of employing the strategy. The strategy can be very flexible and can be used dynamically to extremely good effect. Its main advantage is that, unlike certain other dynamic strategies, it presents far less risk to the company.

ZERO COST STRATEGIES

For many companies, mere cost reduction strategies are not sufficient to satisfy their cost aversion. Using options that are further OTM may not represent a sufficient reduction in cost for these companies, compared to the benefit received. The next step is thus to resort to giving up more of the advantages of options, yet retaining some of the essential advantages insofar as the company might regard it as desirable. The company might then seek a more limited hedge that is curtailed by a strike differential based on put call parity. The meaning of this will become clear during the following discussion.

put/call parity

Put/call parity is a situation where for a given underlying interest rate, the put option at a particular strike has a premium equal to the call option at the same or another strike price. The parity that is referred to is thus a parity of premiums. Premium parity does not occur at only one particular set of strikes. The underlying idea of zero cost strategies is to make use of put/call parity and also any disparities, to achieve a combined option hedge structure that results in zero cost.

Put/call parity, or virtual parity in the case of options on futures, occurs at regular distances from the money, as is illustrated by the figures shown in Table 8-2. The strikes, at which parity will occur, always straddle the money. In other words, the call and the put will both be ATM or at some virtually equal distance OTM. One strike may be somewhat closer to the money than the other, but the strikes will straddle the futures price or the outright forward rate in the case of OTC options. The difference in distance from the money may also be caused by a difference in the volatility of the options at different strikes.

It is difficult to get actual put/call parity in options on futures, due to the standardised nature of the option strikes. With OTC options precise put/call parity can be achieved because the strikes can be selected to give exact parity. This strategy will be discussed in the next section.

Accepting that precise put/call parity is seldom if ever achieved with options on futures, consider the close parities illustrated in Table 8-2. The option prices illustrated in the table relate to a price of 96.125 for the underlying futures contract. In order to come as close to the money as possible, the first put/call parity occurs with the put at strike 96.00 and the call at strike 96.25. The difference in premium is only $2 per option. Observe, however, that total put/call parity is reached with the call at strike 96.50 and the put at strike 95.75. The premiums of both options are equal at $237.50. It also appears from the table that parity will also be reached at the exact price of March futures, but that price lies somewhere between the two available strikes.

If put/call parity were reached at the same strike, then selling the put and buying the call would be equal to a long interest rate futures position. That is to say, the net profit/loss profile of the options would be exactly equal to the profile of a long futures position. Similarly, if the call was sold and the put bought at the same strike rate, the position would amount to a synthetic short futures position.

Table 8-2. Put and call option premiums for CME March 2002 Eurodollar futures, trading at 96.125

Call Premium		Strike Price	Put Premium	
Amount ($)	Quote		Quote	Amount ($)
1,812.50	72.50	95.50	5.50	137.50
1,187.50	47.50	95.75	9.50	237.50
750.00	30.00	96.00	17.00	425.00
475.00	19.00	96.25	27.50	687.50
237.50	9.50	96.50	N/A	N/A
112.50	4.50	96.75	61.00	1,525.00

When put/call parity at different strikes is used, the strategy is sometimes called a zero cost collar. When the strategy is followed using OTC options, there will be put/call parity at the strike where both options are exactly ATM. With OTC options, a zero cost strategy would thus be possible, while it can usually only be approximated with options on interest rate futures.

In practice, the following course of action would be followed to construct a zero cost hedge. To protect against a drop in interest rates, using options on the March Eurodollar contract, calls at strike 96.50 would be purchased, while an equal number of puts would be sold at the 95.75 strike. Conversely, to give protection against a rise in interest rates, the puts will be bought and the calls sold. In either case, this action will result in zero cost because the total premium paid will be exactly equal to the total premium collected. This strategy represents the principal zero cost strategy using a combination of interest rate options.

Such a hedge is obviously not a perfect hedge. The interest rate implied by the futures contract is 3.875% APR. In a hedge against a drop in rates, the calls would give protection against a drop in interest rates only from 3.5% down. The hedger thus assumes the risk of an adverse change in rates down to 3.5%. Any drop after that would be neutralised by the hedge. However, any rise in interest rates would be cancelled out by the loss on the short puts. However, the loss would only come into effect after a rise in rates beyond the interest rate implied by the 95.75 strike of the short puts, which equals 4.25%. Thus, the hedger would be able to enjoy the benefit of any rise in interest rates up to 4.25%.

forward rate locks

When OTC options are used to construct a put/call parity hedge, the strategy is known as a forward rate lock. Although the label seems to indicate a separate product, it is in fact merely a borrower's IRG combined with an opposite position in a lender's IRG at the same strike price. The similarity between this strategy and the one employing options on futures will become evident from the discussion that follows.

A forward rate lock allows a client to 'lock in' a certain interest rate for settlement on a specified date in the future. The interest rate is locked in at the strike price of the combination. In the case of a borrower's interest rate lock, if the actual interest rate is higher than the lock rate on the specified future date the holder of the lock is paid the difference. If the actual interest rate is lower than the lock rate, the holder of the lock pays the difference. The risk manager has no leeway. The company enjoys total protection against interest rate rises beyond the strike price, while it is immediately subject to losses for all interest rate moves below the strike price.

The effect is the same as entering into a standard fixed-against-floating swap. In both cases, there is no premium payable and there is no possibility of profit on a favourable change in interest rates. A forward rate lock is often used by companies that wish to hedge their future borrowing needs.

case study 16: hedging future borrowing rates using a borrower's interest rate lock

❐   THE SCENARIO

Assume a certain company plans to issue long term public debt in 3 months. Assume further that the deal will be priced at a spread over the 10-year Treasury note with a current implied yield to maturity of 4.852%.

The company is concerned that rates might be headed higher. To protect the value of its forthcoming debt issue against an increase in the 10-year Treasury note yield, the company decides to hedge the present yield of the 10-year US Treasury note.

❑   THE OPTION

In execution of this strategy, the company enters into a Treasury lock with, for example, HSBC for value 3 months forward. Assume that the lock is arranged at a rate of 4.9%. There is no premium payable for the lock.

❑   OUTCOME OF THE HEDGE

In 3 months, when the company issues its debt at a spread over the actual 10-year Treasury note yield at that time, it would simultaneously settle its Treasury lock agreement. If the actual 10-year Treasury note yield were higher, the price realised by the company on its debt issue would have been lower. If the 10-year Treasury note yield were higher than the lock rate of 4.9%, HSBC would compensate the company for the difference in rates.

❑   DISCUSSION

The compensation paid by HSBC should approximate the actual shortfall on the issue very closely. Thus, the interest rate lock serves to offset the incremental changes in the 10-year Treasury note yield, making up for the decrease in the price obtained on the company's debt issue.

The hedge is a perfect one and therefore allows for no profit on a favourable change in interest rates. The only 'cost' to the hedger is the dealers spread on the underlying interest rate.

❑   PARTICIPATING CAPS AND FLOORS

The two previous discussions both concerned put/call parity in single interest rate period instruments. It is possible to achieve the same effect by using interest rate caps and floors at par value. A participating cap is similar to a regular interest rate cap. It also provides protection against the rising of a floating interest rate such as Libor or Prime. Were the floating interest rate to rise above the cap level, which is the strike of the linked borrowers interest rate guarantees, the client is paid the difference.

Similarly, participating floors provide protection against a drop in the floating interest rate. Were the rate to drop below the floor level, the client would be paid the difference. A floor is thus a construct of a chain of lenders' interest rate guarantees.

However, participating caps and participating floors require no up front premium. Rather, the client agrees to forgo a portion of the rate benefit when floating rates decline in the case of a participating cap, or rise in the case of a participating floor. In the case of a participating cap, for example, when the floating rate is below the cap level, the client is debited for a percentage of the difference. In effect, the client retains some, but not all, of the rate savings when floating rates fall. This feature will become clearer during the next case study.

case study 17: hedging a borrowing rate with a participating interest rate cap

❐   THE SCENARIO

Assume that a rapidly expanding soft goods manufacturing company just obtained a 5-year lending commitment from its bankers. The loan is for an asset based principal of $15 million at a spread over 3-month Libor. The bank requires the company to purchase interest rate protection at a maximum Libor level of 3.50%.

❐   THE PARTICIPATING CAP

The company prefers the flexibility of an interest rate cap in order to hedge the exposure, but they are reluctant to pay the up front premium. As a result, the company buys a 3.60% Libor participating cap. In order to eliminate the net premium payable on the option, the company agrees to share equally with the bank, half of the difference between the actual 3-month Libor market rate and the strike of the cap. This applies respectively to each period of interest in which Libor is below 3.50%.

❐   LIBOR DECLINES

Assume that, at the start of a particular interest rate calculation period, Libor is set at 3.00%. The company must thus pay out 25% of the difference between 3.50% and 3.00% to the bank, which equals 0.125%. Consequently, the company's interest payment to the bank will be based on the actual Libor rate, plus another 0.125% per annum for 91 days.

   In essence thus, the soft goods manufacturer captures 75% of the downward move in interest rates, against which it forgoes 25%.

❐   LIBOR RISES

In this instance, it is assumed that 3-month Libor resets at 4.00% for the next interest period. Then, the company is credited with the difference between actual Libor at 4.00% and the cap level of 3.5%. The company thus is assured that the interest rate on its loan will never exceed 3.50%, ignoring any borrowing spread. The borrowing spread is not a risk factor since it is a fixed rate per annum over Libor for the period of the loan.

❐   DISCUSSION

A participating cap thus provides exactly the same protection as an ordinary interest rate cap when rates rise above the strike price. However, when rates drop below the cap level, the buyer forgoes some of the benefit of the favourable change. It therefore still represents an improvement over a straight hedge, which allows for no profit on a favourable change in rates.

By the same token, a participating floor will provide exactly the same protection as an ordinary interest rate floor when the base interest rate falls below the floor level. When rates rise favourably for the investor above the floor level, the buyer of the participating floor forgoes some of the benefit of that rise.

The major benefit of a participating interest rate cap or floor is that the buyer of the option does not have to outlay the premium at the start of the hedge. Because the holder will have to give up some of the benefit of a favourable move on a percentage basis, the opportunity cost becomes greater the greater the favourable move becomes. Thus, when there is a big favourable change in rates, the opportunity cost may eventually exceed the premium cost of a comparable interest rate guarantee. This can only be judged retrospectively and can never be prophesied with certainty. A company thus has to base its decision on whether it wishes to use an ordinary interest rate cap or floor, or the participating construct, on the actual facts available to it at the time it makes the hedging decision. It is never wise to be too clever when it comes to calling the markets.

Whenever one is concerned with managing risk, it is never a good idea to continually look over one's shoulder. It serves no purpose to ruminate on what action might have yielded a more favourable result 'if only we had known what was going to happen'. Unfortunately, many companies indulge in this type of after the event analysis. It is unproductive because one actually learns nothing through the process. It does not matter how much one studies the 'might have done if only we knew' scenarios, you will never know the outcome of an uncertain future event. You will therefore not perform better next time for all the study.

What a company needs to do in risk management is to make the uncertain outcomes of future events certain. Once that is done, the risk that was present in the situation has been eliminated and the expected result achieved. It is therefore a good idea to keep the purpose of managing risk in mind. The goals must be set at the start of the exercise, and they must not be moved during the course of the process.

EXOTIC OPTIONS

introduction

The options that have been discussed so far are standard options. That is to say, however they might be combined, they all have standard terms and conditions. Such standard term options are known as vanilla options. This must disclose something about the culinary horizons of those who are responsible for designing and naming financial instruments. It is thus enlightening to note that non-standard options have not been appropriately blessed with names such as 'strawberry chocolate caramel fudge crunch' options. Rather distressingly, the innovative creators of financial instruments seem to have depleted their vocabulary of culinary delights with 'vanilla' and then settled for grouping all the other versions under the umbrella label of 'exotic options'. There you have it then. Options come in two flavours only – vanilla and exotic.

Many exotic options are great gambling tools, but do not present much of an opportunity for risk management. An example of this type of option is the digital option, also known as a binary option. It is an option that pays out a fixed amount if the underlying asset has a value greater than the strike price. It is thus a straightforward casino bet on the value of the underlying asset at expiration. The premium is no more than the stake for a bet that the underlying asset will be worth more than the strike price of the option on expiration day. It does not matter how much more or less than the strike price the value of the asset is at expiration; the payout remains the same. If the value of the asset is equal to or less than the strike price at expiration, the premium is lost. There is not much room there for managing interest rate risk.

The field is growing so fast that it is not possible to deal comprehensively with these options. At best, guidelines can be given by means of which the further developments can be followed. Additionally, not all exotics are available for interest rates. For example, compound options, which are options on options, are only available in the currency markets, because of the often-encountered 'tender-to-contract' potential currency exposure in international commerce.

For these reasons, the subject will be dealt with based on the standard terms of interest rate options that are, or have been changed by such options.

amended exercise style

A standard element that can be varied is the exercise style. It has often been mentioned throughout this book that there are two exercise styles, namely American and European. There is a third possibility that lies in between the two mentioned exercise styles. This third style is named a Bermudan option for obvious reasons.

A Bermudan option does not allow the right to exercise the option continuously, like an American option. However, it allows greater flexibility in the exercise than European options, which can only be exercised on expiration. Typically, it will allow the option to be exercised on specific dates during the life of the option. Such dates will be synchronised with the dates required by the client's underlying interest rate exposure.

If the option is exercised at any one of the available dates, it is obviously extinguished. It must not be confused with multi-period derivatives. There is still only one option for a single period that can end on certain specified dates. Because it allows for more flexibility, Bermudan options are more expensive than European style, but cheaper than American style options.

contingent payment of the option premium

Some options allow the buyer not to pay the premium at the time the option is bought. They fall into a class of options quite aptly referred to as contingent premium options. As the name suggests, the payment of the option premium is subject to a specified contingency.

❐   PAY-LATER OPTIONS

'Pay-later' options are contingency options. In a sense, they also amend the exercise style. Two standard terms are thus amended by these options, as will appear more fully from the discussion hereunder.

When a pay-later option is bought, the premium is only payable if the option is exercised. The catch is however, that the option must be exercised if the option is ITM on expiration. This amends the normal exercise style of OTC options that always leave the exercise of ITM options at the discretion of the holder. As far as their exercise is concerned, these options are thus somewhat similar to options on futures that are automatically exercised upon expiration ITM. The similarity ends there.

As can be expected, the premium for such an option will be higher than for standard options. The main advantage is however, that the premium is always paid from a realised profit. The hedger can thus never be solely out of pocket for the premium.

□   KNOCK-IN CAPS AND FLOORS

This exotic option can be useful in managing interest rate risk. They are multi-interest rate period constructs with their premium contingencies based on 'triggers'.

For example, a knock-in cap on 3-month Libor will have an agreed trigger rate for 3-month Libor. While the rate is below the trigger rate, no cap actually exists.

When the underlying rate hits the 'trigger' rate, the cap comes into existence and the premium is due. The strike rate of the cap will always be higher than the trigger rate. Consequently, when the trigger rate is reached, a cap comes into existence with a somewhat higher strike rate than the trigger rate. A 'knock-in' interest rate floor would obviously have a trigger rate lower than the current interest rate with a strike rate a few ticks lower down.

The important issue with knock-in options is obviously that it depends on the view a company takes of the interest rate market. A company's management might be of the opinion that interest rates are really going nowhere at present. They are therefore reluctant to spend money on a hedge under the circumstances. However, they might believe that should 3-month Libor, for example, rise to 4.00%, it would indicate that interest rates are on the rise and the company must then seek protection against its interest rate exposure. They would then seek an interest rate cap with a strike of say, 4.25%.

In order to give effect to this view, the company enters into a knock-in cap with a trigger of 4.00% and a strike of 4.25%. Should the cap be triggered, the company will enjoy full protection against rising 3-month Libor from 4.25% up. It must also be noted that the premium, if it is paid, will be substantially greater than the premium of a 4.25% strike cap would be at the same moment in time.

Nevertheless, it is also true that by definition, a 4.25% strike cap will be quite far OTM at the time the cap is purchased. That is because even the trigger rate of 4.00% is necessarily OTM at that time. The company is thus at risk of rising rates up to 4.25% immediately after it buys the knock-in cap, even though the cap does not actually exist at the start.

It is also worth noting that the company's view of the interest rate market might be quite wrong. The 4.00% trigger rate might in fact represent nothing more than a spike in an otherwise docile market. It is thus possible that when the company's cap is triggered, they pay the higher premium and then 3-month Libor settles back to its former range below 4.00%. Such are the risks of trading one's market views.

❏   KNOCK-OUT OR UP-AND-OUT CAPS AND FLOORS

The knock-out cap and floor is an amended version of the previous one. This construct requires the premium to be paid up front, but provides for its refund under predetermined circumstances. This is also called an up-and-out cap or floor.

In this case, the 'trigger rate' does not bring the cap or floor into existence as in the previous construct, but has the opposite effect of extinguishing it. The basic structure is thus again that two rates are specified namely, a strike rate for the option and a trigger rate for its extinction.

The cap or floor comes into existence immediately upon its arrangement. It is effective immediately and the premium is due and payable. In the case of an up-and-out cap, the strike rate will be lower than the trigger rate, while the trigger rate will be lower than the floor rate in a knock-out floor.

In practice, this means that the company is prepared to accept the risk of the underlying interest rate if it rises to a very high level. Presumably, the motivation for this readiness to accept very large losses is based on a market view that interest rates actually will not reach such levels.

At each fixing date during the life of, for example a knock-out floor, the underlying interest rate will be compared to its strike and trigger rates. If the interest rate is above the strike rate, nothing is payable. If the underlying rate is lower than the strike rate, but higher than the 'trigger' rate, the company will be paid the difference between the actual rate and the strike rate. If the underlying interest rate is lower than the floor level, the floor is extinguished and the company is refunded the premium for the unexpired period of the floor.

It is evident that this option does not lower the premium of the cap or floor. There is hardly any advantage to this strategy, but many inherent dangers. If the market view of the company is off target, it gets a refund of a portion of the premium paid, but it then has to deal with interest rates that are higher than it anticipated. In other words, the company loses its protection against interest rate exposure at the exact time it would have been of greatest value. It is surprising that there could be a market for such a product.

calculation of the underlying interest rate

Some options have challenged the notion that the holder of an option must be paid out the full difference between the strike rate of an ITM option and its underlying interest rate. Obviously, there cannot be any amendment to this rule when a single interest rate period is at issue. It would no longer be a risk management tool if compensation were not calculated on the full difference in value.

However, the scene changes when products that extend over multiple interest rate periods are considered. Thus, when a company considers buying interest rate caps or floors to hedge a single, multiple-period interest rate exposure, it might be well advised to consider Asian options.

Consider a cap on 3-month Libor. A normal cap will pay out at the end of every quarter, depending on the state of the 3-month Libor market compared to the strike rate of the cap. By contrast, Asian options will calculate the average rate for 3-month Libor over the past year since the start of the option and pay out if, on average, 3-month

Libor was higher than the strike price of the cap. The averaging out of the underlying rate makes for less volatility and consequently less risk to the option seller. It is therefore not surprising that an Asian interest rate Cap can be quite considerably cheaper than a standard interest rate cap.

Asian options can therefore be a valuable tool for companies that have a greater need to meet their annual budgeted interest rate cost than to manage their cash flows on interest rate payments. If the management of interim cash flow is a company's greatest concern, Asian style caps will not be as good a solution as standard interest rate caps would be.

variable strike rates

A very important and popular class of exotic options allows for variable strike rates. That is to say, the strike rate of the option can be varied or reset at certain stages during the life of the option. The strike can always be reset to the lowest rate achieved during the life of the option in the case of a call, or at the highest rate achieved in the case of a put option. There are a few varieties of this type of option in existence, but they are all classed as 'look-back' options.

This sounds much like having the best of all possible worlds and it is, but at a price. The premium of a look-back option is usually around double the premium of a standard option.

☐   A STANDARD LOOK-BACK OPTION

A standard look-back option allows the buyer to 'look-back' over the life of the option and to 'select' a strike rate at the lowest rate if it were a call option. In effect this means that the option will always be 'ITM' or at least 'ATM' upon its expiration. The same holds true for a look-back put option. There the holder will be looking back to find the highest rate of the underlying interest rate to fix the strike of the option at that rate.

Taking a look-back call option as an example, suppose 3-month Libor is at 3.5% when the option is taken out. The initial strike of the option is thus at 3.5%. Suppose that 3-month Libor then goes up to 4.00% before coming down to 2.50%.

At expiration, 3-month Libor is back to 3.5%, where it started. The look-back call option will now be treated as a call option with a strike of 2.5% and will be ITM. The holder will be paid out the difference on the principal.

This can be a very advantageous option to buy, but the premium paid will be high. It would be wrong, however, to assume that the buyer could not lose. If, at expiration of the call, 3-month Libor were at its lowest point for the whole period, the option would expire ATM and the holder would not be receive one cent. There are no free lunches.

a ladder option

This is probably the most popular version of a look-back option, since it is cheaper than the standard look-back. It is nevertheless still appreciably more expensive than a standard call option.

The major difference here is that the right to 'look back' is not continuous so that the actual lowest point of the underlying rate will necessarily be found. The 'look-back' right is restricted to certain pre-specified dates in the life of the option. The option holder, in the case of a ladder put option, would then be able to select the highest rate that say, Prime rate, reached at any of the specified dates. The highest rate on any such day would then become the strike of the put option.

This strategy gets its name from the series of specified look-back dates, which resemble the rungs of a ladder. The price at each rung is available for selection as the eventual strike of the option.

The same comment as with the previous strategy is appropriate. Do not conclude that the holder cannot lose.

conclusion on exotics

It is clearly in any company's interest to investigate and be aware of all the options that are available in the market. Not all of the inventions are necessarily worthwhile, but many variants might serve a company well under particular circumstances. It might thus not be wise to content oneself with the knowledge of only such derivative instruments as are normally used. There may indeed be superior advantages to be obtained in the business of risk management, if the markets are constantly surveyed.

CHECKLIST FOR THE REVIEW OF CHAPTER 8

General overview: the overall control objectives of the material dealt with in this chapter are to acquaint the business with some advanced strategies with interest rate options and their variants. In addition, it is intended to acquaint the reader with some of the uses, advantages and relative disadvantages of certain products encountered in the market place.

	Key Issues	Illustrative Scope or Approach
8.1	Does the company ever consider the use of cost reduction strategies with interest rate option?	Cost reduction strategies exist that will reduce the premium on options The premium of an option can be reduced to zero using the appropriate strategy All cost reduction strategies operate on the basis that some advantage of the standard option arrangement must be sacrificed in order to gain the advantage of a reduced cost The main advantage that is sacrificed always comes down to the level of cover offered by an option and/or the advantage to be gained from a favourable move in the underlying interest rate Cost reducing strategies are available with OTC options as well as options on futures
8.2	What are the main premium reducing strategies?	Buying OTM call or put options Buying interest rate collars Buying vertical spreads

continued

	Key Issues	Illustrative Scope or Approach
8.3	What are the main features of each of these strategies?	With OTM options the company accepts the risk of adverse changes in the interest rate to the strike price of the option, while it retains the full advantage of profit on a favourable move In an interest rate collar, the company accepts the consequences of all moves in the interest rate while it remains between the two strikes of the collar. It enjoys full protection against adverse moves beyond the strike of the long option, while it loses all the advantage of a favourable move beyond the strike of the short option In a vertical option spread, the company gains the advantage of immediate cover against an adverse change in interest rates, but loses further protection beyond the strike of the short option
8.4	What are the main zero cost strategies?	Put call parity with options on futures, which result in either a zero cost collar or a synthetic interest rate future OTC forward rate locks OTC participating caps and floors
8.5	What are the main features of each of these strategies?	When put/call parity is employed with the long option and the short option at different strikes, the result is a zero cost interest rate collar. The company accepts the consequences of all moves in the interest rate while it remains between the two strikes of the collar. It enjoys full protection against adverse moves beyond the strike of the long option, while it loses all the advantage of a favourable move beyond the strike of the short option A borrower's forward rate lock is the equivalent of buying a call and selling a put at the same strike. The holder obtains full protection against a rise in the underlying interest rate, but must pay in the difference when the underlying rate declines A lender's forward rate lock is the equivalent of buying a put and selling a call at the same strike. The holder obtains full protection against a decline in the underlying interest rate, but must pay in the difference when the underlying rate rises

continued

	Key Issues	Illustrative Scope or Approach
		A participating cap is in principle no different from a forward rate lock, except that it covers multi-interest rate periods. Some products allow the holder and the bank to 'share' the difference in interest rate below the cap level. Above the cap level, the company enjoys full protection against a rise in the interest rate
		A participating floor is in principle no different from a forward rate lock, except that it covers multi-interest rate periods. Some products allow the holder and the bank to 'share' the difference in interest rate above the floor level. Below the floor level, the company enjoys full protection against a decline in the interest rate
8.6	What are exotic options?	Exotic options consist of a class of options where the standard terms of options have been amended to suit particular requirements of the market
8.7	What standard features of options are amended by exotic interest rate options?	Exercise styles
When and under what conditions the premium is payable
How the underlying value is calculated in relation to the strike price
The strike rate of the option is not fixed at the start of the option
8.8	What are the main features of each of these amendments?	The Bermudan option introduces a third exercise style between American and European. The option is exercisable at a number of predetermined dates during the life of the option
Contingent premium options make the payment of the option premium subject to a contingency:
• Pay later options provide for payment only upon exercise, but mandates exercise upon expiration ITM
• Knock-in caps and floors provide for a 'trigger' interest rate level to be reached before the options come into existence and the premium then paid. Protection against adverse moves in the underlying interest rate is thereafter given at a strike further OTM
• Knock-out caps and floors provide immediate cover against adverse moves and require immediate payment of the premium. They

continued

Key Issues	Illustrative Scope or Approach
	provide for a 'trigger' interest rate OTM, when the cap or floor will be extinguished, against the return of a pro-rated portion of the premium Asian options provide for averaging out the value of the underlying interest rate over the period of the option. The average value of the underlying rate is then compared to the strike price and the difference, if any, paid to the holder. The options represent a major saving in premium cost Strike rates that are varied over the life of the option are provided mainly by: • Look-back options allow the final strike price of the option to be determined at expiration. Then the value most favourable to the holder that the underlying interest rate achieved during the life of the option, will be selected as the strike of the option. These options are generally twice as expensive as normal options • Ladder options provide a 'ladder' of dates on which the value of the underlying interest rate may be selected as the strike price of the option at its expiration

index